NEW ROUTES FOR
DIASPORA STUDIES

New Routes for Diaspora Studies
IS VOLUME 5 IN THE SERIES

21ST CENTURY STUDIES
Center for 21st Century Studies
University of Wisconsin–Milwaukee
RICHARD GRUSIN, GENERAL EDITOR

Terror, Culture, Politics: Rethinking 9/11
Edited by Daniel J. Sherman and Terry Nardin

Museums and Difference
Edited by Daniel J. Sherman

The State of Sovereignty: Territories, Laws, Populations
Edited by Douglas Howland and Luise White

The Question of Gender: Joan W. Scott's Critical Feminism
Edited by Judith Butler and Elizabeth Weed

NEW ROUTES FOR DIASPORA STUDIES

Edited by Sukanya Banerjee, Aims McGuinness,
and Steven C. McKay

INDIANA UNIVERSITY PRESS
BLOOMINGTON AND INDIANAPOLIS

This book is a publication of

Indiana University Press
601 North Morton Street
Bloomington, Indiana 47404-3797 USA

iupress.indiana.edu

Telephone orders   800-842-6796
Fax orders   812-855-7931

⊖ The paper used in this publication meets the minimum requirements of the American National Standard for Information Sciences—Permanence of Paper for Printed Library Materials, ANSI Z39.48-1992.

Manufactured in the United States of America

Library of Congress Cataloging-in-Publication Data

New routes for diaspora studies / edited by Sukanya Banerjee, Aims McGuinness, and Steven C. McKay.
     p. cm. — (21st century studies volume 5)
  Includes bibliographical references and index.
  ISBN 978-0-253-00217-4 (cloth : alk. paper) — ISBN 978-0-253-00210-5 (pbk. : alk. paper) — ISBN 978-0-253-00601-1 (e-book)   1. Human beings—Migrations.   2. African diaspora.   3. Asian diaspora.   4. Emigration and immigration.   I. Banerjee, Sukanya, [date]   II. McGuinness, Aims, [date]   III. McKay, Steven C. (Steven Charles)
  GN370.N48 2012
  304.8—dc23
                                          2011049670

1   2   3   4   5   17   16   15   14   13   12

CONTENTS

ACKNOWLEDGMENTS

We wish to thank the following individuals for their help and encouragement in putting this volume together: Daniel Sherman, Merry Wiesner-Hanks, Richard Grusin, Ruud van Dijk, Kate Kramer, Michelle Caswell. Special thanks to John Blum for shepherding the manuscript through the final stages. Our thanks to Rebecca Tolen and Indiana University Press for continued support of this project and to the two readers for the press for their valuable feedback. Thanks to Drew Bryan for copyediting the manuscript. We would also like to thank the Center for 21st Century Studies, University of Wisconsin–Milwaukee, for sponsoring the conference "Routing Diasporas: Labor, Citizenship, Empire," which generated many of the discussions reflected in this volume.

Sukanya Banerjee
Aims McGuinness
Steven C. McKay

NEW ROUTES FOR DIASPORA STUDIES

Introduction
Routing Diasporas

SUKANYA BANERJEE

It has often been noted that diaspora is a phenomenon that can be traced to antiquity. Its current ubiquity as a focus of academic study, however, is informed in no small measure by contemporary conditions of global capitalism. *Globalization* and *diaspora,* though, bespeak different histories and modes of experience and should not be conflated. Nevertheless, there is no doubt that the surge of academic interest in diaspora has paralleled, or even been effected by, the emergence of a world that appears to be shaped to an ever-greater degree by the dispersal of peoples and the rise of new forms of connectedness. The growth of interest in matters of a global scope has led many within academia today to rethink the spatial and temporal categories that once constrained much research and writing in the humanities and social sciences. Not only have the nation and its borders been subjected to the most enthusiastic interrogation, but similar categories such as the world region, area, and empire have also come under questioning in recent years. Amid this rethinking of spatial and temporal categories, the term *diaspora* has gained currency as a productive frame for reimagining locations, movements, identities, and social formations that have either been overlooked by earlier modes of analysis or, equally important, stand the chance of being flattened by the homogenizing effects of global capital.

As Khachig Tölölyan recounts in a recent assessment of the current state of diaspora studies, the concept of *diaspora* dates back at least to the period around 250 BCE, when the Jews of Alexandria adopted the term to signify "their own scattering away from the homeland into *galut,* or collective exile."[1] By the early 1930s scholars had applied the term to the Jewish, Armenian, and Greek diasporas, what Tölölyan describes as the three "classical diasporas." The increasingly visible migrations of the twentieth century, however, have extended the semantic domain of *diaspora* such that the term has come to be applied to groups as disparate as "ethnics, exiles, expatriates, refugees, asylum seekers, labor migrants, queer communities, domestic service workers, executives of transnational corporations, and transnational sex workers."[2] Reflecting on the expansion of the discourse of diaspora in the early 1990s, James Clifford had called for a "polythetic definition" of the term, one that would reach beyond more conventional conceptualizations of diaspora as a dispersed community or network oriented around a single point of origin or homeland.[3] Suggesting that scholars of diaspora pay closer attention to what he described as "decentered, lateral connections," Clifford envisaged diaspora as exceeding a "teleology of origin/return."[4] This broader definition of diaspora— one from which we take our cue—gained purchase in diaspora studies over the next two decades. The moving ship so powerfully evoked in Paul Gilroy's mapping of the transatlantic, transcultural histories of a "black" diaspora serves as but one example of the fractal, incomplete, or crosshatched movements and identities that scholars now understand as diasporic.[5]

While Gilroy's particular evocation of the Black Atlantic world has also attracted criticism,[6] it cannot be gainsaid that the "spatially disseminated identity" foregrounded by the rubric of the Black Atlantic continues to lend an added charge to diaspora studies.[7] The study of diaspora today extends to an imaginative rethinking of the effects of migration, dispersal, and displacement—as evidenced in contemporary art, for instance—as well as to the formulation of a methodology of study.[8] In fact, Sudesh Mishra's insightful coining of the term "diaspoetics" indicates not only the prolific scholarship on diaspora, but also the emergence of diaspora as a field and mode of study in its own right.[9] It is precisely this visibility of diaspora that has also engendered its own set of attendant anxieties. R. Radhakrishnan remarked in the early 1990s that the concept of diaspora was in danger of becoming a "virtual theoretical consciousness," one devoid of historical referents or any relationship to material realities.[10] In his more recent assessment of diaspora studies, Tölölyan adds the caveat that the proliferation of meanings ascribed to diaspora has masked important distinctions among groups and kinds of dispersion.[11]

The need to balance the resonant metaphoricity accrued by *diaspora* with an attention to its material histories is a recurrent concern in academic discussions of diaspora.[12] An underlying theme of the present volume is that the continued viability of diaspora studies hinges on an ongoing effort to maintain this balance, such that *diaspora* does not expand into a too-capacious umbrella term for mobility and displacement or crystallize into a prescriptive typological framework. In other words, in acknowledging the significance of the expanded referentiality of *diaspora,* we must also develop a nuanced vocabulary that can pay heed to the specificities of its manifestations. Exercising such mindfulness might well be challenging, but it is a challenge that bears even further weight as we head into the second decade of the twenty-first century, a decade whose advent has already been heralded by the proliferating valence of *diaspora.*

In keeping with the rapid advances made in cyber technology, Robin Cohen had suggested the feasibility of thinking about "deterritorialized diaspora[s]" to indicate the extent to which "space has become reinscribed by cyberspace."[13] The increasing accessibility of online resources has also ushered in a spate of what can be described as "digital diasporas."[14] But 2010 also signaled the extent to which *diaspora* can more broadly infuse a cyber sensibility as well, as evident in the announcement of efforts to create a decentralized social networking service called DIASPORA.[15] The function of DIASPORA is in many ways akin to already existing social networking sites that help maintain connectivity across geographical divides. But by intending to store the user information of its dispersed users in personal web servers called "seeds," DIASPORA resonates with the etymological root of the term *diaspora* (Greek *diaspeirein,* which refers to the "scattering of seeds"). This particular appropriation of *diaspora* is significant in marking the expanded claims that can be made upon the term: if DIASPORA is successful and popular, then a large section of the population could well call itself "diasporic," thereby lending an unprecedented connotation to the term. It is also precisely the possibility of further appropriations of *diaspora* in a milieu in which dispersed individuals and communities are rapidly forming networks around various points of filiation and identity based on a diasporic model that perhaps underlines the following caveat in a 2010 issue of the influential journal *Diaspora:* "when discussing the nature and main issues facing diasporas and transnational entities at the beginning of the twenty-first century, one should avoid generalizations and make very careful and clear distinctions between the origins, identities and identifications, boundaries, organization, and pattern of behavior of the various types of such entities."[16]

As current students and scholars of diaspora, it is imperative that we braid together a study of diaspora that remains sensitive to the multiplicity of global histories and movements, with an examination of the evolving incarnations of *diaspora* and awareness of the concerns and filters that must attend its study. This is the particular burden of "routing" this volume bears, and in so doing, *New Routes for Diaspora Studies* does not focus only on contemporary diasporas but provides a reading of diasporas from the past two centuries in an effort to arrive at a composite understanding of what it means to "read" *diaspora* at the disciplinary crossroads of the twenty-first century.

New Cartographies

By its very name, *New Routes for Diaspora Studies* gestures toward Clifford's resonant use of "routes." For Clifford, diasporas negotiate with both "routes" and "roots." While on the one hand Clifford would emphasize the derootedness of cultural identities (no community is "pure or "discrete") by pointing to the mobility and displacement effected by diaspora, he also underscores how diasporas mark the "local": how diasporic formations are characterized as much by movement as by an attempt to form "distinctive communities [though] in historical contexts of displacement."[17] In this, the homonymous "route" and "root" blend together to disrupt any easy distinction between "rootedness" and "displacement," a distinction that in any case has been reified as but a function of modernity.[18] In the emphasis on "routing" diasporas, therefore, this volume consciously seeks to maintain the multivalence of the term, rendering "routes" and "roots" supplemental to each other. It also emphasizes "routing" as reflecting the scholarly approach most adequate to the study of diasporas, which is to say an approach that is alert and open to the continually changing modes, configurations, and formations engendered by and through diasporas, an approach that maps or routes diaspora as an *ongoing process* rather than one that forecloses its definitional bearings.[19] And a significant part of the scholarly responsibility in "routing" diasporas lies in the entwining—routing together—of different disciplinary approaches in ways that can yield new possibilities of analysis while remaining sensitive, as mentioned earlier, to diaspora as experience, practice, analytical category, and metaphor. In other words, by bringing together what have too often been parallel approaches to the study of diaspora, this volume looks to the new directions diaspoetics can take by illuminating the vital if underexamined interplay between the historical, sociological, affective, somatic, and aesthetic manifestations of diaspora.

In keeping with the emphasis on "routes," the essays in this volume are attentive to how diasporas—both as historical experience and category of analysis—reorient conventional cartographies and spatial configurations. Although the concept of diaspora frequently arises in discussions of "the transnational," the term, as Jana Evans Braziel and Anita Mannur are right in pointing out, "is not synonymous with transnationalism."[20] For Braziel and Mannur, the difference between diaspora and transnationalism is that transnationalism refers more to "macroeconomic and technological" flows, whereas diaspora speaks more to the "migrations and displacements of subjects."[21]

This volume etches the distinction between the two terms further by suggesting that diaspora offers something that the category of the transnational does not, in that it goes beyond evoking the transcendence or absence of the nation and directs attention to specific, historically located networks that have often escaped the attention of scholars working within the framework of individual nations or area studies.[22] For instance, in studying the literary output of the Hadrami diaspora that spanned the Indian Ocean for five hundred years, Engseng Ho has remarked, "One of the main obstacles to discovering the narratives has been the fact that they were written in different parts of the ocean, such as Zanzibar, Mecca, Hadramawt, Surat and Malabar in India, and the Malay Archipelago. The texts were thus known as belonging to different national literatures, separated from each other, rather than as parts of a unified phenomenon in dialogue with each other."[23] In this context, the utility of diaspora as a category of analysis lies in part in its capacity to gather together what conventional academic demarcations have tended to divide. Among the significant contributions of the new wave of investigation into diaspora has been the fostering of conversations among what had previously been largely separated areas of academic expertise, including national and area studies. The emergence of the African diaspora as a subject of inquiry has enabled the building of bridges among scholars working on both sides of the Atlantic as well as the Indian Ocean, the Mediterranean, and beyond.[24] The growth of interest in diaspora has similarly enhanced collaborations between specialists in other area studies (including East Asian, South Asian, Southeast Asian, and Latin American Studies) and scholars working in Asian American and Latino studies.[25] Moreover, given that with the emphasis on globalization, there is, as Tejaswini Niranjana comments, the strong possibility that "the paths to the First World will be defined more clearly than before"; a foregrounding of diasporic networks yields more possibilities for exploring and strengthening South-South collaborations and cartographies.[26] Recent studies of diasporic networks forged across and through the Indian Ocean, for instance, tilt the trajectory of migration and mobility away from a North-West orientation, as is often the case when diaspora is viewed through the paradigmatic lens of globalization.[27] In fact, as will be further discussed in the afterword, in contrast to the concept of globalization, which purports to name a process by its promised endpoint (a "globalized" present or future), *diaspora* carries no implication of its own inevitable teleology, allowing therefore for a reckoning of temporal and geographic connections that are otherwise rendered disjunctive, if not impossible.[28]

Yet even as the concept of diaspora has been deployed as a way of thinking beyond accustomed units of analysis, much of the scholarly discourse on diaspora has ironically remained confined within conventional academic boundaries in the humanities and social sciences. As is readily recognized, the topic of diaspora presents a pedagogic challenge on account of its immense disciplinary reach that is otherwise curtailed by the administrative exigencies of academic disciplinarity. As Ato Quayson put it, "How does one teach about a phenomenon that seems to fall into so many disciplines and fields at the same time (history, sociology, political science, ethnic studies, international relations, public health, human rights, and literary and cultural studies are just a few that come to mind)?"[29] From the perspective of research, this predicament is compounded further by what is often a divide in the scholarship on diaspora studies, one that demarcates a typologically oriented positivistic study of diasporas from an approach that is attuned to the constitutive role played by subjective and discursive acts of identity formation integral to the shaping of diasporic experience.[30]

New Routes for Diaspora Studies presents one response to this academic quandary, and the essays in this collection reflect the spatial and temporal reconfigurations germane to the academic study of diaspora not just by foregrounding cartographies or imaginings that remain relatively unexplored (migrations from China to Panama or the "diasporic" status of Algerians in France), but also by fostering a conversation across disciplinary divides. In this, rather than imposing a homogenous framework, the collection deliberately includes essays written in different rhetorical modes and deploying a range of analytical approaches. The different methodologies used range from literary and cultural analysis to ethnographic fieldwork and archival research. While some essays distance themselves from "discourse analysis," others seek specifically to underscore discursive modes of identity formation; while for some authors the object of study is the written text, others focus on oral testimony or the built environment. And even if the ensuing conversation sounds dissonant at times, such dissonance testifies to the robustness and the heterogeneity of diasporic practice. Moreover, while the individual contributions bespeak their respective disciplinary grounding (art history, anthropology, ethnic studies, history, literature, and sociology), it is worth noting how they converge around common nodes of interest or analysis. An attentiveness to the narrative constituents of diasporic experience, for instance, assumes as much importance in Lok Siu's analysis of her ethnographic findings as it does in Jenny Sharpe's and Betty Joseph's studies of the literary and cultural formations of diaspora, though the authors take up the question of narrative in very different ways. In vivifying the necessarily interdisciplinary scope of diaspora studies, the essays highlight the polyvocal nature of diasporic experience in ways that render diaspora an "expressive configuration," the richness of which is otherwise shorn as it is parceled out across disciplinary academic divisions.[31]

Although the authors in this collection may take different geographical, temporal, methodological, and disciplinary routes, they share questions and concerns in common. One of the themes that cuts across the essays in this collection is that of labor. At a time when globalization is often glossed in terms of disembodied processes, electronic flows, and virtual worlds, it becomes all the more important to recall the importance of "real" labor and actual laborers, be they indentured Indian laborers in nineteenth-century South Africa, Chinese laborers in late nineteenth- and early twentieth-century Panama, U.S. military personnel in East Asia, or Haitian "boat people" struggling to gain access to low-paying jobs shoring up the U.S. economy.[32] This is not so much to fetishize the "reality" or the physicality of labor (which, as Marx reminds us, is precisely what gets overlooked in commodity fetishism) as to draw attention to the various networks and nodes of experience that emerge when labor is re-embodied, so to speak. A close interrogation of these formations not only unearths forms of gendered labor that are otherwise rendered invisible in global economies, but it also illuminates how gendered identities critically constitute and are constituted through diasporic formations.[33] A focus on labor also links the economic roles and material constrictions of diasporic subjects with resultant forms of belonging, exclusion, and network (re)production. As the essays in this volume collectively suggest, even though diasporas may be characterized by displacement and dispersal over time and space, it is erroneous to imagine that the subjects of diaspora are therefore necessarily deterritorialized, unmoored, or free-floating.[34] In fact, part of the value of diaspoetics as a collective if sometimes contentious enterprise has come from explorations of the tensions between material and economic conditions that foster and condition diasporas and the multiple negotiations through which diasporic subjects struggle to forge their own forms of identification and/or networks of labor in ways that complicate any transparent sense of agency, individuality, or even cohesive notion of diasporic identity. Part of this book's own labors lies in the routing together of these multiple strands of diaspora.

A consideration of diasporic labor also directs our attention to the reconfiguration of abiding forms of inequality across geographical scales and historical periods. The relatively recent focus on histories of African, South Asian, Chinese, and other diasporas have much to teach us about how colonial domination and the geopolitics of global commerce foster different trajectories of displacement and dispersal. They remind us that the apparent upswing in global migratory flows in the present build on long-standing inequalities between locales, communities, and regions. But reinserting the "labors" of diaspora into the consideration of global migration also significantly recasts who or what is considered diasporic. For instance, an emphasis on labor as an important constituent of diaspora also helps us understand how British bureaucrats and military personnel in British India occupied an uncertain diasporic space. Such an understanding helpfully reveals the asymmetries of colonial paradigms that are/were otherwise propped up by colonial self-assurances of dominance; it unhinges the colonial dynamic by highlighting the (white) colonizer too as a "diasporic subject," an incarnation that has too often been ignored by scholars of diaspora.[35]

Reinserting the centrality of labor in the consideration of diasporas also expands our understanding of labor to include its intellectual, emotional, sexual, physical, and aesthetic relays. The range of focus in this volume therefore varies widely: from how the phenomenon of diaspora registers on the built environment, as revealed in the animated debates about incorporating a "Jewish" architectural design into the building of the Pennsylvania Academy of the Fine Arts, to the convoluted processes through which French Algerians defied legal ascriptions to conceive of themselves as "French" in the aftermath of the Algerian Revolution; from the legislations monitoring conjugal relations and the sexual labor of Asian women in the post–World War II United States, to how the crosshatching of seemingly disparate narratives aids in the self-styling of the bourgeois (and significantly technocratic) South Asian diaspora in the contemporary United States. While the essays focus on specific contexts, they, individually and collectively, point to an interlinking—through various labor economies—among slaves, freed people, coolies, planters, professionals, merchants, domestic workers, and colonial officials across imperial and interoceanic networks, illuminating what Lisa Lowe describes in a broader context as "global intimacies."[36] By adding a layered interpretation to the term "intimacy," such that it encapsulates connotations of spatial proximity as well as modes of contact between laboring populations, in addition to the more conventional usage of the term with reference to bourgeois notions of privacy, Lowe points to "global intimacies" as that "out of which emerged not only modern humanism but a modern racialized division of labor."[37] Tracing these "global intimacies," therefore, can serve a heuristic purpose for limning the boundaries and constitutive experiences of diaspora, in which labor plays such a central role.

Interrogating Terms

As Brent Hayes Edwards has reminded us, any effort to conceptualize diaspora entails a rethinking of the "politics of nominalization."[38] Who names whom "African," with what justification, and with what purpose? Even as the study of diaspora has been increasingly divorced from teleologies of return, diasporas are frequently identified and distinguished with reference to a singular node of affiliation or origin, as with the "Chinese diaspora" or the "Haitian diaspora." By identifying complex configurations and hybrid networks as elements of a particular diaspora, we run the risk of reifying the relationship between those elements and their purported "home" or "point of origin." What kinds of spatiality, territoriality, temporality, or cartography must be interrogated to avoid tethering what we have denominated as "diasporic" to inaccuracies of autochthony, or confining them to national, social, regional, religious, or continental paradigms that they otherwise exceed? At what point do the disadvantages of gathering up disparate peoples into a given conceptual category of diaspora begin to outweigh the advantages? Admittedly, there can be no single answer to these questions, but if, as Kim Butler suggests, "diasporan identity be not defined by the group itself but by the types of research questions asked," then the first three essays in this volume further develop the ground for inquiry by interrogating diasporic labels and categories and reflecting on the contingent nature of the eponymous diasporas they consider.[39]

These three essays (Sharpe, Shepard, and Bates and Carter) in part 1 interrogate fundamental ideas of "displacement," "return," or "place-of-origin" that play such a crucial role in assigning diasporic identities. Located across different sites—the Middle Passage juxtaposed with contemporary migrations from Haiti, the repatriation of French Algerians in the aftermath of Algerian independence, and the formation of indentured Indian communities in colonial Natal—the essays variously posit the salience of a "diasporic imaginary," which, as Brian Axel, among others, describes, shifts the emphasis in diaspora studies from a privileging of place of origin more to "the process of identification generative of diasporic subjects."[40] This is not to discount the importance that questions of return and reclamation may hold out for diasporic communities. Rather, it is to enhance our understanding of the multiple ways such trajectories and identities are charted. Moreover, it is also to remain mindful of the ways such trajectories can become problematic because the teleological arc ascribed to diasporas is often dependent on a "genealogical, implicitly heteronormative reproductive logic" that imposes its own exclusionary practices.[41]

Jenny Sharpe's essay, "The Middle Passages of Black Migration," recalls Stuart Hall's observation that "Africa" coheres as a composite identity only through the experience of diaspora[42] to further her suggestion that "the transatlantic black diaspora also includes and impacts Africans 'at home' and not just those who experience the homelessness of migration."[43] In extending the framework for understanding the "African diaspora," Sharpe provides a reading of Caryl Phillips's *A Distant Shore* (2003), juxtaposing it with an analysis of Edwidge Danticat's short story "Children of the Sea." By doing so, the essay suggestively highlights how the normative association between mobility, displacement, and diaspora can be troubled—as in Danticat's story—through the linked homelessness of Haitians both at "home" and at sea. In fact, by re-examining the key analytical categories of "home," "travel," and "mobility," Sharpe asks us to reconsider the valences we attribute to these terms, thereby providing an important frame for reviewing the contours and constitutive features of diaspora. Moreover, even as the essay emphasizes how the Middle Passage of the transatlantic slave trade provides a focal point for contemporary writers, the argument is also sensitive to how invocations of the Middle Passage are reconfigured in ways that unsettle any originary moment of displacement or point of return. In this, Sharpe's essay provides a literary framework for reconceptualizing the contours of diaspora.

Todd Shepard's essay, "Making the Exodus from Algeria 'European': Family and Race in 1962 France," further complicates the notion of "return" or "repatriation" through a historical examination of decolonization in Algeria in the 1950s and 1960s. The French government originally devised its policy of "repatriation" as a way of encouraging Algerians with French citizenship to remain in Algeria at a time when French officials feared that continental France might soon be flooded with refugees who opposed Algerian independence and yet who were not themselves considered sufficiently "French" by the metropole. By tracing the intertwined assumptions of racial and heterosexual familial identity that underwrote the process, Shepard recovers how those who "failed" the test of French citizenship as devised by metropolitan authorities found themselves in a kind of limbo, with no guarantee of citizenship in France despite the promises inscribed earlier in French law and colonial policy. Drawing attention particularly to the exilic status of the Muslim French citizens from Algeria, the *harkis,* Shepard outlines how the exodus from Algeria complicated ideas of repatriation and return, revealing the contingent discourses of citizenship and national belonging.

Crispin Bates and Marina Carter's essay, "Enslaved Lives, Enslaving Labels: A New Approach to the Colonial Indian Labor Diaspora," furthers the examination of diasporic nominalism by proposing that reclamation of the term *coolie* (a name commonly and often pejoratively assigned to indentured Indian laborers in the nineteenth century) can identify a commonality among diasporic subjects without essentializing the "Indian-ness" of those subjects.[44] Bates and Carter acknowledge the centrality of exploitation to the practice of indenture. In a departure from much recent scholarship on indentured labor, however, they shift attention to the ways in which the location of indentured laborers within a coercive global system opened up, at least for some of those laborers, the possibility of translocal economic and social realignment. Their essay recounts how colonial powers tapped into a "circulatory system of labor" that predated colonization and also how this colonial appropriation extended networks among subaltern migrants, enabling them in some instances to gain more control over their migratory patterns. To be sure, the voyages of the indentured laborers destroyed familial networks and tore commonalities asunder, but, as Bates and Carter suggest, they offered, if only inadvertently, the possibility for the forging of new visions of long-distance, translocal solidarity.[45] A consideration of particular modes of indentured affiliation is timely because 2010 marked the 150th year of the first arrival of Indian indentured labors to South Africa, an event that has been commemorated with due sobriety in both countries. Interestingly, however, the Indian indentured labor diaspora has until recently only been a matter of limited interest (and that too, largely academic) in India, a country that has otherwise actively laid a more proprietary claim on its wealthier diasporic populace, especially in Europe and North America. The question of the nineteenth-century "coolie diaspora," therefore, brings home the problems of "return" and "reclamation" even in cultural and historical memory making.[46]

Maps of Intimacy

The questions of nominalism raised by the first three essays also open up a consideration of how shorthand terms such as "Jewish diaspora" or "South Asian diaspora" bring with them the temptation to think of these abstractions as if they were stable, neatly bounded entities or transcendent, homogenous groups. But as Rogers Brubaker urges, "We should think of diaspora in the first instance as a category of practice . . . used to make claims, to articulate projects, to formulate expectations, to mobilize energies. . . ."[47] Brubaker's comment on recognizing diaspora as a porous practice, rather than the reification of an always-already status, in some ways echoes Axel's notion of a "diasporic imaginary," a view shared by many scholars of diaspora. For the purposes of this volume, it has also been important to build upon these overlapping frames to underline how diasporas both reflect and are forged through a panoply of practices—indeed, through *intimate* practices that become the grounds for contesting and consolidating notions of identity and difference. The realm of the intimate, as Ann Stoler, taking from Foucauldian biopolitics, reminds us, offers "strategic sites for assessing the contingent and convergent strategies of governance."[48] In this, the essays in part 2 by Parama Roy and Rachel Ida Buff respectively draw attention to how intimate relations, be they of commensality or conjugality, become the site upon which anxieties and imperatives of statist import are addressed in and through diasporic contexts. For both these essays, the diasporas under study constitute in some way "imperial diasporas," in that they are sanctioned and sustained in the interests of a state power; for Roy, it is the nineteenth-century British colonial state, for Buff it is the twentieth-century U.S. state in its imperial incarnation.[49] However, even as these two essays momentarily shift attention away from questions of disenfranchisement and dispossession that often provide the starting point for studies of diasporic communities, they effectively point to how anxieties of governance and power are addressed and assuaged through relations of intimacy forged through contexts of diaspora. Matters of sexuality, appetite, and consumption, these essays suggest, play a key role in forging dispersed networks and identities that become key in upholding state practice, yet often times also exceed it.[50]

Roy's essay, "Empire, Anglo-India, and the Alimentary Canal," re-examines the so-called "Indian Mutiny" of 1857–58, but with an emphasis on the figure of the Anglo-Indian, the resident Briton in India. Through an emphasis on seemingly mundane details of diet, ingestion, and consumption, the essay provides a different lens for viewing the events of 1857, a view that centers, unexpectedly enough, on the "alimentary canal." Such a focus is important in that it allows the analysis to depart from conventional readings of British assertions of a stark and irremediable difference between colonizer and colonized that emerged in the aftermath of 1857. Roy shows how concerns related to ingestion and pollution actually linked the categories of Anglo-Indian and Indian through what she insightfully describes as a "shared affective and corporeal circuit."[51] Roy's reconstruction of this circuit in the mid-nineteenth century illuminates the amorphous relation between Indians and Anglo-Indians, teasing the avowedly discrete identity that the imperial metropolis attempted to foist upon its diasporic "Anglo" Indian population. In doing so, the essay adds to the growing literature that posits the British colonial presence in diasporic terms.[52] It also demonstrates how a textured reading of the quotidian practices of everyday life can be brought to bear effectively upon a reading of diaspora in ways that highlight the intricacies of the relations forged through it.

The intersection between empire and intimacy is also the subject of study for Rachel Ida Buff in "Domestic Internationalisms, Imperial Nationalisms: Civil Rights, Immigration, and Conjugal Military Policy," which analyzes U.S. imperialist discourse and debates about citizenship in the era following World War II. Adding to Shepard's essay, which examines the interplay between imperial discourse and struggles over the boundaries of citizenship in the context of French decolonization, Buff directs our attention toward debates over immigration policy at a time when the United States was dramatically intensifying its overseas power, in the immediate aftermath of World War II. She highlights how the remaking of the racial limits of the national U.S. body politic after World War II was bound up with a reimagining of constructions of gender and sexuality during the early years of the Cold War. Immigrant women from Asia, including China and Korea, emerge in her analysis as critical actors in the fashioning of diasporic networks that connected the continental United States to new zones of U.S. influence above, even as they helped force a reshaping of U.S. immigration policy from below. Yet if Asian immigrants were able to find a "home" in the United States to a greater degree than the *harkis* discussed earlier by Shepard, it was in part because of successful efforts in the United States to portray Asian women as "marriageable" and Asians more generally as available for assimilation to a body politic, which continued to be figured in official terms as implicitly "white."

Nation, Narrative, Diaspora

While the essays by Roy and Buff variously outline how the formation of diasporic communities is often corollary to colonial practice and state policy, the final three essays shift focus to particular narrative and aesthetic forms that emerge through the context of diaspora. As scholars of diaspora widely recognize, affective and imaginative modes of articulation are key to the formation of diasporic subjectivities. In fact, in attempting to map the Indian diaspora in the post–World War II U.S. and U.K., Sandhya Shukla goes further to ask rhetorically, "how can we confidently distinguish the material from the symbolic, or, for that matter, experience from fiction?"[53] In part 3, three essays by Lok Siu, Martin Berger, and Betty Joseph point to the centrality of various modes of cultural production in inscribing the diasporic experience. The different texts of study include oral testimony, architectural design, and the epic novel, respectively. While Siu and Berger underscore the importance of acknowledging how "much of diaspora experience is [actually] unwritten," Joseph's analysis is attentive to how the consumption of the written text—in this case, the "epic novel"—is heavily mediated by cyber technologies of virtual communication.[54] Taken together, the essays gesture to how such modes of cultural formation and identification reframe notions of space and territoriality in ways that set up differential relations with ideas of nationhood and national belonging. Whereas in Berger's essay, what is labeled "diasporic" becomes itself an important way to mark the parameters of the U.S. nation-state, for Siu and Joseph, one effect of a diasporic sensibility is that it maps a geographic imaginary that both contends and colludes with that of the nation.

In Siu's study of oral narratives that seamlessly transition between Panama and the United States, there is an explicit rejection of national labels, whereas Joseph's study foregrounds the mythic space of a "Hindu nation" as constructed through diasporic notions of Indian nationhood. In reading these three essays, it is worth keeping in mind that even though the salience of diaspora studies is often posited as a correlative of the supposed demise of the nation-state,[55] the relation between the two, as is widely recognized, is never mutually exclusive; at the very least, as we know from Benedict Anderson's influential treatise, the nation itself is of diasporic provenance.[56] But even as the notion of "long-distance nationalism," for instance, has become something of an aphorism, what still demands attention are the novel, shifting, ever-changing cultural and narrative forms that are produced at the intersection of nation and diaspora. Tracking these configurations is important not only for the purposes of detailing the literary and cultural imaginary of various diasporas but for also dispelling what has been rightly described as a "facile or premature model of nationlessness that, however unwittingly, answers to the neoliberal fantasy of a borderless world."[57] But in directing attention to the particular narrative and aesthetic modes that diaspora engenders, the final set of essays offers not only a considered reflection of what is the ongoing, jostling relation between nation and diaspora, but also of how the valences of those categories are continually considered anew. In other words, they not only underline diaspora as process, but also foreground the transactional nature of national belonging and nationhood that can be both salutary and insidious in effect.

Lok Siu's "Serial Migration: Stories of Home and Belonging in Diaspora" provides an ethnographic study of Panamanian Chinese subject formation. Focusing on the phenomenon of "serial migration," Siu argues that even when multiple migrations have begun with forced displacement, subsequent moves have often been shaped by migrants' own decisions, the motivations for which have included a quest for cultural capital. Siu's case studies make it clear that diasporic subjects may reject racial or national labels in favor of "locating home in diaspora." Her foregrounding of "serial migration" emphasizes how establishing narrative continuity—representing diaspora in terms of a *serial* migration—plays an instrumental role in normalizing the rupture usually attributed to diaspora, in ways that render the experience of diaspora more "familiar." In doing so, Siu's essay raises the important question of whether diaspora must always be conceived of as an effect or cataclysmic aftermath. In other words, how do we balance an understanding of the disorienting effects of displacement with a recognition of the idioms that enable its naturalization? By reminding us of the centrality of transnational migrations to the advanced state of capitalism, Siu's narratives of "serial migration" prompt a reconsideration of whether diaspora need necessarily be cast as an exception to a rule of stasis.

Martin Berger's "Building Associations: Nineteenth-Century Monumental Architecture and the Jew in the American Imagination" draws attention to aesthetic and narrative forms emerging from and within diasporas. Examining the debates surrounding the design for the Pennsylvania Academy of the Fine Arts, Berger's interests as a historian of visual culture include an interrogation of how the "*idea* of particular diasporic peoples" shaped and was shaped by elite architectural spaces. Rather than focus on migrant constituencies as such, he draws our attention to "resident" U.S. designers and architects who sought to channel architectural forms associated with the Jewish diaspora and other purportedly "oriental" groups into the design of a building. The symbolic purpose of the academy, Berger points out, was not to celebrate but rather to assert superiority over Jews, Muslims, and other allegedly inferior or less civilized groups, while simultaneously portraying white, Protestant "America" as the culmination of civilization. Berger's essay bridges two areas of study that have flourished in recent years but have rarely intersected in practice: the scholarship on constructions of "whiteness" and that on diaspora. Although scholarly debates surrounding the discursive formation of whiteness have often been framed in national terms, Berger's essay suggests how an attention to diasporic contexts and the labeling of diasporas might help to trace the emergence of whiteness in the United States within the formation of racial discourse on a transnational level.[58] Read within the broader context of U.S. nationalist discourse, Berger's essay calls for a consideration of the role played by the label "diasporic" in portraying peoples and practices as "exceptional," "exotic," or "extraneous" in ways that may actually be integral to national formation in the United States and its forging of global economic linkages.

Betty Joseph's "Cultural Forms and World Systems: The Ethnic Epic in the New Diaspora" further underscores the link between diasporas and discourses of nationalism by examining how the diasporic framework has been integral to the reimagining of race and history in ways that have been critical to strident discourses of Indian (predominantly Hindu) nationalism in the contemporary United States. In her examination of Bhagwan Gidwani's novel *Return of the Aryans* (1994), she asks why Gidwani's celebratory narrative of an idealized Aryan past has found such purchase among the South Asian diaspora, particularly in North America. Expanding upon earlier studies of the novel that have argued for its imbrication with the rise of nationalism, Joseph's essay offers an important reconsideration of the novel as a vehicle of diaspora, as "a shuttle," she describes, "between archaic and new forms; between the pre-national orality of the epic . . . and the transnational, time-space compressed simultaneity of new technologies like the Internet."[59] In tracing the interface between print culture and the Internet, Joseph analyzes how notions of purity and authenticity—notions that are successfully appropriated by chauvinistic nationalisms—are insidiously incarnated in and through diasporas. While the relation between sections of the South Asian diaspora and the rise of right-wing Hindu ideologies in India has been fairly well-documented, Joseph's essay reminds us that the ongoing *narrative* negotiations between print and cyber culture compel careful attention, if only as an ethical response—on our part—to the limitations and pitfalls of diasporic imaginaries that are being made and remade.

———

As the following essays will make evident, the contributors to this volume are all mindful of the dangers of reifying, abstracting, or overgeneralizing about diaspora as a phenomenon, even as they identify and analyze the historical, material, and cultural routes of particular diasporas. Although the essays have been arranged in different groupings, this categorization is by no means binding or discrete. Readers are encouraged, in fact, to trace the multiple areas of overlap and complementarity among the essays. Such a reading in itself will be one way to "route" the richness of diasporic experience. A gathering at the crossroads, the collection reminds us how the historical experience of diaspora is constituted through a complex ensemble of affective, emotional, and imaginative practices that make it reductive to limit the study of diaspora to only one aspect of the multifacetedness it otherwise marshals. Diasporas are not merely effects of history but producers of history in their own right, and this volume presents one attempt to underline the fact that how we read diasporas plays no small role in shaping this unfolding history and our understanding of it.

NOTES

My thanks to Aims McGuinness and Steve McKay for their help with this essay.

1. Khachig Tölölyan, "The Contemporary Discourse of Diaspora Studies," *Comparative Studies of South Asia, Africa and the Middle East* 27, no. 3 (2007): 648. For an earlier statement on the meanings of diaspora by the same author, see Khachig Tölölyan, "The Nation-State and Its Others: In Lieu of a Preface," *Diaspora* 1, no. 1 (1991): 3–7.

2. Tölölyan, "Contemporary Discourse," 648.

3. James Clifford, "Diasporas," *Cultural Anthropology* 9, no. 3 (1994): 306. Also see Brian Keith Axel, "The Context of Diaspora," *Cultural Anthropology* 19, no. 1 (2004):

26–60; and Evelyn Hu-Dehart, "Afterward: Brief Meditation on Diaspora Studies," *Modern Drama* 48, no. 3 (2005): 428–39.

4. Clifford, "Diasporas," 306. In this, Clifford departs from a potentially rigid interpretive grid through which William Safran, for instance, identifies diasporic communities. William Safran, "Diasporas in Modern Societies: Myths of Homeland and Return," *Diaspora: A Journal of Transnational Studies* 1, no. 1 (1991): 83–99. For a discussion and extension of Safran's diasporic framework, see Robin Cohen, *Global Diasporas: An Introduction,* 2nd ed. (London: Routledge, 2008).

5. Paul Gilroy, *The Black Atlantic: Modernity and Double Consciousness* (London: Verso Press, 1993).

6. Paul Tiyambe Zeleza, "Rewriting the African Diaspora: Beyond the Black Atlantic," *African Affairs* 104 (2005): 35–68, 37. See also Laura Chrisman, "Journeying to Death: Paul Gilroy's *Black Atlantic*," *Race and Class* 39, no. 2 (1997): 51–64.

7. The phrase "spatially disseminated identity" is from Ian Baucom, "Charting the Black Atlantic," *Postmodern Culture* 8, no. 1 (1997).

8. I refer here to contemporary artwork that focuses on the motif of the moving ship to highlight the composite, de-essentialized nature of identities in diaspora. Examples include Marsha Pearce's mixed media artwork described in Marsha Pearce, "Transnational/Transcultural Identities: The Black Atlantic and Pythagoras' Theorem," *Callaloo* 30, no. 2 (2007): 547–54. In a related context, British-Nigerian artist Yinka Shonibare's commissioned sculpture "Nelson's Ship in a Bottle," unveiled in London's Trafalgar Square in May 2010, highlights not only the crosshatched nature of Britain's colonial history but also the imprint of diasporic communities in contemporary Britain. For a recent rendition of diaspora as a mode of study, see Christina Sharpe, *Monstrous Intimacies: Making Post-Slavery Subjects* (Durham, N.C.: Duke University Press, 2010).

9. Sudesh Mishra, *Diaspora Criticism* (Edinburgh: University of Edinburgh Press, 2006), 7.

10. R. Radhakrishnan, "Postcoloniality and the Boundaries of Identity," *Callaloo* 16, no. 4 (1993): 763. See also Jana Evans Braziel and Anita Mannur, "Nation, Migration, Globalization: Points of Contention in Diaspora Studies," in *Theorizing Diaspora: A Reader,* ed. Jana Evans Braziel and Anita Mannur, 3 (Malden, Mass.: Blackwell, 2003).

11. Tölölyan, "Contemporary Discourse," 649.

12. For a synthesis of these various viewpoints, see Kim D. Butler, "Defining Diaspora, Refining a Discourse," *Diaspora: Journal of Transnational Studies* 10, no. 2 (2001): 189–219. For an earlier iteration of this point, see Stuart Hall, "Cultural Identity and Diaspora," in *Identity: Community, Culture, and Difference,* ed. Jonathan Rutherford, 222–327 (London: Lawrence & Wishart, 1990).

13. Cohen, *Global Diasporas,* 8.

14. For a delineation of the term "digital diaspora" and its limits, see Michael S. Laguerre, "Digital Diaspora: Definition and Models," in *Diasporas in the New Media Age,* ed. Andoni Alonso and Pedro J. Oiarzabal, 49–64 (Reno: University of Nevada Press, 2010).

15. Announced in April 2010, DIASPORA is a project undertaken by four students of New York University who intend to create a decentralized social networking system

that allows users to retain more control over their privacy and the information they share. The project is still underway but has attracted considerable attention and a fair amount of funding as it is being developed. The current website for the project is www.joindiaspora.com.

16. Gabriel Sheffer, "Transnational and Ethnonational Diasporism," *Diaspora: A Journal of Transnational Studies* 15, no. 1 (Spring 2006): 130. Sheffer's essay argues for differentiating between transnational networks and ethnonational diasporas, and he concludes his essay by emphasizing the need to create "'theoretical islands' that will eventually serve as bases for a more comprehensive theoretical exploration of diasporism and transnationalism, two phenomena that are not going to disappear but, rather, will continue to grow" (141). Though dated 2006, this journal issue was published in Spring 2010.

17. Clifford, "Diasporas," 308. For an analysis of the diasporic production of the "local," see, for instance, Jacqueline Nassy Brown, *Dropping Anchor, Setting Sail: Geographies of Race in Black Liverpool* (Princeton, N.J.: Princeton University Press, 2005).

18. See Clifford, "Diasporas," 309. For the perils of employing a "sedentarist" approach to the "local," see Liisa H. Malkki, "Refugees and Exile: From 'Refugee Studies' to the National Order of Things," *Annual Review of Anthropology* 24 (1995): 495–523. In a related context, Rey Chow has noted how enhanced speed in global technology alters relations between time and space such that data operators in India and the Soviet Union, for instance, also become "migrants," as their "useful labor" is "extracted and fed into the global media machine" (Rey Chow, *Writing Diaspora: Tactics of Intervention in Contemporary Cultural Studies* [Bloomington: Indiana University Press, 1993], 180).

19. Such an approach enables a study of diaspora that posits it, as Avtar Brah has described, as a "relationality of . . . migrancies across fields of social relations, subjectivity, and identity." Avtar Brah, *Cartographies of Diaspora: Contesting Identities* (London: Routledge, 1996), 16.

20. Braziel and Mannur, "Nation, Migration, Globalization," 8. For an extended discussion of the relation between diaspora and transnationalism, see Aihwa Ong, *Flexible Citizenship: The Cultural Logics of Transnationality* (Durham, N.C.: Duke University Press, 1999) and Karen Leonard, *Locating Home: India's Hyderabadis Abroad* (Stanford, Calif.: Stanford University Press, 2007).

21. Braziel and Mannur, "Nation, Migration, Globalization," 8.

22. For a discussion of the need to go beyond nationally demarcated units of study, see C. A. Bayly, Sven Beckert, Matthew Connelly, Isabel Hofmeyr, Wendy Kozol, and Patricia Seed, "AHR Conversation: On Transnational History," *American Historical Review* 111, no. 5 (2006): 1441–64.

23. Engseng Ho, *The Graves of Tarim: Genealogy and Mobility across the Indian Ocean* (Berkeley: University of California Press, 2006), 29.

24. The outpouring of works specifically about the African diaspora over the past two decades is too vast to survey in any meaningful way in note. Examples of scholarship that examine the emergence of the African diaspora as a field of inquiry from different perspectives include Brent Hayes Edwards, *The Practice of Diaspora: Literature, Translation, and the Rise of Black Internationalism* (Cambridge, Mass.: Harvard University

Press, 2003); Earl Lewis, "To Turn as on a Pivot: Writing African Americans into a History of Overlapping Diasporas," *American Historical Review* 100, no. 3 (1995): 765–87; and Paul Tiyambe Zeleza, "Rewriting the African Diaspora: Beyond the Black Atlantic," *African Affairs* 104 (2005): 35–68. Recent works that examine and exemplify bridge building across area studies include Michael A. Gomez, *Reversing Sail: A History of the African Diaspora* (Cambridge, UK: Cambridge University Press, 2005); Ruth Simms Hamilton, ed., *Routes of Passage: Rethinking the African Diaspora* (East Lansing: Michigan State University Press, 2006); Kristin Mann and Edna G. Bay, eds., *Rethinking the African Diaspora: The Making of a Black Atlantic World in the Bight of Benin and Brazil* (London: Routledge, 2001); Patrick Manning, "Africa and the African Diaspora," *Journal of African History* 44, no. 3 (2003): 487–506; Isidore Okpewho, Carole Boyce Davies, and Ali A. Mazrui, eds., *The African Diaspora: African Origins and New World Identities* (Bloomington: Indiana University Press, 2001); and Ben Vinson III, "Introduction: African (Black) Diaspora History, Latin American History," *The Americas* 63, no. 1 (July 2006): 1–18.

25. See, for example, Jesse Hoffnung-Garskof, *A Tale of Two Cities: Santo Domingo and New York after 1950* (Princeton, N.J.: Princeton University Press, 2007); Madeline Y. Hsu, *Dreaming of Gold, Dreaming of Home: Transnationalism and Migration Between the United States and South China, 1882–1943* (Stanford, Calif.: Stanford University Press, 2000); Roger Rouse, "Mexican Migration and the Social Space of Postmodernism," *Diaspora* 1, no. 1 (1991): 8–23; Kristin Ruggiero, ed., *Fragments of Memory: The Jewish Diaspora in Latin America and the Caribbean* (East Sussex: Sussex Academic Press, 1995); and Rhacel Salazar Parreñas and Lok C. D. Siu, eds., *Asian Diasporas: New Formations, New Conceptions* (Stanford, Calif.: Stanford University Press, 2007). For an elaboration of this point with reference to the South Asian diaspora, see Susan Koshy, "Introduction," in *Transnational South Asians: The Making of a Neo-Diaspora,* ed. Susan Koshy and R. Radhakrishnan (New Delhi: Oxford University Press, 2008).

26. Tejaswini Niranjana, *Mobilizing India: Women, Music, and Migration Between India and Trinidad* (Durham, N.C.: Duke University Press, 2006), 14.

27. In addition to Ho, *Graves of Tarim,* see Sugata Bose, *A Hundred Horizons: The Indian Ocean in the Age of Empire* (Cambridge, Mass.: Harvard University Press, 2006); and Pamila Gupta, Isabel Hofmeyr, and Michael Pearson, eds., *Eyes Across the Water: Navigating the Indian Ocean* (Pretoria: Unisa Press, 2010).

28. On the teleology of globalization, see Frederick Cooper, "Globalization," in *Colonialism in Question: Theory, Knowledge, History* (Berkeley: University of California Press, 2005), 91–112.

29. Ato Quayson, "Introduction: Area Studies, Diaspora Studies, and Critical Pedagogies," *Comparative Studies of South Asia, Africa, and the Middle East* 27, no. 3 (2007): 589.

30. Ibid.

31. The phrase "expressive configuration" is from Quayson, "Introduction," 589.

32. For a productive alternative to the idealization of flows, see Paul A. Silverstein's concept of transpolitics as discussed in Paul A. Silverstein, *Algeria in France: Transpolitics, Race, and Nation* (Bloomington: Indiana University Press, 2004).

33. The scholarship on this subject is immense, but for an illustration of the forms of gendered labor rendered invisible, see Rhacel Salazar Parreñas, *Servants of Globalization: Women, Migration, and Domestic Work* (Stanford, Calif.: Stanford University Press, 2001). For an analysis of the modeling of gendered identities in and through diaspora, see, for example, Jana Evans Braziel, *Artists, Performers, and Black Masculinity in the Haitian Diaspora* (Bloomington: Indiana University Press, 2008); with reference to the South Asian diaspora in the United States, see Annanya Bhattacharjee, "The Habit of Ex-Nomination: Nation, Woman, and the Indian Immigrant Bourgeoisie," *Public Culture* 5, no. 1 (1992): 19–43; and more recently, Monisha Das Gupta, Chapter 5, "Subverting Seductions: Queer Organizations" in *Unruly Immigrants: Rights, Activism, and Transnational South Asian Politics in the United States* (Durham, N.C.: Duke University Press, 2006).

34. Yen Le Espiritu, *Home Bound: Filipino American Lives Across Cultures, Communities, and Countries* (Berkeley: University of California Press, 2003).

35. See Radhika Mohanram, *Race, Diaspora, and the British Empire* (Minneapolis: University of Minnesota Press, 2007), xxi.

36. Lisa Lowe, "The Intimacies of Four Continents," in *Haunted by Empire: Geographies of Intimacy in North American History,* ed. Ann Stoler, 192 (Durham, N.C.: Duke University Press, 2006).

37. Ibid. For Lowe's delineation of the various meanings she ascribes to "intimacy," see 195–203.

38. Brent Hayes Edwards, "The Uses of Diaspora," *Social Text* 19, no. 1 (2001): 46.

39. Kim Butler, "From Black History to Diasporan History: Brazilian Abolition in Afro-Atlantic Context," *African Studies Review* 43, no.1 (2000): 127.

40. Brian Keith Axel, "Diasporic Imaginary," *Public Culture* 14, no. 2 (2002): 412.

41. Gayatri Gopinath, *Impossible Desires: Queer Diasporas and South Asian Public Cultures* (Durham, N.C.: Duke University Press, 2005), 10. Gopinath foregrounds the ways in which a queer diasporic framework can unsettle the normalizing effects of diaspora. See also Martin F. Manalansan IV, *Global Divas: Filipino Gay Men in the Diaspora* (Durham, N.C.: Duke University Press, 2003).

42. See Stuart Hall, "Cultural Identity and Cinematic Representation," in *Black British Cultural Studies: A Reader,* ed. Houston A. Baker, Jr., Manthia Diawara, and Ruth H. Lindeborg, 214 (Chicago: University of Chicago Press, 1996). See also Michael Gomez, "Introduction," in *Diasporic Africa: A Reader* (New York: New York University Press, 2006).

43. Jenny Sharpe, this volume.

44. See also Marina Carter and Khal Torabully, *Coolitude: An Anthology of the Indian Labor Diaspora* (London: Anthem Press, 2002), 15.

45. As Rhacel Salazar Parreñas and Lok Siu have argued in a broader context, it may be this long-distance connection or shared belonging that most usefully distinguishes diaspora as a phenomenon rather than a shared point of origin or homeland. Parreñas and Siu, "Introduction," in *Asian Diasporas,* 1–28.

46. Primarily due to the efforts of organizations such as the Global Indian Diaspora Heritage Society, which largely comprises the descendants of indentured laborers, in

January 2011 the Kolkata Memorial was unveiled at the Kidderpore Docks in Kolkata, India, to commemorate the thousands of laborers who departed from there over the course of the nineteenth century.

47. Rogers Brubaker, "The 'Diaspora' Diaspora," *Ethnic and Racial Studies* 28, no. 1 (2005): 12.

48. Ann Stoler, "Intimidations of Empire: Predicaments of the Tactile and Unseen," in *Haunted by Empire: Geographies of Intimacy in North American History,* ed. Ann Stoler, 15 (Durham, N.C.: Duke University Press, 2006).

49. For a delineation of a definition of "imperial diaspora" in this context, see Butler, "Defining Diaspora," 202. For a broader discussion of "imperial diaspora," see Cohen, *Global Diasporas.*

50. In mapping various trajectories of intimacy through commensality as well as conjugality, one is mindful of Ballantyne and Burton's caveat that a study of the realm of the intimate is not reducible to sexuality alone (8). Rather, as they rightly point out, it is important to acknowledge the "broader investigative possibilities that attention to the body and/or the history of intimacy" yields, given, as they point out, that "bodies are not inscribed with meaning only through sexual desire" (8–9). Tony Ballantyne and Antoinette Burton, "Introduction," *Moving Subjects: Gender, Mobility, and Intimacy in an Age of Global Empire,* ed. Tony Ballantyne and Antoinette Burton (Urbana: University of Illinois Press, 2009).

51. Parama Roy, this volume.

52. For an examination of the "British diaspora," see Mohanram, *Race, Diaspora, and the British Empire,* and Leonard Tennenhouse, *The Importance of Feeling English: American Literature and the British Diaspora, 1750–1850* (Princeton, N.J.: Princeton University Press, 2007).

53. Sandhya Shukla, *India Abroad: Diasporic Cultures of Postwar America and England* (Princeton, N.J.: Princeton University Press, 2003), 5.

54. The point about the "unwritten" nature of diaspora is made in Butler, "Defining Diaspora," 212.

55. While this has been variously discussed, for one iteration of this point see Inderpal Grewal, *Transnational America: Feminisms, Diasporas, Neoliberalisms* (Durham, N.C.: Duke University Press, 2005), 80.

56. Benedict Anderson, *Imagined Communities: Reflections on the Origin and Spread of Nationalism* (London: Verso Press, 1983).

57. Ania Loomba, Suvir Kaul, Matti Bunzl, Antoinette Burton, and Jed Esty, "Beyond What? An Introduction," in *Postcolonial Studies and Beyond,* ed. Ania Loomba, Suvir Kaul, Matti Bunzl, Antoinette Burton, and Jed Esty, 21 (Durham, N.C.: Duke University Press, 2005). For this point, see also Jana Evans Braziel, *Diaspora: An Introduction* (London: Wiley-Blackwell, 2008).

58. For an example of the fruits that such a global approach can offer, see Carl H. Nightingale, "The Transnational Contexts of Early Twentieth-Century American Urban Segregation," *Journal of Social History* 39, no. 3 (2006): 667–702.

59. Standard references for the constitutive relation between nationalism and the novel include Homi Bhabha, ed., *Nation and Narration* (London: Routledge, 1990); and Patrick Parrinder, *Nation and Novel: The English Novel from its Origins to the Present Day* (Oxford: Oxford University Press, 2006), among others. But literary scholars are also tracing the reconfiguration of the novel form in a transnational setting: see, for instance, Bishnupriya Ghosh, *When Borne Across: Literary Cosmopolitics in the Contemporary Indian Novel* (New Brunswick, N.J.: Rutgers University Press, 2004); Betty Joseph, this volume.

PART 1
INTERROGATING TERMS

CHAPTER ONE

The Middle Passages of Black Migration

JENNY SHARPE

The *middle passage* is a particularly charged signifier within a black literary imagination. Carl Pedersen calls it "arguably the defining moment of the African-American experience."[1] He identifies a literary geography that extends the signification of the middle passage beyond the historical moment of the African slave trade, when the term narrowly referred to the second or "middle" portion of the triangular trade route between Europe, Africa, and the Americas. In response to a Eurocentric perspective that considered the middle passage as a rupture with African culture, there developed an Afrocentric one that sought to establish continuity with Africa. Pedersen, however, is interested in those writers who charted a third path. For Afro-Caribbean intellectuals such as C. L. R. James, Edward Kamau Brathwaite, George Lamming, Wilson Harris, Édouard Glissant, and Derek Walcott, the transatlantic passage of enslaved Africans did not signify the absence of black creativity, as it did for European colonizers. Rather, it signaled the beginning of a new creolized and hybridized culture.[2] To the Afro-Caribbean writers that Pedersen identifies, one can add black British writers such as Caryl Phillips and Fred D'Aguiar, who have fictionalized the lives of slaves who journey back and forth along the transatlantic trade route, and artists such as Keith Piper and Lubaina Himid, whose seascapes memorialize the death and suffering of slaves who experienced the middle passage. These black British writers and artists not only resurrect middle passage images in order to let the dead bear witness to the past, they also transform those images so that they can speak to the more recent migration of people from Africa and the Caribbean. If, during an era of black power and nation building, the middle passage signified a fundamental connection with Africa, the term has more recently been deployed to describe multiple crossings that transform the meaning of diaspora into a vital and ongoing process.[3] The routes traveled by black migrants do not necessarily retrace the same paths of the slave ships: they cross continental Europe, the English Channel, and the Caribbean Sea. The theoretical "routing" of a transatlantic black diaspora thus involves not making the multiple crossings cohere into a single narrative but rather maintaining their temporal and spatial disjunctures and discontinuities.

This new imaginative geography is present in Paul Gilroy's *The Black Atlantic: Modernity and Double Consciousness* (1993), which invokes the ship as a chronotope for charting the temporal and spatial axes of a transatlantic culture.[4] The ship, for Gilroy, represents the crisscrossing of travelers and cultures along the triangular slave trade route, which is a movement that complicates a simple, linear narrative of a black diaspora originating in Africa. Instead of denoting a foundational connection with Africa, the middle passage in Gilroy's black Atlantic model represents a "catastrophic rupture" that hurtled diasporic space into a linear temporal order.[5] Alluding to Gilroy's explanation, James Clifford suggests that the middle passage does not simply exist as a past moment in time because its trauma continues to be repeated. "For black Atlantic diaspora consciousness," he observes, "the recurring break where time stops and restarts is the Middle Passage. Enslavement and its aftermaths—displaced, repeated structures of racialization and exploitation—constitute a pattern of black experiences inextricably woven in the fabric of hegemonic modernity."[6] Time, for a transatlantic black diaspora, is broken; the past can, and does, coexist with the present.

The simultaneity of past and present is incorporated into the narrative structure of two literary works that metaphorically extend the middle passage to contemporary conditions of black migration. Caryl Phillips' novel *A Distant Shore* (2003) tells the story of an African refugee who is smuggled into post-9/11 Europe as a traumatic journey that mirrors the middle passage and ends in death.[7] Edwidge Danticat's short story "Children of the Sea" (1993) allegorizes the middle passage for conveying the present hardships and future uncertainties experienced by Haitian boat people fleeing the political instability of their nation.[8] Both works suggest that although the waters modern migrants cross may not be as vast as the Atlantic Ocean, their voyages are no less perilous than the ones made by slaves. They transform received images from the past in order to critique the present treatment of black refugees. They also, however, harness the symbolic value of the middle passage as the beginning of a transatlantic black diaspora for rethinking its meaning. Both works expose the limitations of a diaspora model that suggests a unified history and destiny of all peoples of African descent. *A Distant Shore* revives a middle passage memory to show the isolation of the black man living in the diaspora, while "Children of the Sea" frames that memory with a Haitian worldview that offers a counternarrative to the middle passage's broken temporality.

Phillips often deploys the middle passage as a metaphor for the psychological state of homelessness associated with migrancy.[9] In *A Distant Shore,* two intersecting narratives about an African refugee and a divorced English woman show how the term "stranger" does not apply to immigrants alone. "England has changed," observes Dorothy, a retired schoolteacher, about the former mining town where she grew up and to which she has now returned. "These days it's difficult to tell who's from around here and who's not. Who belongs and who's a stranger. It's disturbing. It doesn't feel right" (3). Here the sense of homelessness applies to a middle-aged English woman who is estranged from a hometown that offers her no asylum, equal to its treatment of the lone black inhabitant, Solomon Bartholomew. Their shared state of mind makes them shipmates in the turbulent national waters. The white woman is also connected to the black man as the potential recipient of his story. "This is a woman to whom I might tell my story," he thinks. "If I do not share my story, then I have only this one year to my life. I am a one-year-old man who walks with heavy steps. I am a man burdened with hidden history" (266). Since Solomon is beaten to death before he has the opportunity to share his story with Dorothy, the moment for bridging the colonial divide through an unburdening of history is lost. The English nation remains broken and disjointed, like the novel's narrative. Only in the second half does the reader learn that Gabriel, an African refugee, and Solomon, the night watchman at the housing development in which Dorothy lives, are one and the same person.

Solomon, whose real name is Gabriel, comes from a war-ravaged African country that is not explicitly identified. He claims to have belonged to a smaller tribe that was disliked for controlling most of the businesses in the capital city and their tribal land in the south. After a member of his tribe becomes president, there is a military coup and soldiers begin killing his people. His father sends him to join rebel troops in the south, where he trains in the bush for guerilla warfare. Although Gabriel refuses to kill the villagers his captain denounces as traitors, government troops destroy his entire family in revenge anyway. After witnessing the massacre of his family from the concealed space of a cupboard, he pays his uncle to smuggle him out of the country.

Phillips places Gabriel's journey out of Africa within the memory of the middle passage. The discomfort Gabriel experiences evokes images of the hardships slaves were made to endure in their long and arduous trip to the

Americas. The first leg of his journey is in the back of a truck, where he is made to lie down alongside other people concealed under a heavy tarpaulin:

> As the engine roars to life, Gabriel realizes that, trussed as they are like cargo, this first part of their journey is not going to be pleasant. He can feel the dampness of other men's perspiring bodies, and it is not possible to distinguish whose arm or leg is pressing up against him (84).

The truck's cramped quarters conjure up that infamous line drawing from Thomas Clarkson's *History of the Rise, Progress, and Accomplishment of the Abolition of the Slave Trade* (1808) of a cross-section of the slave ship *Brookes* depicting shackled slaves packed sardine-style into its hull. Whereas in the past, African slaves had only further misery awaiting them on the other side, Gabriel anticipates a better future: "He knows that if he is lucky the past will soon be truly past, and that with every gasp of the acrid air beneath the heavy tarpaulin, life is taking him beyond this nightmare and to a new place and a new beginning" (84). These words, which allude to a linear model of history underpinning post-Enlightenment narratives of progress, are undermined by the novel's temporal structure.

The subsequent paragraph jumps to a future point in time after Gabriel has reached England, where he finds himself in a state that differs little from the cramped conditions aboard the truck. Sedated and strapped to a bed by his hands and feet, he is confined to a filthy immigration cell where he receives little food or water. The story of one African man's journey to England is interspersed with scenes of his detention, which is a narrative structure that undermines the character's own belief that he is escaping to freedom. The England of Phillips' novel is not a liberating space where the chains of slavery are broken, as British abolitionists once claimed; rather, it exists as a xenophobic nation where new invisible bonds are introduced. The movement back and forth in time between scenes of Gabriel's escape from his warring nation and his immobilization in a British jail prolongs the nightmarish crossing from which there appears to be little escape. The novel extends the middle passage trauma from sea to land in order to undermine the perception of Europe as a safe haven.

Each stage of Gabriel's journey echoes the harrowing experience of the African slave's transatlantic crossing except that continental Europe acts in the place of the Atlantic Ocean. The truck delivers Gabriel to a cargo aircraft that carries approximately one hundred men and women from Africa to an unknown destination in Eastern Europe. On their arrival, the refugees are made to strip naked so they can be hosed down with icy cold water, just as

African slaves were when they disembarked from slave ships on the other side of the Atlantic. The migrants are loaded onto a bus and then a boat, which crosses a small body of water to place them in "Europe proper" (90). Gabriel subsequently boards a train for France. For the final leg of his journey across the English Channel, he is forced to stand on a small ledge on the outside of a ferry's hull while hanging on to a metal chain. His entry into England is reminiscent of the *Zong* incident recounted by Quobna Ottobah Cugoano in *Thoughts and Sentiments on the Evil of Slavery* (1787). While journeying from Africa to Jamaica in 1781, the unscrupulous captain of the *Zong* slave ship ordered that 133 sick and dying slaves be thrown overboard so he could collect insurance for the human "cargo" lost at sea. Cugoano records that one slave was believed to have survived being thrown overboard by hanging on to a rope extended by slaves from inside the ship's hull.[10]

Despite Gabriel's success in avoiding drowning at sea (his Chinese companion is not so fortunate), he meets an unnatural end at the hands of racist skinheads. On being bound and held captive by a gang of threatening youths, he thinks, "I am a man who has survived, and I would rather die like a free man than suffer my blood to be drawn like a slave's" (251). Gabriel manages to free himself and attack them "like a madman" (47), for which he is mercilessly beaten to death. The gang's action, which is to dump the African man's body in a canal to make his death look like an accident, repeats that of the *Zong* ship captain. The image of Gabriel's lifeless body being found face down in a canal allegorically alludes to his drowning at sea. Phillips uses the symbolic value of the middle passage as a space of death to launch a critique of Britain as a free and democratic nation.

The middle passage in *A Distant Shore* does not simply refer to the journey from one coastline to another, but it is extended spatially and metaphorically to the interior of Britain. Gabriel discovers on his arrival that he has not arrived anywhere, but remains a castaway at sea: "This is not the England that he thought he was traveling to, and these shipwrecked people are not the people that he imagined he would discover" (155). Scarcely does the thought flit through his mind when he realizes that the fellow countryman who befriended him has made off with his money. The novel's model of diaspora is a bleak one of homelessness and isolation; there are no signs of a black community.

The England of *A Distant Shore* belongs to a post-9/11 Europe in which some people, generally those with darker skins and a different religion, are stripped of their humanity. The novel's dark vision reflects Britain's growing hostility toward asylum seekers during the 1990s, as European refugees escaping communism gave way to Asians and Africans fleeing civil war. The xenophobic response to asylum seekers, flamed by the British press, resurrected images from Enoch Powell's 1968 "Rivers of Blood" speech.[11] Gabriel is befriended by a teenage girl but is sent to a detention center for illegal immigrants after her father accuses him of raping her. He shares his cell with an Iraqi man who eventually dies from neglect: "He died in the cell and they let him lie there on the floor like a dog" (104). Gabriel is eventually released from the detention center and settles down in the former mining town of Weston, located halfway between Manchester and Birmingham. The specificity of this location is a direct allusion to the 1999 Asylum and Immigration Act that instituted a policy of dispersing asylum seekers throughout Britain, an act intended to avert their overcrowding in London and the South East but which increased their racial victimization in the newly settled areas.[12] Weston is in the West Midlands, one of the ten consortia contracted for the resettlement of asylum seekers.

While London is now recognized as the multiethnic, multiracial city that it is, the West Midlands of Phillips' novel appears locked within a time warp.[13] Native-born English exhibit a tribal attitude toward the presence of a black man in their midst as they make it clear that Gabriel is not welcome. He is sent seven threatening letters, one of them with razor blades sewn into the paper, and dog excrement is shoved through his letter-slot.[14] Rather than endorsing modernity's narrative of progress, *A Distant Shore* shows how time is stuck in a cycle of repetitions. It suggests, through the end or *telos* of Gabriel's journey, that the trauma of the middle passage continues to be repeated some two hundred years after the African slave trade ended. Phillips wants to remind his readers of a history that cannot be relegated to the past so long as its racist legacy continues to exist. The death of Gabriel's Iraqi cellmate adds a new layer of violence, one in which a history of slavery and empire intersects with the more recent war on Islam.

But even as the novel records with great precision the time and place of post-9/11 Europe, it actively refuses to similarly locate the civil war of Gabriel's African nation. The country from which Gabriel escapes could be any of several war-torn African nations: Liberia, Sierra Leone, Rwanda, Angola, or the Republic of Congo. The brief exchange he has with an African man who approaches him in London—the stranger says "I think you are from my country," to which "Gabriel says the name of his country" (153)—demonstrates an intentional withholding of his nationality from the story. On a different occasion he is asked whether he is Afro-Caribbean, to which he responds that he is "from Africa" (169). The novel seeks to demonstrate that details concerning the name and location of Gabriel's homeland are immaterial to a racist immigration system that classifies him by his outsider status derived, in part, from the color of his skin. Like Olaudah Equiano centuries before him, he is known simply as "the African." Yet Equiano does identify his people as Igbo and opens his slave narrative with a detailed ethnographic description of their culture, practices, and beliefs.[15] This act of self-identification is the sign of a refusal to accept an identity that was imposed upon him by slavery and to establish, within a narrative form that begins with "I was born a slave," the memory of freedom in Igboland.

The novel's presentation of Gabriel as "African" both subsumes the continent's diverse history under a single, homogenous name and extends to continental Africa a cultural identity that was born of slavery. As Stuart Hall explains, there was no place called "Africa" except in its absence, for it is only after linguistically and culturally diverse peoples were transported overseas and mixed together with each other that they came to be known, and identify themselves, as "African."[16] While Britain is presented as being haunted by its slave past, "Africa" exists as a place outside of that history. The only memory of his homeland Gabriel possesses is that of the tribal war he is trying to escape. In the absence of any explanation for the intertribal wars in which soldiers "drink and kill, and kill and drink" (122), we are left with a "rivers of blood and mountains of skulls" vision of African culture. Gabriel's generic African identity not only extends to Africans an identity that was the effect of diasporic displacement, it also locates African nations outside the imperial violence through which the novel's critique of the mistreatment of asylum seekers is being made.

Charles Piot argues that we need to consider Africa as "diaspora-derivative," a term he uses to draw attention to how the transatlantic slave trade altered the culture and political dynamics of West Africa.[17] In order to place Phillips' novel within the frame of a diaspora-derived Africa, I want to propose that the political circumstances of Gabriel's story are based loosely on those of Sierra Leone, which perhaps more than any other African country, with the exception of Liberia, was a nation born of the British abolition of the African slave trade. Initially established in 1787 as a refuge for rescued slaves, Sierra Leone became a British Crown colony in 1808. The original British freemen who settled in Freetown were later joined by African American slaves who had escaped to Canada during the American War of Independence and Jamaican maroons who had been deported to Nova Scotia for resisting the British colonial government. By the middle of the nineteenth century, tens of thousands of Africans captured from French, Spanish, and Portuguese slave ships intercepted by the British navy were relocated in Sierra Leone around Freetown. These repatriated Africans, who came from different tribal groups across West Africa, intermarried with the original settlers to form their own ethnic group. The new tribe became known as the Krio, which is a contraction of the Yoruba expression *Kiriyo* for "to walk about" and "be satisfied." The Krio—whom the British called "Creole," thereby conflating them with island-born Caribbean slaves—developed their own language and a hybridized culture that combined African and Western elements. They were able to acquire some wealth through trading.[18] When the British began to expand their business interests into the interior of Sierra Leone, they favored the Krio, thus sowing the seeds for Temne and Mende resentment of the minority group's economic dominance.

Gabriel's life story inhabits a (albeit unnamed) Sierra Leonean history to which the novel, as a postmodern work of fiction, is not entirely faithful. He belongs to a minority tribe much like the Krio, one that he claims "formed the backbone of the economy" (122) because it ran the businesses. The army that he joins resembles Sierra Leone's Revolutionary United Front (RUF) led by Foday Sankoh, a rebel leader in the country's ten-year-long civil war that ended in 2002. The RUF was notorious for funding its war with smuggled diamonds and using armies of child soldiers. The boys, often orphaned or kidnapped from their families, were injected forcibly with cocaine to numb them to their war of terror that included such atrocities as amputating the limbs of villagers who supported the government.[19] Although child soldiers have been used in Liberia and the Democratic Republic of Congo, the spectacular imagery of the RUF army appears in Phillips' novel by way of the surreal world Gabriel enters when he travels south to join his people's rebel forces. He commands boy soldiers who are given cannabis mixed with gunpowder to make them feel invincible, and he witnesses villagers "with swollen stumps where their arms and legs used to be" (126). The youths carry teddy bears and wear Donald Duck masks or pink lipstick as signs of their invincibility, while their leader, Captain JuJu, wears Ray-Ban glasses and Nike sneakers and adorns his hut with glossy pinups of American movie stars.

Through its acknowledgment of the globalization of commodity culture, the novel avoids an ethnographic writing that freezes Africa's interethnic conflict in some timeless tribal past. Yet in the absence of any historical context for the "savagery" (131) that Gabriel as narrator refuses to endorse, the reader is left with disembodied acts of violence that reattach themselves to stereotypical images of African barbarism. Although the novel suggests that European nations exhibit the same tribal mindset that is generally associated with Africa, it does not overturn or complicate the idea of a tribalized Africa. In this regard, it extends the modernist vision of Conrad's *Heart of Darkness,* which depicts Europeans committing acts as savage as any African but only inasmuch as Africa serves as the model for its savagery.[20] Whereas Gabriel's presumed journey to freedom in Europe is disrupted by images of a slave past and a post-9/11 future, the images that disrupt his quiet life in postindustrial England are the nightmarish memories of his country's civil war:

> I remembered my mother lying on a floor in my now far-off country with blood pouring from her wounds. I remembered my father and my sisters being shot like animals. My dreams contained my history. Night and day I tried not to think of these things anymore. I tried not to think of these people any more. I wanted to set these people free so that they might become people in another man's story (263).

The history from which Gabriel is trying to escape involves the dehumanization of his family at the hands of a warring tribe. The ghosts haunting his private dreams belong to his nation's interethnic war.

I am interested in reading Sierra Leonean history as a *supplement*—an excess contained within, rather than a social reality that exists outside—to the text of Phillips' novel. To consider Gabriel as Krio is to see that the transatlantic black diaspora includes Africans at home and not just those who experience the homelessness of migration. The Krio are undeniably African, no less than African slaves transported to the United States are American. At the same time, their hybridized culture, which combines elements of not only European and African civilizations but also different African tribes, bears the signature of the West's benevolent effort to reverse the violent effects of the middle passage, to undo its own savagery through the utopian vision of returning freed slaves to their homeland.

A Distant Shore critiques the abolitionist presentation of England as a refuge for escaped slaves while simultaneously exposing the fissures in a present-day government program that presents itself as helping asylum seekers. By extending the space of the middle passage from sea to land, the novel exposes the racism that still exists in Britain. The middle passage does not simply refer to the experience of black people living in the diaspora; it also places the British nation itself under its sign. Past and present are linked through a history of slavery and the lingering effects of the dissolution of empire. The novel also reflects on the absence of community that derives its symbolic value from the middle passage as that which connects people in the diaspora with Africa. However, even as it redraws the lines of the second or middle portion of the triangular slave trade route to include continental Europe and Great Britain, Africa exists outside of that imperial geography.[21]

Danticat's "Children of the Sea" takes a more localized approach to redrawing the map of the African slave trade by extending the Atlantic Ocean to the Caribbean Sea. The short story was initially published under the title of

"From the Ocean Floor" in October 1993, which was at the height of the Haitians' exodus from their country. It is set in the period following the September 1991 military coup that resulted in President Jean-Bertrand Aristide's exile to the United States.[22] This was an era when the U.S. government distinguished Haitian from Cuban boat people by defining the former as economic rather than political refugees, a distinction that allowed the Coast Guard to return Haitians to the civil war they were escaping. Danticat's story makes it evident that the distinction was not only politically motivated—since it was based on Cold War politics that led the United States to support anticommunist dictators such as "Baby Doc" Duvalier, the Haitian president whom Aristide replaced—but also racial, since Cubans tend to be white-identified.[23] While hundreds of Haitian boat people drowned in the Caribbean Sea, thousands more were tortured and murdered by a military government that restored the Duvalier dynasty's secret police. Through its metaphoric extension of a middle passage geography to Haiti, Danticat's short story suggests that Haitians remain chained to a slave past from which they are struggling to break free. At the same time, the story stages how the idea of a black diaspora that traces its beginnings to a shared origin in Africa has given way to one of transnational diasporas rooted in national cultures.

"Children of the Sea" opens with an unidentified Haitian man on a small makeshift boat making his way, along with thirty-six other people, to the United States. It unfolds via alternating journal entries made by the man and his girlfriend in Haiti. The reader learns that he belonged to a federation of youth who denounced the military regime on a radio show. When soldiers began rounding up other members of his group, he decided to attempt the hazardous trip to Miami by sea. He teases his girlfriend in his unmailed letters to her about the sheltered life she has lived and suggests that if he had been born a girl, he might not be in the situation in which he finds himself. By the end of the story, however, she learns that soldiers are coming for her as a member of the same youth federation to which her lover belonged. In the meantime, the boat is slowly sinking as it springs a number of leaks, which its occupants attempt to patch with tar. When the girlfriend hears that a boat has sunk off the Bahamian coast, she knows, through the prophetic image of a black butterfly, that her lover has died. As the recipient of the news of his drowning, she is connected to his watery grave.

The literary device of an epistolary exchange allows for the parallel stories of the circumstances of the man's escape from and the woman's confinement within Haiti to be told. Phillips makes a similar move in *A Distant Shore* when he splits its narration between an African refugee and an English woman. However, since his dual narration is in the interest of showing what Homi

Bhabha characterizes as "the [English] nation split within itself, articulating the heterogeneity of its population," it does not explicitly address the male-gendering of black Atlantic narratives.[24] There is a black female refugee, Amma, who belongs to the group Gabriel travels with across Europe, but she steals away during the night once they arrive in France and in the process leaves the story. Amma serves more as a marker for the absent black women in transatlantic narratives than as a character with a story of her own to tell. Danticat's short story intervenes more strongly into pre-existing narratives in which diasporic travel is associated with a mobility that is gendered as male.

"Children of the Sea" exposes the male gendering of black Atlantic narratives by extending the uncertainty of undocumented travel to the presumed sanctity of domestic space. The two lovers are not only linked by the un-mailed letters they write to each other but also by parallel circumstances in which they find themselves. Since the army has taken over the streets and public institutions, the woman is "cramped inside all day" (4), just as for the man there is no escape from the cramped quarters of the small boat. The presence of a fifteen-year-old pregnant girl, Célianne, on the boat breaks down the opposition between home as a place of sanctuary and the open sea as a space of risk. Although the boat people think Célianne is escaping the disgrace of an illicit affair with a married man, they later learn that she had been raped by ten to twelve soldiers after they forced her brother to sleep with their mother and subsequently arrested him for his moral crime. The military's use of rape and incest as instruments of terror shows that women are not exempt from the trauma of civil war. Célianne's face is covered with scars, the result of self-inflicted razor wounds in her futile effort to conceal her shame. When she gives birth to a stillborn baby, her fellow passengers force her to throw its tiny body overboard to lighten the boat's load. She does so unwillingly and jumps into the water after it.

Behind the drowning of Célianne and her baby flits the ghosts of African women who were the victims of rape and who drowned themselves or their mixed-raced babies. But Célianne's situation both is and is not the same as that of raped slave women, for her body was violated in her homeland at the hands of fellow Haitians. The story alludes to the middle passage in order to acknowledge Haitian soldiers' engagement in a violence that repeats the criminal acts of European slave traders. As Elizabeth DeLoughrey explains in her reading of the story, "the middle passage must be 'charted' by contemporary Caribbean migrants, but without a recognition of the ways in which state-sanctioned violence (either in European slaving or Haitian autocracy) is repeated, Caribbean peoples are destined to reproduce the same violent diaspora."[25]

The middle passage as metaphor is Janus-faced. As a signifier for the beginning of a black diasporic culture, it embodies mobility and creativity; as the path toward enslavement, it represents stasis and social death. Writing from within the milieu of black Britain as a hybridized, transatlantic culture, Gilroy emphasizes the former meaning, positing "the image of ships in motion . . . as a central organizing symbol" of the black Atlantic, whose waters denote fluidity, movement, and transcultural exchange.[26] Joan Dayan is critical of Gilroy's symbolic ship for not considering political and economic migrants "who do not choose to leave their homes in celebration of 'nomadism.' "[27] Danticat uses the image of a small and leaky boat that sinks before it reaches land for disengaging migrancy from its association with mobility. The words penned by her character aboard the boat—"From here, ships must be like a mirage in the desert" (27)—highlights the different perspective from each seafaring vessel. For Haitian boat people, the dispossession of the past meets "the hopelessness of the future" (5) in a present journey to nowhere. The middle passage here is depicted as the state of limbo in which *all* Haitians find themselves—between freedom and bondage, the human and spiritual world, earth and air. The story, however, also interrupts the stasis of a middle passage temporality with the prophetic time of Vodou culture. I want to suggest that Danticat's integration of popular ways of knowing into her story offers an alternative perspective on the middle passage to the one belonging to the historical records. I will proceed by way of Diana Taylor's concept of "repertoire," which offers a methodological lens for reading textual representation as a performance that destabilizes archival memory.

Taylor uses "repertoire" in *The Archive and the Repertoire: Performing Cultural Memory in the Americas* to designate a form of memory that does not presume stable objects in the archive but ones whose meanings change across time. Although she proposes the term for addressing those ephemeral forms of knowledge that are repeatable in dance, theater, song, and ritual, she also insists that the distinction between ephemeral and enduring memory is a conceptual one based on the archive as a privileged site of historical memory.[28] "The repertoire," she continues, "allows for an alternative perspective on historical processes of transnational contact and invites a remapping of the Americas, this time by following traditions of embodied practice."[29] The concept of repertoire can be borrowed usefully from performance studies for reading Danticat's incorporation of popular ways of knowing into her short story. I want to present this popular Haitian perspective—grounded in ritualized religious practices—as a way of rethinking a black Atlantic cartography derived from the enduring records of the middle passage.

If I had to name a single nineteenth-century memorialization of the middle passage that carries currency in contemporary black Atlantic studies it would have to be J. M. W. Turner's rendition of the *Zong* ship drownings in *The Slave Ship (Slavers Throwing Overboard the Dead and Dying, Typhoon Coming On)* (1840), painted almost sixty years after the event. For Marcus Wood, the mixed reception of the painting illustrates the difficulty of coming to terms with the memory of slavery that his book, *Blind Memory: Visual Representations of Slavery in England and America,* addresses.[30] Gilroy considers the painting's transatlantic movement from London to Boston to be emblematic of the cultural exchanges his book describes.[31] The picture of slaves being thrown overboard constitutes for Ian Baucom in *Specters of the Atlantic: Finance Capital, Slavery, and the Philosophy of History* a haunting of the *Zong* tragedy that continues into the present. Baucom considers the painting as an effort to transform an "indescribable, unrepresentable middle passage" into a representative image of the evils of the African slave trade.[32] Yet Turner does so, he argues, only through an artistic abstraction that depicts the dying and drowned slave's suffering less than it does the *idea* of suffering, thus painting a picture for the contemplative mind of the liberal humanist. "We stand as spectators before it," he writes of Turner's painting, "not as witnesses in it."[33]

"Children of the Sea" places the reader within its scene of drowning, not simply to give visibility to the misery and suffering of Haitian boat people, but also to suggest a worldview that exists outside of the oceanic cartography of liberal humanism. When the male narrator records that he overhears the captain whispering that he had to "*do something* with some of the people who never recovered from seasickness" (20), the reader is reminded of the *Zong* ship captain who threw sick slaves overboard. When he claims that he has to defecate as they did on slave ships, he is suggesting that they are repeating that primordial journey from Africa. As the brutal sun blackens his skin further with the passing of each day, he says he is becoming "African," a statement that suggests a journey backwards in time. When he is "finally an African" (11), he has a prophetic dream that he has died and gone to heaven, except that it is not the heaven he expected because "it was at the bottom of the sea" (12). The sea space is explicitly named in his journal as *Guinin.* "I feel like we are sailing for Africa," he records. "Maybe we will go to Guinin, to live with the spirits, to be with everyone who has come and has died before us" (14). To become African, then, does not assert a stalled temporality or even a narrative of return so much as an arrival at Guinin, a sea space whose *kreyòl* name is derived from the European term for the African west coast, Guinea. As an imaginative geography, Guinin refers to a spiritual place that is reached after death from under the sea. The Haitian belief in *en bas dio* (the gods below) was born of the middle passage. There is no single explanation for or agreement on the exact location of Guinin, but the idea behind Guinin is that the spirits of the dead did not have to be stranded in a hostile and foreign land even if their bodies could not be returned to Africa. In "Children of the Sea," Danticat places a middle passage memory within the framework of a Haitian worldview, thereby emphasizing a diasporic Caribbean perspective over a European one. She also rewrites this Haitian imaginary born of the middle passage in order to account for the shifting dynamics of pan-Caribbeanness.

Whereas in the past the spirits of slaves could at least find refuge in Guinin, Haitian migrants are so unwelcomed that the male narrator ironically remarks they would probably be turned away from Guinin as well (14). He writes about sacrificing his two gourds of coins to Agwé, the Vodou *lwa* of the water and protector of ships, as objects are thrown overboard one by one in an effort to lighten the boat's load. He is finally forced to throw his notebook into the sea. Whatever written record of the journey that exists—an old man requests that he write down his full name, the wonderfully elaborate Justin Moïse André Nozius Joseph Frank Osnac Maximilien—is committed to the ocean floor. Vodou offerings to Agwé are often floated out to sea on handmade rafts, the sinking of which is a sign that the *lwa* has accepted the offering. The story suggests, through the eventual sinking of the boat, that Haitian people are being sacrificed.

Forced to take the longer route to Miami because neighboring islands will not accept them, Haitian boat people are at greater risk of drowning. One of the refugees expresses how they are not wanted in the Bahamas despite the similarity of their cultures:

> They treat Haitians like dogs in the Bahamas, a woman says. To them, we are not human. Even though their music sounds like ours. Their people look like ours. Even though we had the same African fathers who probably crossed these same seas together (14).

The woman's words allude to a colonial mindset that undermines the formation of a pan-Caribbean identity. The dehumanization of Haitians by their neighboring Caribbean islanders ("To them, we are not human") is placed within the memory of the middle passage ("Even though we had the same African fathers who probably crossed these same seas together"). Instead of looking to Haiti as the first black republic, neighboring Caribbean nations look down on it as the poorest country in the Western hemisphere, whose people are victims of poverty, violence, and superstitious beliefs. The short story also implicates the United States in the racial denigration of Haitians. The male narrator speaks of how the U.S. Coast Guard distinguishes Haitians from Cubans by their color—a distinction that the Cubans share "even though some of the Cubans are black too" (8).

"Children of the Sea" shows how a pan-Caribbean identity remains a distant ideal so long as mestizos do not consider themselves black and Caribbean peoples disassociate themselves from their Haitian neighbors. "Haiti free but cut off from the world," writes Édouard Glissant about the missed opportunity for a pan-Caribbean revolutionary consciousness following the Haitian revolution, "the process of exchange that could have *created* the Caribbean dried up."[34] Glissant nonetheless deploys the image of slave bodies lining the ocean floor for establishing the heterogeneity of submarine, multiple connections between the islands and as a sign of the transcultural nature of the black diaspora.[35] In "Children of the Sea," the ocean floor contains not only slave bodies but also the corpses of Haitian boat people. These latter bodies are the sign of the transnational nature of *dyaspora* or people of the Haitian diaspora through the formation of subterranean connections between Haiti and the American mainland.

In view of the failure of pan-Caribbean unity, Danticat's story favors a national diaspora over an African or even pan-Caribbean one. A veiled allusion to the scene of drowning in "Children of the Sea" appears in "Caroline's Wedding," the last story of the collection of short stories to which "Children of the Sea" belongs and which takes place in New York. In a Brooklyn church a Haitian priest calls on the congregation of "transients" and "nomads" to pray for 129 refugees who had drowned at sea that week—a number that approximates the 133 slaves thrown overboard the *Zong*.[36] As he reads off a list of their names, the people who knew them express their grief. Two of the victims the priest mentions even though he does not have their names are Célianne and her stillborn baby. "A young woman," he recounts, "who was pregnant when she took a boat from Haiti and then later gave birth to her child on that boat. A few hours after the child was born, its precious life went out, like a candle in a storm, and the mother with her infant in her arms dived into the sea" (167). The priest's knowledge (how could he know?) and commemoration of the dead suggests that the Haitian boat people who drowned were not completely lost at sea. Unlike the Africans aboard the *Zong*, for whom all records of their identities have been lost, the names of the drowned Haitians are remembered and recorded.[37] Here the present does not repeat the past because there are people who *did* make it over to the other side in the past, just as there are others who surely will in the future. There may be no "end" to the violence of the middle passage, but neither is its death scene the end of the story.

"Children of the Sea" ends with the female narrator recording that the sea is endless like her love for her boyfriend, words that echo the ones recorded in the notebook that he committed to the ocean floor. The words suggest that the story does not end with his death; indeed, it continues in a different story, the story of Caroline's wedding. The narrator of "Caroline's Wedding" tells of how in her mother's village in Haiti, people "believe that there are special spots in the sea where lost Africans who jumped off the slave ships still rest, that those who have died at sea have been chosen to make that journey in order to be reunited with their long-lost relations" (167–68). The Haitian belief in a preordained reunion under the sea explains why the male narrator of "Children of the Sea" dreamt he was drowning. Just before his boat sinks, he realizes that the dreams were a prophecy and that he "was chosen from the beginning of time to live there with Agwé at the bottom of the sea" (27–28). The stasis of middle passage temporality is interrupted by a prophetic time in which a diasporic future is already written. By placing a middle passage scene of drowning within a Haitian spiritual belief system and its prophetic temporality, the story claims the sea as the site of a collective memory rather than simply a space of death. Inasmuch as the drowned man's girlfriend in Haiti and the boat people's relatives in Brooklyn are the recipients of the news of the boat's sinking, it also shifts the signification of drowning from the dead who lie at the bottom of the Caribbean sea to Haitians both at home and in the *dyaspora*.

By characterizing the desperate journeys undertaken by African and Haitian refugees as today's "middle passages," *A Distant Shore* and "Children of the Sea" complicate the idea of a singular and originary moment of a transatlantic black diaspora. Their fictional chartings of multiple passages remind us that the diaspora is shifting and changing as populations continue to move and be displaced. Both works suggest that diasporic cultures are the products of discrete moments in time that are related but also irreducible to each other. Whereas *A Distant Shore* invokes the middle passage as a trauma that is endlessly repeated, "Children of the Sea" suggests that the story is more openended. In Danticat's story, prophetic time severs the narrative link between death and narrative endings so that the hold the past has on the present can be broken.

NOTES

This essay appeared in slightly different form as Jenny Sharpe, "The Middle Passages of Black Migration," Atlantic Studies 6, no. 1 (April 2009): 97–112. It is reprinted with the permission of Taylor & Francis, Ltd.*

1. Carl Pedersen, "Middle Passages: Representations of the Slave Trade in Carib-bean and African-American Literature," *The Massachusetts Review* 34, no. 2 (Summer 1993): 225. For a review of the appearance of the middle passage in African American literature, see Wolfgang Binder, "Uses of Memory: The Middle Passage in African American Literature," in *Slavery in the Americas,* ed. Wolfgang Binder (Wurzburg, Ger-many: Konigshausen & Neumann, 1993); and Maria Diedrich, Henry Louis Gates, Jr., and Carl Pederson, *Black Imagination and the Middle Passage* (New York: Oxford Univer-sity Press, 1999), 5–13.

2. Carl Pedersen, "Sea Change: The Middle Passage and the Transatlantic Imagi-nation," in *The Black Columbiad: Defining Moments in African American Literature and Culture,* ed. Werner Sollors and Maria Diedrich, 44–45 (Cambridge, Mass.: Harvard Univer-sity Press, 1994).

3. Since I am examining the role of the middle passage in conceptualizations of "diaspora," I am speaking primarily about a transatlantic black diaspora. For a critique of the equation of global African diasporas with slave diasporas, see Paul Tiyambe Zeleza, "Rewriting the African Diaspora: Beyond the Black Atlantic," *African Affairs* 104, no. 414 (2005). In his important essay "The Uses of Diaspora," *Social Text* 19, no. 1 (2001), Brent Hayes Edwards locates its emergence as a conceptual framework in the 1960s, when black intellectuals showed an interest in Pan-Africanism as a political and cultural movement during an era of decolonization.

4. Paul Gilroy, *The Black Atlantic: Modernity and Double Consciousness,* reissue ed. (Cambridge, Mass.: Harvard University Press, 1993), 4.

5. Ibid., 197.

6. James Clifford, *Routes: Travel and Translation in the Late Twentieth Century* (Cam-bridge, Mass.: Harvard University Press, 1997), 264.

7. Caryl Phillips, *A Distant Shore* (New York: Alfred A. Knopf, 2003; New York: Vintage Books, International Edition, 2005). Parenthetical page references are to the Vintage edition.

8. Edwidge Danticat, "Children of the Sea," in *Krik? Krak!* (New York: Vintage, 1995), 3–29. Parenthetical page references are to this edition.

9. See, for instance, his first novel, *The Final Passage* (London: Faber & Faber, 1985), and his travel memoir, *The Atlantic Sound* (New York: Alfred A. Knopf, 2001).

10. Ottobah Cugoano, *Thoughts and Sentiments on the Evil of Slavery,* ed. Vincent Car-reta (New York: Penguin, 1999), 85. Fred D'Aguiar tells the story of the *Zong* episode from the perspective of this survivor, imagined as a woman, in his novel *Feeding the Ghosts* (New York: Ecco Press, 2000).

11. Roy Greenslade, *Seeking Scapegoats: The Coverage of Asylum in the UK Press* (Lon-don: Institute for Public Policy Research, 2005). I am grateful to Joe Bristow for bringing Britain's increased hostility toward asylum seekers to my attention.

12. Alice Bloch, *The Migration and Settlement of Refugees in Britain* (London: Palgrave Macmillan, 2002), 51–54; Vaughan Robinson, Roger Andersson, and Sako Musterd, *Spreading the 'Burden'? A Review of Policies to Disperse Asylum Seekers and Refugees* (Bristol: The Policy Press, 2003), 121–48.

13. One of the criticisms made of Britain's dispersal policy is that it cuts off asylum seekers from the informal social networks made available to them in the cities, which are crucial to their successful adjustment to a new environment. See Bloch, *Migration and Settlement of Refugees,* 194–95; and David Griffiths, Nando Sigona, and Roger Zetter, "Integrative Paradigms, Marginal Reality: Refugee Community Organisations and Dispersal in Britain," *Journal of Ethnic and Migration Studies* 32, no. 5 (July 2006). In *A Distant Shore,* even an urban center such as London offers no sanctuary for Gabriel, which is why I am arguing that its vision of diaspora is more strongly equated with "homelessness" than "community."

14. This is a direct allusion to Enoch Powell's claim in his "Rivers of Blood" speech that West Indian immigrants terrorized an English widow by pushing excreta through her letter-box.

15. Olaudah Equiano, "The Interesting Narrative of the Life of Olaudah Equiano, or Gustavus Vassa, The African," in *The Classic Slave Narratives,* ed. Henry Louis Gates, Jr. (New York: Penguin, 1987). Vincent Carretta's argument that Equiano invented his African-born identity does not negate its strategic value as a narrative device.

16. Stuart Hall, "Cultural Identity and Cinematic Representation," in *Black British Cultural Studies: A Reader,* ed. Houston A. Baker, Jr., Manthia Diawara, and Ruth H. Lindeborg (Chicago: University of Chicago Press, 1996), 214.

17. Charles Piot, "Atlantic Aporias: Africa and Gilroy's Black Atlantic," *South Atlantic Quarterly* 100, no. 1 (Winter 2001): 155–70.

18. Although the British called the resettled Africans "Creole," which was derived from the Spanish term for American-born settlers and slaves, the Krio identify themselves by the Yoruba term, which alludes to their practice of visiting each other after church. See Akintola Wyse, *The Krio of Sierra Leone: An Interpretive History* (London: C. Hurst, 1989), 6.

19. Many observers consider the Sierra Leone war to be over its diamonds, which were first discovered in 1930. Sankoh's trade in diamonds, known as "blood" or "conflict" diamonds valued in 1998 at $15 billion, has been with European businessmen, which demonstrates the difficulty in characterizing Sierra Leone's civil war as simply an internal affair. See Greg Campbell's investigative reporting in *Blood Diamonds: Tracing the Deadly Path of the World's Most Precious Stones* (Boulder, Colo.: Westview Press, 2004), where he demonstrates how the London-based DeBeers cartel laundered money for Al Qaeda.

20. As Terry Eagleton explains in *Criticism and Ideology: A Study in Marxist Literary Theory* (London: Verso, 1976), "the 'message' of *Heart of Darkness* is that Western civilization is at base as barbarous as African society—a viewpoint which disturbs imperialist assumptions to the precise degree that it reinforces them" (135).

21. Yogita Goyal, "Theorizing Africa in Black Diaspora Studies: Caryl Phillips' *Crossing the River,*" *Diaspora* 12, no. 1 (2003): 5–38, makes an excellent case for the problematic representation of Africa as a mythic space in Phillips' earlier novel *Crossing the River.*

22. The metaphoric implications of the middle passage are less pronounced in "From the Ocean Floor" and the political circumstances, perhaps due to the currency

of events, are made more explicit. For instance, Aristide is mentioned by name, whereas in "Children of the Sea" he is referred to simply as "the old president."

23. Gilber Loescher and John Scanlan, "Human Rights, U. S. Foreign Policy, and Haitian Refugees," *Journal of Interamerican Studies and World Affairs* 26, no. 3 (Aug. 1984): 313–56; Christopher Mitchell, "U. S. Policy Toward Haitian Boat People," *Annals of the American Academy of Political and Social Science* 534 (July 1994): 69–80.

24. Homi Bhabha, *The Location of Culture* (New York: Routledge, 1994), 149.

25. Elizabeth DeLoughrey, "Tidalectics: Charting the Space/Time of Caribbean Waters," *Span* 47 (1998): 24.

26. Gilroy, *The Black Atlantic*, 4.

27. Joan Dayan, "Paul Gilroy's Slaves, Ships, and Routes: The Middle Passage as Metaphor," *Research in African Literatures* 27, no. 4 (1996): 11.

28. Diana Taylor, *The Archive and the Repertoire: Performing Cultural Memory in the Americas* (Durham, N.C.: Duke University Press, 2003), 19–27. Taylor argues that both archival and embodied memories are mediated, and that repertoire, like the archive, does survive into the present.

29. Ibid., 20.

30. Marcus Wood, *Blind Memory: Visual Representations of Slavery in England and America* (New York: Routledge, 2000), 41–68. Also see Alan J. Rice, *Radical Narratives of the Black Atlantic* (New York: Continuum, 2003) 69–81, and Mary Lou Emery, *Modernism, the Visual, and Caribbean Literature* (Cambridge, UK: Cambridge University Press, 2007), 19–35, for black textual and visual responses to Turner's painting.

31. Gilroy, *The Black Atlantic*, 14.

32. Ian Baucom, *Specters of the Atlantic: Finance, Capital, Slavery, and the Philosophy of History* (Durham, N.C.: Duke University Press, 2005), 288.

33. Ibid., 292.

34. Édouard Glissant, *Caribbean Discourse: Selected Essays,* trans. J. Michael Dash (Charlottesville: University Press of Virginia, 1989), 7.

35. "Whenever a fleet of ships gave chase to slave ships," writes Glissant in *Poetics of Relation,* trans. Betsy Wing (Ann Arbor: University of Michigan Press, 1997), "it was easiest just to lighten the boat by throwing cargo overboard, weighing it down with balls and chains. These underwater signposts mark the course between the Gold Coast and the Leeward Islands" (6). Baucom understands Glissant's description to be a response to Turner's painting, one that situates the drowning of slaves less as an end in itself, as does liberal humanism, than the beginning of globalized cultures of modernity (312–21).

36. Edwidge Danticat, "Caroline's Wedding," in *Krik? Krak!* (New York: Vintage, 1995), 155–216. Parenthetical page references are to this edition.

37. Baucom, *Specters of the Atlantic,* 11.

CHAPTER TWO

Making the Exodus from Algeria "European"
Family and Race in 1962 France

TODD SHEPARD

Does every exodus lead to a diaspora? The biblical stories linked to both terms do not, of course, support such a causal claim. Yet looking at one moment at the height of the mid-twentieth-century collapse of European empires, a phenomenon that contemporary French observers dubbed "the exodus," offers some telling clues about how popular understandings, official decisions, and the rush of events can consolidate a shared sense of exile and fabricate a diasporic community. This chapter looks at a short period of several months, when the end of the Algerian War, which brought to a close 132 years of French rule over Algeria, forced many people to make decisions about what their identities were and what their connections to Algeria and to France meant, and required the public elaboration—via debates, accusations, and decrees—of stories that explained what was going on.

The French government first defined the term "repatriate" to name French people who came to live in continental ("metropolitan") France from territories that had been part of the French empire, as long as they were *not* from Algeria. Throughout the 1950s, in Egypt, Pondichery, and Indochina, and then in other colonies and protectorates where anticolonial agitation ended or diminished direct French domination, French government decisions obligated most "overseas French" to leave their homes.[1] Among officials in Paris, these officially incited and desired repatriations were the object of concern and, occasionally, action. It was in the name of helping these people from already decolonized areas that, in the fall of 1961, the government acted to establish a legal definition of "repatriate status."

Public explanations in the French Parliament that preceded the December 1961 approval of the so-called Boulin Law on Repatriate Status contained almost no references to Algeria. The only legislators who did invoke Algeria were those who opposed the law on the grounds that it was yet another Gaullist subterfuge on the road to the abandonment of French Algeria. The law was in fact meant to address the Algerian situation, to help put an end to the now seven-year-long Algerian Revolution, and to prepare for a cease-fire with Algerian nationalists and eventual Algerian independence.[2] The Evian Accords—the agreement for an immediate cease-fire and measures that would quickly lead to Algerian independence, which the French government and representatives of the provisional government of the Algerian Republic, based in Tunis, both signed—formalized these efforts less than three months later on March 18, 1962. To focus on the debate *manqué* as evidence of Gaullist subterfuge, however, would ignore the more important reasons why Algeria was not part of the Boulin Law debates. Unlike with previous repatriations, which they thought of as necessary elements of government efforts to manage the French retreat from overseas empire, officials' attempts to make plans for potential repatriates from Algeria sought to reduce dramatically, and hopefully avoid, any departures from Algeria. Government planners, in considering potential repatriates from Algeria, were consistent with official thinking about Algeria since the 1830s: Algeria was a wholly unique overseas possession.

Repatriate status was announced as helping people from former colonies as they returned to their French homeland. It was meant to prevent French citizens in Algeria from coming back to the metropole. To be more explicit, the government wanted to guarantee that the vast majority of so-called European Algerians—the mosaic of non-Muslim people whose ancestors had come to Algeria from France, Malta, Italy, and Spain since the French invasion of 1830, as well as various Jewish migrations, most importantly of the Sephardim—would remain in Algeria after independence. Government planners saw the establishment of repatriate status as a way to reassure this group of some one million people (who had, by the last years of the war, become more widely known as *pieds noirs*) that because they would be welcomed in the metropole, they did not have to come. As one *haut fonctionnaire* (high-ranking civil servant) remarked, "The certainty given to French people who feel threatened in Algeria that they will find an efficient welcome, available housing and, above all, the possibility of [jobs], would work to calm the distress of most of them."[3] To deal with the evident contradictions government experts discerned in planning this aspect of Algeria's future, the office of Minister of State for Algerian Affairs prepared a special repatriate status to "intervene at the governmental level in order to ameliorate" the spotty assistance afforded existing repatriates from Tunisia, Morocco, and elsewhere. In addressing the situation of people who had already left decolonized French colonies, the note summarizing the minister's concerns continued, "the apprehensions of our compatriots from Algeria over their future situation" will be "calmed."[4] Repatriate status, then, was first and foremost a guarantee, meant to placate people in Algeria, and not the important category of political and social identity it would become.

Rather than a recognition of any existing identity, repatriate status aimed to dissipate connections to Frenchness and permit the consolidation of a specifically Algerian identity. In conjunction with widespread certainty that this and other guarantees would succeed in keeping almost all "Europeans" in Algeria, official discussions of repatriate status, and the Boulin Law of 1961, made no distinction among potential repatriates based in national origin, ethnicity, race, or religion, hewing to republican "color-blindness." By avoiding any invocation of questions of national origin, ethnicity, race, or religion, discussions of repatriate status, like other preparations for Algerian independence, avoided any explicit engagement with the central argument of die-hard supporters of keeping Algeria French: Algerian territory, unlike other colonies, was legally an extension of the French Republic. Since 1865, French law had proclaimed all Algerians to be French nationals; after World War II, they were given citizenship; finally, in trying to combat the Algerian revolution, the Fifth Republic in 1958 had extended political rights equal to other French citizens to all Algerians, Europeans, and Muslims—which is to say that when government officials sought to encourage Algeria's one million Europeans to stay in Algeria, they simply acted as if all of Algeria's eight million "Muslim French citizens" would also stay in Algeria. Officials, in fact, presumed that all of them, Europeans and "Muslims," would become Algerians if they remained in what was to become the Algerian Republic.

Yet with everyone certain that Algeria and Algerians were not French, nothing had been done to exclude them from France or from citizenship. People in Algeria would become Algerians; Algerians in France would leave. Events confounded these presumptions and wishes. Between mid-April and September 1962, a chaotic rush to escape Algeria—a migration that commentators immediately named the "exodus"—brought close to one million people to the Hexagon. No one in France predicted the exodus of the quasi-totality of so-called *pieds noirs*. Many people and organizations forecast what they considered large numbers of departures, yet even the most perceptive assumed that the majority would end up living in Algeria. An article on plans for "Operation Dunkirk" that *France-Observateur* published in summer 1961, for example, spoke of plans for a massive air- and sea-lift to bring back almost all French Algerians, but made clear that they meant only the minority of "Europeans" who had "French" ancestry, rather than those with Spanish, Jewish, Italian, Maltese, or other ancestors.[5] The subtitle of a magazine article in the summer of 1962, "From Predictions (400,000 Repatriates in Four Years in 90 Departments) to Reality (400,000 repatriates in Four Weeks in Four Departments)," gives a sense of the distance between what was planned for and what happened.[6]

Recognizing the Exodus

The arrest of ex-general Raoul Salan, the head of the *Organisation de l'armée secrète* (OAS) (Organization of the Secret Army)—the terrorist organization that since spring 1961 had fought to keep Algeria French—marks, empirically and symbolically, the beginning of what would be recognized as more than a variety of discrete phenomena but rather as an event: the exodus. *Empirically* because, from April 20 on, what would prove to be definitive departures to the metropole went up markedly and "continued with no slow-downs" until the exodus ended.[7] As a year-end chronicle asked, "Coincidence or consequence? On 21 April 1962, and for the first time ever, the constabulary had to refuse entrance to the Maison-Blanche airport, where numerous *Algérois* [inhabitants of Algiers] sought to board. Two thousand people were able to leave. The rest, pushed back, camped in their cars."[8] And *symbolically* because Salan's arrest not only removed the individual who had embodied *pieds noirs'* hopes for the victory of the forces supporting French Algeria; it ended "European" certainty that they would triumph.

Once the exodus began, the influence of the OAS collapsed; its brutish methods, widely accepted in the early crucible of French Algerian resistance to Algerian independence, now inspired anguish among *pieds noirs* who did not want to leave Algeria but were desperate to remain French. Official reports remained vague on the causes of this *pied noir* anguish. In early April, officers noted a growing feeling among "Europeans" that they were being "rejected by the Nation" as "*Pieds Noirs,*" which inspired "their stupor, their shock, their desperation, or their anger." In mid-May, other military observers noted for the first time "a certain queasiness among the general population." "The masses," wrote Col. Cousin, "particularly in Algiers, have a sinking, sickened feeling as they face accusations made against the whole European community." The claims concerned accusations widespread in the metropole that the *pieds noirs* as a group were responsible for terrorism, torture, colonial racism, and ongoing violence in general.[9] Besides moral qualms, however, the same report also pointed to "fear of Muslim reprisals" inspired by the "machine-gun attack" of May 14, 1962 (by the *Front de Libération Nationale* [FLN] [National Liberation Front] commander Azzedine in Algiers), to explain a "timid" movement "to separate themselves from the OAS."[10]

After Salan's capture, the exodus began, did not stop, and was definitive. Even in the midst of the exodus, however, the belief that the *pieds noirs* necessarily would remain in Algeria was tenacious. Gendarmerie Commander Koch reported that while movement within Algeria concerned "entire families," that toward the metropole, although affecting "all social classes," was "primarily women and children. The head of the family generally stays behind." He made clear that his attention to *pied noir* men was not a warning about continued OAS violence, but a hopeful sign that those who had left would return.[11] The government continued to believe that repatriate status would encourage most who had fled Algeria in fear to return and, more important, that official presumptions about what "Europeans" wanted were correct. After their vacations, politicians and press secretaries repeated, "Algerians" would return to their now independent homeland.[12] Even internal government documents referred straightforwardly to vacations, perhaps envisioning the summer as a cooling-down period. In late May, the Oran prefecture, calling attention to the masses of people "descending on the port of Oran and waiting day and night on the docks," urged the minister of the interior "to organize the transportation to France of thousands of women and children for summer vacation."[13] Others, although asserting that Europeans were "pretending to go on summer vacation" in order "to save face," still drew attention to "their hope that they will be able to return." Just as experts in the Hexagon continued to plan on no more than three hundred thousand repatriates from Algeria staying for good in Europe, official reports from Algeria maintained that, as the head of gendarmes in Oran wrote in early June, "Although many Europeans try to convince themselves that staying in an independent Algeria is impossible, it is certain that in their heart of hearts they hope to stay." Noting the "massive exodus of Europeans towards the metropole," he highlighted the "small number of them who declare that they are giving up and leaving definitively."[14] In July 1962, the Coordinating Commission for the Reinstallation of Overseas French did insist that "it seems reasonable to expect that some 50% of civil servants . . . will reinstall themselves in the metropole."[15] This reasonable estimate was made even though 80 percent had already requested a transfer to the metropole. Once the current "climate" had passed, the commission presaged, the conditions for most civil servants to remain in Algeria would reassert themselves.

Elements of the OAS, too, disputed the reality of the "exodus" long after the movement had become a veritable groundswell. The OAS group "Zone III" (Oran) refused to accept the early June Susini-Mostefaï agreements—which called for an end to fighting and the participation of "Europeans" in the independence process—and sought to establish a "territorial platform" governed by the OAS and independent from the French Republic as well as from Algeria. In mid-June, a communiqué explained that "we have asked that certain zones be evacuated, and the slightly more numerous departures of the last few days are the result of the evacuation of some families from the interior." Their definition of families, they specified, meant women and children: "THE MEN ARE STAYING PUT. THEY ARE READY TO FIGHT." An ever smaller group of die-hards still argued that (part of) Algeria would remain French, and the French of Algeria would return.[16]

"The Massive Effort Asked of the Nation"

On May 30th, a *Section Française de l'Internationale Ouvrière* (SFIO) (French Section of the Workers' International) deputy insisted in the National Assembly that what was occurring was an "exodus." "The truth is, there is a wave of panic sweeping over Algeria. Why deny it?" he questioned Gérard Wolff, secretary of state for repatriates; "everyone wants to leave."[17] At the May 23 cabinet-level meeting that prepared for this debate, Wolff had told his colleagues that "at this time the situation has changed profoundly." Now, and in the months to come, "circumstances lead us to predict massive arrivals at a rhythm that could easily be greater than 100,000 to 150,000 per month."[18]

The Pompidou government immediately decided that its most important task was shaping public understandings of what was going on, rather than committing resources or formulating new measures. At the May 23 cabinet-level meeting, after enumerating the diverse measures that had or needed to be taken (and paid for), Secretary Wolff emphasized that "for psychological and political reasons" it now was "essential to go before the Parliament to detail the massive effort asked of the Nation." What was most important, Wolff reiterated, was not what was going to be done: In addressing the National Assembly, the goal was to prevent the legislators from demanding that more be done—or more money spent—than the government recommended. As he said, "any other policy" except appealing to "the Nation" in apocalyptic terms "might lead the Assembly to reject the budget we propose as ridiculously small."[19]

There was widespread and powerful resistance to taking any action to assist the repatriates. The archives of two interministerial committees chaired by President de Gaulle reveal the intense conflict among the Fifth Republic's leaders over the way to respond. De Gaulle himself disdained the *pieds noirs,* a group he considered only slightly more French than Algerian "Muslims." As Alain Peyrefitte reminds us, de Gaulle simply did not believe that people from Algeria could be made French. The president privileged police responses to the exodus: the repatriates were a vector of OAS criminality and banditry and a potential locus for political upheaval. The attention to law enforcement met, as well as inspired, public concerns: during the summer of 1962 much of the popular press identified the repatriates as the source of a wave of banditry in the south and around Paris. Many on the left drew attention to potential political violence. Socialist (SFIO) leaders were, according to the *Renseignements Généraux* (RG) (Central Directorate of General Intelligence), "preoccupied" by "the problems posed by the repatriation of refugees from North Africa," while the *Confédération française des travailleurs chrétiens* (CFTC) (French Confederation of Christian Workers) union warned its locals to be on guard against the threat of "infiltration by repatriates."[20] A communist deputy warned against letting "the retreated from Algeria become a reservoir of fascism."[21] In *France-Observateur,* the letters to the editor page was filled each week of early 1962 with criticisms of the *pieds noirs,* the repatriates, and what many readers felt was the left-leaning weekly's too-sympathetic coverage of their situation. Mr. H. C. from Paris, "one of your earliest subscribers," questioned whether the "exodus" was well-founded, given that "the French government has done everything to guarantee their safety and their property."[22] Opposed to assisting the repatriates, he worried that they would "reinforce metropolitan [OAS] activism, which the press tells us is growing stronger and more violent."[23] Against such concerns, Prime Minister Georges Pompidou successfully played on de Gaulle's concerns about political upheaval to overcome scorn for the *pieds noirs* and to establish a more varied response to the exodus.

The plans officials put in place under duress, however, worked most efficiently to eliminate the complicated set of definitions and structures that had emerged since the conquest of Algiers in 1830, and in particular since 1958. In place of existing subtle subsets of French citizens—with Koranic Status, with double nationality, protected by European minority status, etc.—the government embraced a simple division between "Algerians" and "French." The former were "Muslims"—a term that never appeared in official reports as a religion but always in reference to the majority "community" in Algeria—the latter were not. These categories did not accurately capture some obvious reality, and they did not respect republican principles or French law. They were, however, easier to understand and easier to explain to a metropolitan population that had tired of trying to figure out what was happening with Algeria.

The abrupt transformation of the application of repatriate status captures this effort to clarify who was French. On April 2, 1962, the government had extended the status of "repatriate" to people who arrived in the metropole from Algeria.[24] While the December 1961 law that had created the category of "repatriates" did so in the name of standardizing treatment, it had individualized the process of obtaining benefits: potential repatriates would need to prove they left under duress in order to receive full assistance. Officials in the metropole were to assess each case, and this judgment would affect directly the amount of benefits for which each repatriate was eligible. The exodus destroyed this individualized system, creating a uniform class of "repatriates from Algeria." All repatriates now were eligible to receive specified benefits. As distinctions within repatriate status disappeared, the division that emerged instead was between those inside and those outside of membership. "Repatriates" came to refer almost exclusively to "Europeans," while "Muslims" became "refugees."[25]

The government responded to the exodus of "Europeans" with an ardent reaffirmation of the classic French theory of assimilationism and of policies meant to assimilate the new arrivals. French authorities at all levels reiterated this principle and made clear their reasoning: the need to avoid the danger of any *"pied noir* community" emerging in the metropole. Some articulated this imperative as necessary to overcome bitterness and homesickness (*le mal de pays*), while others feared the implantation of a far-right pro-OAS constituency in the nation. Both positions shared the same remedy: economic assimilation. Published proposals and popular discussions of the repatriates repeatedly raised cultural problems to the assimilation of a "Mediterranean" and "colonial" population. To address this threat, policies were planned to avoid *pied noir* ghettos and to disperse families from Algeria. Officials worked, as one late August 1962 memo to de Gaulle explained, "to incite the repatriates to settle themselves throughout the metropole."[26] Cultural and political particularities, the planners presumed, would melt away in the rising tide of 1960s French economic growth.

Numerous journalists and commentators encouraged the government to act aggressively to assimilate the new arrivals. Philippe Hernandez, a journalist at *France-Observateur,* explicitly linked a call for assimilation and anticommunitarian (more accurately, anticorporatist) language. In April 1962, presenting a group interview with recently repatriated *pieds noirs,* the self-identified *pied noir* writer called on "Frenchmen" to "lend an ear," to argue that "tomorrow, the thousands of *pieds noirs* who are going to arrive will group together and organize themselves because no one will help them, I don't like that one bit."[27] He urged that action should be taken by the nation to address their problems because, as he wrote, "I would rather that any future associations made up of French of Algeria have nothing better to do than to organize an annual cocktail party."[28]

Observers attributed responsibility for metropolitan resentment, dislike, or suspicion of the *pieds noirs* to the *pieds noirs*. Accusations varied; what one witness referred to as "the black legend of the *'pied noir,'* vain and exploitative" grounded certain accusations. A call for understanding published in the pages of *France-Observateur* inspired one reader to write that bad feelings between metropolitans and new arrivals could be avoided, "but on one condition: once he sails for France, the *Pied Noir* throws overboard his superiority complex, that of the colonist," offering as an example "that driver with the 9A [Algiers] license-plate who, when I signaled for room to pass him, told me 'I'm in the right!' while hogging the middle of the road." This complaint was joined by references to their use of the racial epithet *bougnoule* and similar belittling references to "Arabs." It ended with the correspondent's bitter memory of being "refused bottles of water by *Pieds Noirs* . . . during the long marches of our military service."[29] Even the most serious and thoughtful observers held any and all signs of *pied noir particularisme*, or difference, responsible for metropolitan reactions. One volunteer charged with organizing efforts to respond to the exodus argued that while "the misery and the disarray of most of those arriving today" largely had undermined the credibility of the "black legend," to end it would necessitate "making *'pied noir'* particularities disappear, on the one hand by breaking up all concentrations of refugees, on the other hand, by re-registering as soon as they arrive all automobiles brought over from Algeria."[30] Separate them one from another and separate them from all signs that they were from Algeria. That way, French drivers, for example, would see rude drivers as just bad eggs and not as embryos of a coming fascist plague identifiable by their license plates.

Previously certain that Europeans would not leave, yet having failed to convince them that they could remain French in Algeria, French officials encountered enormous difficulties in mobilizing transportation and accommodations to counter the "psychosis of the exodus." Over the summer, the government put in place aggressive social and political responses to the exodus. The government, supported by a broad range of media sources, private agencies, and politicians, addressed metropolitan opinion to insist on the importance and the necessity of massive mobilization to help "French people in distress." What, in the eyes of planners and officials, were the conditions that would make this population assimilable? What made them seem enough like other French people that assimilation would work? The *pieds noirs* were, after all, deeply distrusted and resented. It is a question that must be posed at the very moment that the Fifth Republic abandoned France's most ambitious attempt at assimilation, that directed at Algerian "Muslims." It was not their status as citizens; this the history of the exodus makes clear. It was less their legal rights than the "European" origins they shared with metropolitan French people.

Press discussions of the exodus, joined by government policy choices, presented the "Europeans" of Algeria as part of the same family as other French people. To make this argument, representations of the "Europeans" themselves as part of normal, heterosexual families proved critical; this normalizing representation of gender relations countered the widely publicized media discussions of "European" Algeria as a male, homosocial society that bred violent male perversion, representations that had shaped metropolitan rejection of the *pieds noirs* in the months leading up to the exodus.

Pied Noir Men into French Families: Reaffirming the Frenchness of (European) Repatriates

Metropolitans and the French press were fixated on the exodus. The reactions varied enormously, although overall the press was much more welcoming than the people. The emerging official line, cobbled together once the collapse of all previous predictions became undeniable, urged metropolitans to welcome the *pieds noirs*. The mythic heterosexual family was the principal register that legitimated such appeals. Days after the "exodus" exploded, *Paris-Match* responded to "the announcement that some families from North Africa have begun to settle in the metropole." The editors dragged old-time natalism out of its post-1945 *bébé boum* (baby boom)–provoked retirement with an editorial titled, "There are not enough French people." The editors wrote that "today, economic progress depends on abundant manpower and the number of solvent consumers." In these months, "Have confidence in the future," the editorial's final line, was the mantra of *Paris-Match*.[31] *Paris-Match* consistently urged its readers to embrace "the repatriates of Algeria," and its editorials, photos, captions, and, less singularly, its articles struggled to fabricate "the friendship of French people for French people."[32] Every element of the photo weekly's June 2, 1962, cover worked to produce compassion: a blond baby holding a stuffed animal, a young, tall, dark (but not too dark) and handsome man, a young, petite, Jean Seberg–coiffed woman in a suede vest, both in profile, leaning on a railing, eyes fixed on land. The headline reads "FRANCE, DOES SHE STILL LOVE US?," with the promise of a "Major Report" not *on,* but "with the repatriates from Algeria." The front-page caption explains, "They met and were married in Algeria, he, a military man, she, *pied noir.* They were teachers, today they return to the coasts of the *mère patrie*." Who could think they were in any way connected with France's enemies? A white band at the top of the page, the bold-faced caption "The Judges of Salan," reminded readers that the enemies were being dealt with, the relevant article beginning with the observation that the judges had "looked to the future."[33]

Images of "whole" families, men with women and children, were repeatedly produced to describe the people coming to France. While not historically unprecedented, the use of familial descriptions to explain official responses to the exodus was particularly intense, working to extricate OAS from *pieds noirs* and acting to reinsert the latter in classic, comforting, and hierarchized gender relations. Men joined their women and children in metropolitan France. The separation between men, fighting for the OAS in Algeria, and women and children in France waiting to return to Algeria, had too successfully convinced metropolitans that the *pieds noirs* were un-French. Both pro-government and pro-*Algérie française* deputies worked to distinguish the innocent French refugees flooding into the metropole from recent and vivid descriptions of violent anti-French fanatics, who like the refugees were "Europeans" and from Algeria. Deputies from all sides, except the far left, called for French fraternity and solidarity. One Gaullist deputy urged, "It is necessary for those who returned with pain in their souls, with bitterness on their lips, who are somewhat maladroit because they suffer—they must be welcomed like distressed members of the same family."[34] More than mere words, there was an institutional vector to this discursive deployment, as the state sought to cement depictions of the refugees as French families.

The government announced that its repatriation program had opened "15,000 dossiers for heads of families." "We have had 19,000 families, about 50,000 people . . . ; each head of family receives 50,000 old francs, each person in their charge 20,000."[35] One Algerian deputy called into question the functionality of such a system: "I would like the Minister for Repatriation to note that in order to receive these allocations, it is necessary that the head of the family be in the metropole. It would be just and it would be reasonable if these benefits were equally available to repatriated families where the head of the family has not come."[36] The genealogy of this dispute is compelling. Directing payments to the male head of the family was not the norm for French social spending. Only in the late 1930s, after the collapse of the Popular Front, did the Daladier government, under great pressure from the traditionalist Catholic and royalist right, begin to utilize familial allocation. Earlier in the twentieth century, the French government had opted repeatedly to give money to needy mothers directly, whether married or not. Thus while the deputy's complaints made sense within the recent history of France, their political origins were novel. The pro—French Algeria right, not the secular left, was calling for a policy that ignored family status.[37]

Rather than a reflection of ahistorical privileging of the traditional familial order, or a choice made on the basis of efficiency, this criterion was forged in discursive necessity. Indeed, within weeks, certain payments to repatriates began to be distributed whether or not the male "head of the family" had arrived. Yet the government's initial policy, insofar as it broke with standard practice, political and bureaucratic, suggests how critical it was for responses to the unexpected "exodus" of "Europeans" to present them as grouped in heterosexual families. Representations of the *pieds noirs* as deviant men had been widely convincing, understandings that offered vivid proof that they were not French and were a threat to France. To be male and *pied noir* was enough to be associated with "fascist" OAS terror. Although French Algerian men on their own were undeniably citizens, legally entitled to enter the metropole, only as "heads of family" could they be welcomed. In late 1961 and January 1962, government reports on departures from Algeria had specified how many of those concerned were "Israelites," which reflected official concerns that Zionist groups were trying to scare Jewish Algerians into moving to Israel; in June and July 1962, RG reports on "repatriates from Algeria arriving in France" distinguished the number of "men older than seventeen."[38]

Counterrepresentations that normalized these men as healthily heterosexual were at the heart of efforts to provoke metropolitan solidarity with people who although from Algeria were, it needed to be proven, French. This familial language worked to assert that the *pieds noirs* were linked directly to other French people, feeding into affirmations that they were "members of the same family." Familial images were readily articulated to disentangle the mass of *pieds noirs* from the actions of the OAS. As one Algerian deputy noted, "Already, in spite of official declarations and proclaimed optimism from the higher ups, stories abound of facts that shame us. . . . In Marseilles, the [repatriates] have to sleep on the roadside before packed hotels or ones that refuse to accept refugees."[39] Through the multiple resonances of familial imagery, the repatriates were positioned not as violent, but as weak, as themselves children, and as profoundly French, all exemplified in the words of one deputy urging his audience to look at the exodus and understand:

> Today, you can see the French who arrive on the docks of Marseilles, or the grounds of our major airports, poor and often miserable, their only baggage several sacks in which they were able to save the modest belongings that, over there, was all they owned. You need only to look at them to know that these are lower middle class Frenchmen, little people

for whom life consists of work, of effort, and suffering. . . . Do not forget that these French people, our compatriots, our brothers, are the children of those who went before, pushed more by the need to give [to France] than greed.[40]

The family—and above all the necessary place of males within it as fathers, brothers, and even children—was a privileged trope, mobilized to cleanse the *pieds noirs,* in particular the men, of the OAS stain and to guarantee their Frenchness. Familial discourse offered tentative resolution to one of the key questions the Algerian revolution forced France to address: who could be French and why?

Excluding the "Muslims"

When the Evian Accords were announced in March 1962, there was no official hesitation concerning what they meant for Muslim French citizens from Algeria. A telegram from the National Defense Headquarters in Paris to army headquarters in Algeria "conveys the Prime Minister's instructions" concerning their future. "Question: Will they have the same possibilities as the French of [European] Origin to settle in the metropole with French citizenship and the benefits of the Law on Assistance to French repatriates? Response: YES." "Question: Will this possibility remain available to French Muslims? Response: Yes, by returning to the metropole at any moment after self-determination they can reclaim French nationality under French law and benefit from the Law."[41] One month before, a six-page message from minister of the armies Pierre Messmer to all officers instructed them to assure "French Muslims serving in the Armed Forces and as auxiliaries that their legitimate interests as soldiers and citizens will be guaranteed."[42] After the announcement of the accords, Radio France broadcast across the metropole the official affirmation that continued French nationality and all measures of the Boulin Law would be available to "every inhabitant of Algeria," whether "French Muslims or Europeans." In the metropole, propaganda in support of the April 8, 1962, referendum to approve the Evian Accords also specified that "French nationality would be maintained for all in Algeria who currently have it, Europeans or Muslims, and who do not explicitly renounce it."[43]

The exodus confronted republican bromides about the irrevocability of French citizenship—these legally binding facts—with their implications. Charles de Gaulle left no doubt as to his own conception of what should be done with Muslims from Algeria, signing on June 21, 1962, a document concerning "The Nationality Problem." While de Gaulle affirmed that "Algerians of European Origins" should have their French nationality as before, each individual "Muslim" should be required to file an application, which French bureaucrats could either accept or reject.[44] It was left to Christian Fouchet, high commissioner in Algeria, to remind the government that "the nationality question is strictly the domain of the law." Thus, he explained, "it does not seem possible, however desirable, to have a very general text that would give total liberty of appreciation to the administration."[45] Putting these legal quibbles aside, de Gaulle's government unilaterally altered one of the primary elements of the Evian Accords via the Ordinance of July 21, 1962: the right of all people from Algeria to keep French citizenship. A June 8, 1962, draft project for what would become the Ordinance of July 21, 1962, affirmed that

> French citizens with Common Law Civil Status [Europeans] living in Algeria on the date of the official announcement of the vote for self-determination will keep French nationality even if, at the close of the three-year period posited by the General Declaration of 19 March 1962 they acquire Algerian nationality.[46]

The opposite was done for Muslim French citizens from Algeria, whose access to French citizenship was heavily restricted and dependent on the government's discretion. They could keep their French nationality only if they submitted "a declaration accepted by the Judge responsible for the area where they live on the territory of the French Republic."[47] Not only did Muslim French citizens have to file a claim to obtain a nationality they already possessed, and do so while living outside of Algeria (and on French territory), but (1) they would lose their nationality if this declaration was not accepted by a judge and then registered with the Ministry of Public Health and the Population by January 1, 1963, and (2) the ministry had the right to refuse to register the declaration or, for a period of three years, to reject the declaration for "reasons of unworthiness."[48] What these reasons might be remained vague, but ranged from suspected or known nationalist activity to moral or personal character flaws. The government actions stripped Algerian "Muslims" of their right to hold onto their French nationality.[49]

This ordinance—which for reasons I will not go into had the force of law and was elaborated without any public debate whatsoever—transformed French law to coincide with illegal government actions in the preceding months. Already in late April and early May 1962, a period when it was still publicly denying the existence of the exodus and hoping that its previous efforts to keep Europeans in Algeria would take effect, the government acted to stop only certain people from coming to the metropole: Muslim French citizens from

Algeria. Or, as military orders and government decrees increasingly put it, "*harkis*" or simply "Muslims" ("*harkis*" was a term that originally only referred to members of "self-defense" units, which the French army established in Muslim areas to fight against the forces of the FLN). Officials charged with assisting Algeria's "Muslim" population, a top secret note of May 23 from de Gaulle's office explained, must "cease all initiatives linked to the repatriation of *harkis*." To be "welcomed in the metropole, Muslims" must leave under the control of the Algerian high commissioner, and "their names must be on a list established to this end."[50] By late May, an officer directed that "Muslims" who were "too old, physically handicapped, or too young" as well as "single women" should not be transported. Such people, he remarked, "are destined effectively either to live off public charity or, with the young women, to turn to prostitution; all will become deadweights."[51] At the cabinet level, the shift in terms was more subtle, and as such became easier to interpret. The secretary of state for repatriates' April report to the government referred to "Muslims" only as "auxiliaries"—*harkis,* whom the army would be in charge of dealing with; the May report split them into two distinct categories: "repatriates of European origin [*souche*]" on the one hand, and "repatriates of Muslim origin [*origine*]" on the other. With these categories, the government abandoned previous references that tied identity to territory (Algeria), and instead identified people from Algeria on the basis of descent, or ethnicity.[52]

When confronted with the exodus of "Muslims," the government did not treat them as French citizens with rights; instead, it presented and classed the *harkis* as outsiders whom the French Republic welcomed and assisted only out of charity and only in unavoidable circumstances. Still referred to in May 1962 as "Muslim repatriates," Muslim French citizens from Algeria would increasingly be named not just "*harkis,*" but "refugees," a semantic shift that effaced their status as "repatriates"—and as "citizens." This was inextricably linked with another shift, in which the adjective "Muslim" was no longer appended to "French," and became instead an "origin" (*origine*). If the April report to the cabinet noted, regarding "Muslim families whose head served in the French Army in Algeria," that their "lack of preparedness for metropolitan life poses special problems," the May report adopted a new tone and recommended a new approach. "As these Muslims are not prepared for European life, it would be inopportune to give them the aid reserved for repatriates as individuals."[53] De Gaulle pretended on July 25 that "the term repatriates obviously does not apply to the Muslims. In their case, we are dealing only with refugees." His statement completely disregarded the Evian Accords and the definition of "repatriate," both of which still had the force of (French) law.[54]

Classing the *harkis* as a group, rather than as individuals, legitimated this shift. Summarizing the difference between its activities in 1958 and in 1963, one agency that had been set up to integrate "Muslims" spoke of "320,000 legally French citizens" before Algerian independence; afterwards, they were dealing with "a group of 480,000 foreigners."[55] The definition of the *harkis* as a group placed them outside the nation. Their fellow French citizens from Algeria (of European origin), "repatriates of European origin [*souche*]," were able to avoid this fate. With "Muslims" moved into their own particular category, references to "Europeans" would disappear from official documents, replaced by references to a geographic origin (from North Africa) or, more usually, simply to the legally defined status "repatriates." The nation offered "repatriates from North Africa" its solidarity, as the discussions preparing the Boulin Law had announced. "Europeans," while part of a group (repatriates) that the government recognized in order to facilitate state solidarity, were above all French individuals. This was the type of solidarity that all French citizens could expect from the nation, rather than any form of special privileges given to a specified group. In the years to come, government efforts to assist the *pieds noirs* would constantly present their efforts as having national implications, not as directed at any "sub-national group." As minister of repatriates François Missoffe stated in May 1963, addressing himself to "*pieds noirs*":

> The future of other French people is in your hands. If you make good use of the grants, contracts, the exceptional institutions put in place especially for you, perhaps they will become permanent. Perhaps other people in need will be able to use them.[56]

His "wish" appeared in a newsletter destined to "repatriates," in which each page was imprinted with images of black feet.

Shifts in government terminology, which excluded all "Algerian Muslims" from French citizenship, aligned bureaucratic rules with the assumptions about people from Algeria that now dominated popular metropolitan discussions. As a late 1962 report emphasized, the French "man in the street would welcome with relief the return of Algerians to their country and he does not hide his surprise that new immigrants are arriving."[57] In acting aggressively to keep "Muslim" Algerians, in particular the *harkis,* out of the nation, de Gaulle's government affirmed a racialized exclusion. While government officials and the mass media struggled to convince the metropolitan public that the *pieds noirs* were really French and not Algerian, nor all "fascists," they concurrently denied any right to French identity for French Muslim citizens from Algeria. The image of the isolated, unrooted, and violent *harki* man displaced descriptions of *harki* families seeking refuge. Policy makers, for example, began to focus on the former. Throughout the 1950s, civil servants and academics in France grappled explicitly with the growing number of Algerian "Muslim" families who were settling in the metropole. One historian argues that 1962 saw a development that had lasting effects: "Algerian families became so invisible that [subsequently] social welfare administrators and the general public commonly denied their existence in France." This decision to focus on the *harkis* primarily as men was in stark opposition to how the government addressed the "European" exodus. Such gendered definitions directly affected the process in which popular presumptions about the foreignness of all "Muslim" Algerians began to take legal form, in the shift of *harkis* from repatriating citizens to a group of refugees.[58]

Shifting Algerian "Muslims" out of the category of repatriates and into the category of refugees, of course, had dramatic material effects. The most immediate concerned the tens of thousands of actual or suspected *harkis* who, abandoned by their government, the French Republic, were killed in Algeria during these months. Whether the act of armed groups, units associated with the FLN, or the result of local settlings of accounts, Algerians claiming to punish traitors to the nation assassinated, using often inhumane measures, other Algerians accused of collaborating with the French. When, in September 1962, Prime Minister Pompidou gave instructions to the minister of the armies to "guarantee the transfer to France of former auxiliaries currently in Algeria who have sought protection from French Forces," he made clear that they were not French. They were "under threat of reprisal from their compatriots."[59] Pompidou's directive was grounded in humanitarian concern for human beings, not in fraternity or national solidarity for French nationals. A "personal note" in late October from the high commander of French armed forces in Algeria to all French generals in Algeria reinforced this point and made clear the limits this placed on humanitarian concern. Despite previous reminders, he observed, "the number of Muslims housed in our camps in Algeria grows steadily." It was thus necessary "as of now to suspend all new admission to our centers." In November 1962, official documents and the newspaper *Le Monde* estimated that more than ten thousand Algerians had been killed for being *harkis* since the cease-fire. It remains difficult to ascertain verifiable numbers for these killings.[60]

Those who made it to the metropole experienced other effects of being refugees in their own country. By early 1963, the head of one agency charged with dealing with *harkis* went further than denying their repatriate status, arguing that "Muslim Algerian refugees in the metropole who have chosen French nationality cannot, *ipso facto,* be considered refugees." A January 1963 circular affirmed that they could benefit from refugee status only if they could "prove that they left their country of origin because in danger or for political reasons."[61] This was exactly the kind of obligation the establishment of repatriate status had aimed to eliminate. While those whose "departure was arranged by the Army automatically have this status," all others were required to establish a dossier, which would be examined by government counselors.[62]

By 1964, government legal experts affirmed that it was the combination of submitting a declaration and official acceptance of that declaration that determined the French nationality and citizenship of *harkis*. It was a result of the government's generosity, not the fact that they previously held French nationality and citizenship. This decision broke with earlier interpretations, which presented the accepted declaration as confirmation of the "maintenance of French nationality."[63]

This bureaucratic gesture—the affirmation that the so-called *harkis* had French nationality and thus citizenship only as a result of official acceptance of their declaration—swept away the entire history of French Algeria and the (failed) assimilation of "Muslims."[64] Government policy emerged as a series of experts and jurists interpreted texts and then interpreted their implications. Without any public debate or even a single sweeping decision, the French citizenship of Algerian "Muslims" came to seem nonsensical. Distinct from the French, "not prepared for European life," they now appeared virtually inassimilable. Just months before, it still had seemed reasonable, at least to some.[65] Official reports in early 1963 still asserted that, as one stated, "The *harkis* and their sons, when they re-establish a normal life here, can integrate perfectly into the French national community."[66] On the copy stored at the *Bibliothèque nationale* in Paris, two vertical lines and a question mark score this passage. The frequency of such written interrogations next to similar assertions suggests more than one unfriendly reader. They indicate that "integration" no longer made sense for the *harkis*. Historians, *harkis* themselves, and their sons and daughters have only begun to recount the isolation, poverty, and misery to which their fellow citizens would submit this group of French people. The *harkis'* status as marginalized outsiders—and what would become their long-term exile in the supposedly temporary camps in abandoned corners of the "French desert" where they were placed—came to seem normal, natural, as they were considered no longer citizens, but refugees. By insisting during the exodus that all Muslim French citizens from Algeria prove their suitability to have French citizenship, the republic institutionalized what had been an uncodified, if widely held, suspicion: "Muslims" were so different from the French that only exceptional individuals (and their families) could be assimilated into the nation.[67]

This history highlights the role of the state—in particular how the centrality of empire in the constitution of modern states, in this case, France and Algeria, created routes of movement and connection, which the end of empire closed off or rerouted. More important, efforts on both sides to erase the complication of empire from national histories forced people to come up with new explanations of who they were. It was within such limits that *harkis* had to define their relationship to France and to Algeria. *Pieds noirs* came with far more resources and received many more options. Yet they, too, had to imagine or make bridges between their French and Algerian pasts and presents. Rather than presume communities and links that cross over or overcome state borders, this history shows how the creation of legal definitions and institution-backed assertions that borders matter framed connections to a lost homeland.

NOTES

Parts of this essay appear in slightly different form as Todd Shepard, Part III: The Exodus and After, in his book The Invention of Decolonization: The Algerian War and the Remaking of France *(Ithaca, N.Y.: Cornell University Press, 2006).*

1. Jean-Jacques Jordi and Emile Temime, eds., *Marseille et le choc des décolonisations* [Marseille and the impact of decolonization] (Paris: Edisud, 1996).

2. For both transcripts of committee meetings and parliamentary debates, see Centre des archives contemporaines, Fontainebleau, France (hereafter CAC): 780058/206. [F/60/01980].

3. G. de Wailly, Mission d'Etudes, Ministère d'Etat chargé des Affaires Algériennes, "Notes sur le rapatriement éventuel des Français—européens et musulmans—d'Algérie" (Paris, March 28, 1961), 1 and 2, in Archives du Ministère des Affaires étrangères, Paris, France (hereafter MAE): 100.

4. Ibid.

5. René Delisle, "L'operation 'Dunkerque' est-elle possible?" *France-Observateur,* July 20, 1961, 6.

6. Philippe Hernandez, "Les pieds noirs de Montpellier," *France-Observateur,* August 2, 1962, 9.

7. Gen. Cherasse, Commandant de la Gendarmerie en Algérie, "Bulletin Quotidien des Informations et renseignements . . . Période du 28 au 29" (Algiers, June 29, 1962), 7, in Service historique de l'Armée de terre, Vincennes, France (hereafter SHAT): 1H/1784/4.

8. *Année Politique 1962,* 282.

9. Col. Cavard, "Bulletin de renseignements mensuel. Mois de mars 1962" (JCM/JD, April 6, 1962), 43, in SHAT: 1H/2716/2; Col. Cousin, "Bulletin Hebdomadaire de renseignements. Semaine du 12 au 18 mai 1962" (SP 87.000, May 19, 1962), 27, in SHAT: 1H/1437/1.

10. Rémi Kauffer, "OAS: la guerre franco-française d'Algérie," in *La guerre d'Algérie, 1954–2004, la fin de l'amnésie* [The war in Algeria, 1954–2004: The end of amnesia], ed. Mohammed Harbi and Benjamin Stora, 472 (Paris: Robert Laffont, 2004).

11. Capt. Koch, "Annexe à joindre au rapport n. 555/4 du juin 1962" (June 5, 1962), 2, in SHAT: 1H/3086/1; Col. Cavard, "Bulletin Hebdomadaire de renseignement psychologique (semaine 16–22/5/62)" (Algiers, May 24, 1962), 4, in SHAT: 1H/2549/2.

12. "Special Report of the Government, without debate, on the Algerian Situation," *Journal officiel de la République française* [The official journal of the French republic] (hereafter *JO*), 1962.

13. Parat, for Biget, Préfet de Police d'Oran "Note à l'attention de M. le Ministre" (May 21, 1962), 1–2, in CAC: 770346/08.

14. Capt. Koch, "Rapport . . . sur les événements survenus pendant la periode du 16 au 31 juin [*sic,* should read May] 1962" (Oran, June 2, 1962), 7, in SHAT: 1H/3086/1.

15. Commission de coordination pour la réinstallation des Français d'Outre-Mer, Commissariat général du Plan, "Rapport de la Commission. Annexe 3: Note relative au problème des fonctionnaires" (Paris, July 18, 1962), 16, in CAC: 80 AJ/254 [930275/94].

16. OAS Zone III, "Texte de l'émission réalisée sur les ondes de la TV le 16/6," in SHAT: 1H/3167/1.

17. René Schmitt, in *JO* (May 30, 1962), 1409.

18. Secrétariat d'Etat aux Rapatriés, "Comité des Affaires Algériennes du Mercredi 23 Mai à 15h30. OBJET: Personnes rentrant d'Algérie" (undated), 2, in MAE: 39.

19. Ibid. On the various agencies put in place, see Vincent Viet, *La France immigrée: Construction d'une politique, 1914–1997* [Immigrant France: Construction of a policy, 1914–1997] (Paris: Fayard, 1998), 163–302; Jean-Jacques Jordi, *1962: L'arrivée des pieds-noirs* [1962: The arrival of the *pied noirs*] (Paris: Autrement, 2002), and *De l'exode à l'exil. Rapatriés et Pieds-Noirs en France* [From exodus to exile: Repatriates and *pieds noirs* in France] (Paris: L'Harmattan, 1993); and Jordi and Temime, *Marseille et le choc*. For an excellent study of how these agencies worked, see Sarah Sussman, "Changing Lands, Changing Identities: The Migration of Algerian Jewry to France, 1954–1967" (PhD diss., Stanford University, 2002), 143–251.

20. Direction centrale des RG [Renseignements Généraux], "Sommaire Générale" (Paris, April 18, 1962), 1; Ibid. (Paris, April 9, 1962), 2; both in CAC: 800280: article 216.

21. François Billoux, *Humanité,* June 5, 1962.

22. H. C., de Paris, "Nos lecteurs écrivent. Pourquoi cet exode?" *France-Observateur,* May 24, 1962, 2.

23. Ibid.

24. See Maurice Faivre, *Les combattants musulmans de la guerre d'Algérie: Des soldats sacrifiés* [Muslim fighters of the Algerian war: Sacrificed soldiers] (Paris: L'Harmattan, 1995), 195.

25. Jean Vacher-Desvernais, *L'avenir des Français d'outre-mer* [The future of the French from overseas] (Paris: Presses universitaires de France, 1962), 140.

26. Secrétaire d'Etat aux Rapatriés, "Note pour Monsieur le Président de la République" (Paris, August 1962), 2, in MAE: 117.

27. Philippe Hernandez, "Quatre Pieds-Noirs en métropole," *France-Observateur,* April 12, 1962, 10.

28. Ibid.

29. M. J. Rosny, "Nos Lecteurs Ecrivent. Ça pouvait s'éviter aussi!" *France-Observateur,* March 15, 1962, 18. 9A was the license plate code for the department of Algiers.

30. Philippe Hernandez, "Les pieds-noirs de Montpellier," *France-Observateur,* August 2, 1962, 10.

31. "Il n'y a pas assez de français" (editorial), *Paris-Match,* April 28, 1962, 7.

32. "La seule garanté" (editorial), *Paris-Match*, March 3, 1962, 27.

33. Cover (photo by Maurice Jarnoux), *Paris-Match,* June 2, 1962; "Editorial: La paix anticipée," in *Paris-Match,* June 2, 1962, 6.

34. *JO,* 1440.

35. Ibid., 1404.

36. Ibid., 1488.

37. See Françoise Thébaud, *Quand nos grand-mères donnaient la vie. La maternité en France dans l'entre-deux guerres* [When our grandmothers gave life: Motherhood in France in the interwar] (Lyon: Presses universitaires de Lyon, 1986); Susan Pedersen, *Family Policy and the Origins of the Welfare State: Britain and France, 1914–45* (Cambridge, UK: Cambridge University Press, 1993); Ann Orloff, "Gender in the Welfare State," *Annual Review of Sociology* 22 (1996): 51–78.

38. Direction centrale des RG, "Sommaire Générale" (Paris, June 27, 1962), 1, in CAC: 800280: article 218.

39. *JO,* 1427.

40. Ibid., 2353.

41. DEFNAT PARIS, "Télégramme au Bureau Moral" (received March 15, 1962), in SHAT: 1H/2467/6.

42. Commandement Supérieur des Forces en Algérie, "MESSAGE n. 0560/CSFA/EMI/MOR" (February 22, 1962), 3, in SHAT: 1H/1260/1.

43. Radiodiffusion Française, "Texte de l'émission diffusée au Bulletin de France II (13h) le 4 avril 1962: A qui s'appliquent les Accords d'Evian?" (April 4, 1962), 2–3, in Centre d'accueil et de recherche des archives nationales, Paris, France (hereafter AN): F/1a/5055.

44. Charles de Gaulle (signed), "Séance du jeudi 21 juin 1962. Rélève des décisions" (June 21, 1962), p. 6, in MAE: 40.

45. Service des Affaires politiques, "Note pour le Ministre a/s Comité des Affaires Algériennes du 21 juin" (June 21, 1962), 2–3, in MAE: 40. This note summarizes Christian Fouchet, Haut Commissaire de la République en Algérie, "Traduction Du Message Chiffré n. 7859/51. Objet: Prochain Comité des Affaires algériennes-Questions de nationalité" (June 19, 1962), 1–2, in MAE: 117.

46. de Gaulle, "Séance du jeudi 21 juin 1962. Rélève des décisions."

47. "LE PRESIDENT DE LA REPUBLIQUE Sur le rapport . . . ORDONNE" (Paris, June 8, 1962), 1–2, in MAE: 117.

48. Ibid.

49. A. Bacquet, "A/S Acquisition de la Nationalité Française par un citoyen Algérien de statut civil local" (Rocher Noir, September 29, 1962), in SHAT: 1H/1260/D3.

50. J. J. de Bresson, "Extrait du rélève des décision du Conseil des Affaires algériennes du 23 mai 1962: Rapatriés Musulmans" (May 28, 1962), 1, in MAE: 39.

51. Bureau du moral, Commandement Superieur des forces en Algérie, "Recasement des supplétifs et civils F.S.N.A. menaces" (SP 87.000, May 26, 1962), 2, in SHAT: 1H/1260/2.

52. Secrétariat d'Etat aux Rapatriés, "Comité des Affaires Algériennes du 28 Avril 1962: Accueil des rapatriés," 6, in MAE: 39; Secrétariat d'Etat aux Rapatriés, "OBJET: Personnes rentrant d'Algérie," 5–6, in MAE: 39.

53. Secrétariat d'Etat aux Rapatriés, "Comité des Affaires Algériennes du 28 Avril 1962: Accueil des rapatriés," 6, in MAE: 39; Secrétariat d'Etat aux Rapatriés, "OBJET: Personnes rentrant d'Algérie," 5–6, in MAE: 39.

54. Faivre, *Les combattants musulmans,* 197.

55. Service des affaires musulmanes (SAM), "Bilan des Réalisations . . ." (November 28, 1963), 1, in AN: F/1a/5055.

56. Minister of Repatriates François Missoffe, "Votre exemple" (editorial), *Bulletin special édité par la Ministre des rapatriés pour la campagne printemps 1963 "Priorité d'Emploi aux rapatriés"* 4 (May 7, 1963), 1, in SHAT: 1H/1130/3.

57. SAM, "Synthèse des rapports trimestriels . . . 1è trimestre (1/1–31/3/62)," 34–35, in AN: F/1a/5014. According to SAM statistics, the months after the announcement of the Evian Accords did witness a new tendency for more "French Muslims" to leave the metropole for Algeria than vice versa. By September, this had ended, and once again more "Algerians" or Algerian "Muslims" were coming to the metropole than were leaving.

58. Amelia Lyons, "Algerian Families and the French Welfare State in the Era of Decolonization (1947–1974)" (PhD. diss., University of California, Irvine, 2004), 286.

59. Prime Minister Georges Pompidou, "Note pour Monsieur le Ministre des Armeés. Objet-Transfert en France d'anciens supplétifs menacés" (Paris, September 19, 1962), in SHAT: 1H/1397/8.

60. On estimates of numbers of Algerians killed in the months following the cease-fire because they were accused of being pro-French, see Guy Pervillé, *Pour une histoire de la guerre d'Algérie* [For a history of the Algerian war] (Paris: Picard, 2002), 243–44. Estimates range from more than 10,000 to close to 150,000.

61. G. Lamassoure, chef du Service des Affaires Musulmanes, "à M. le Préfet de l'Isère. Objet: Anciens supplétifs et réfugiés musulmans" (February 26, 1963), 1, in AN: F/1a/5125.

62. Ibid.

63. See the September 28, 1962, letter from Marceau Long, secretary of state attached to the prime minister in charge of the civil service, "FP/1 n. 4330, à

M. Messaoud DJEGHLOUL, attaché de Préfecture, Poitiers (Vienne)," in CAC: 19770007, article 210.

64. Henri Le Corno, "Application de l'ordonnance n. 62–825 du 21 juillet 1962 . . ." (February 4, 1963), 2; and, in response, Bernard Lory, Ministère de la Santé Publique, "Réponse à . . ." (February 18, 1962), 1; both letters in AN: F/1cII/517.

65. Commission de coordination pour la réinstallation des Français d'Outre-Mer. Commissariat général du Plan, "Rapport Général du 5 decembre 1962" (December 5, 1962), 14, in CAC: 80 AJ/254 [930275/94].

66. SAM, "Synthèse des rapports trimestriels établis par les conseillers techniques pour les affaires musulmanes—4e trimestre/1/10–31/12/62," 41, in AN: F/1a/5014.

67. SAM, "Synthèse des rapports trimestriels établis . . . 3è trimestre/1/7–30/9/62," 25, in AN: F/1a/5014. On the metropolitan welcome of the *harkis,* see Abderahmen Moumen, *Les Français musulmans en Vaucluse. Installation et difficultés d'intégration d'une communauté de rapatriés d'Algérie 1962–1991* [French Muslims in the Vaucluse 1962–1991: Installation and integration problems of a community of Algerian repatriates] (Paris: L'Harmattan, 2003); Mohand Hammoumou, *Et ils sont devenus harkis* [And they became *harkis*] (Paris: Fayard, 1994); and Mohand Hammoumou, with the collaboration of Abderahmen Moumen, "L'histoire des harkis et Français musulmans: la fin d'un tabou?" in *La guerre d'Algérie, 1954–2004, la fin de l'amnésie* [The war in Algeria, 1954–2004: The end of amnesia], ed. Mohammed Harbi and Benjamin Stora, 317–44 (Paris: Robert Laffont, 2004).

CHAPTER THREE

Enslaved Lives, Enslaving Labels

A New Approach to the Colonial Indian Labor Diaspora

CRISPIN BATES AND MARINA CARTER

India has seen some of the largest labor migrations in the modern world, with the annual emigration of Indians overseas fluctuating between 240,000 to 660,000 in the period from 1870 to 1930, and totaling some 2,483,000 between 1911 and 1915 alone. This chapter highlights what are termed "subaltern networks" in the Indian labor diaspora, with particular reference to the Indian Ocean region, and argues both that an analysis of the migration and settlement patterns of groups variously categorized as coolies, servants, or sepoys is crucial to an understanding of the dynamics of overseas labor flows and that rather than occupying discrete categories rooted in South Asia, they may be viewed as a composite itinerant class that may be better understood from a global perspective.

Consequently, it is argued that while the subaltern networks functioned ostensibly as a vehicle for the subordination of labor, they were, over time and with varying degrees of success, appropriated by the subordinated, becoming both a means of sociocultural reassertion and an economic strategy, linking together forest, field, factory, and plantation. The evolving stereotypes about the servant classes in India and their migratory counterparts are revealing of these broader changes but inadequate to provide an understanding of the realities of the diaspora experience. Closer study of the appraisals, projects, and strategies helps to deconstruct the labels that essentialize the status of the coolie, the domestic worker, the convict, and the sepoy, and reveals how such individuals survived and even flourished within the interstices of the colonial system.

The Context

Rural-rural and rural-urban migration within India is an ancient phenomenon that, along with nomadic and shifting systems of agriculture, has been in most parts integral to the functioning of the rural economy. Rarely, if ever, were villages able to meet all the requirements of production and reproduction. The payment of taxes and tributes imposed a degree of circulation even in tribal areas. In many parts of India, particularly the less fertile or more densely populated regions, seasonal labor migration was a common resort at times of harvest, as it continues to be up to the present day. Likewise, Indian migration to Indian Ocean states, East Africa, South Africa, and in particular to Mauritius and surrounding islands (the Mascarene group) is as old as European colonization of those regions. Indeed, they could be said to constitute the beginnings of a circulatory system on an oceanic (if not global) scale well before the establishment of plantations in Assam, Sri Lanka, and Malaysia, as well as the establishment of the later colonial systems of free and indentured migration. The involvement of Indians in almost every phase of Mascarene and South African development, to name but two examples, thus belies the subordinate role that is often accorded the non-British migrant in assessments of empire building.

The process of incorporation of these groups into their host societies has been inadequately explored. In eighteenth- and nineteenth-century Indian Ocean colonies, Indian subaltern groups, such as slaves and later convicts and coolies, all found means of circumventing and rising above the status with which they had been saddled. The nineteenth-century indentured immigrants, in particular, used and extended networks of support and organization put in place by their compatriots in the overseas context. This chapter argues that as a result, Indians themselves increasingly took control of their migratory patterns in the Indian Ocean region, instituting kin and family regroupment, organizing repatriation and terms of settlement onto and off the plantations. And many, once freed from indenture contracts, would re-emigrate to other overseas destinations (e.g., South Africa), establishing new settlements often semi-autonomously. Some would otherwise re-engage on indenture contracts and head for destinations as far away as the Caribbean, although such longer-distance migrations were more largely motivated by the pressure of poverty than adequate information about the opportunities available. Even in these instances, however, a network of contacts and facilitators was indispensable.

Research into the subaltern networks of Indian contract laborers demonstrates that the indenture system did not operate simply or wholly as a European-sponsored importation of a non-white workforce, but tapped into a wider circulatory system of labor. This requires us to challenge the reified, fixed category that the coolie represents for so many orthodox histories of the Indian diaspora.

The Debate

There is little doubt that the lives of slaves, convicts, and indentured laborers were, in many respects, analogous. Despite supposed advances in welfare legislation and juridical control, it was as easy for unscrupulous employers to imprison and ill-treat their Indian indentured workers as it had been for the owners of Indian slaves to confine them in chains and stocks decades earlier. The tools of oppression changed over time, but the operation, magnitude, and effect did not. Resistance was also analogous. Running away was termed "marooning" in the slave era; indentured laborers who adopted the same tactic were categorized as deserters and vagrants. The lash could not, in theory, be used against the recalcitrant coolie, but physical coercion was as present in the camp of the indentured worker as it had been in the slave lines. Yet coolie, convict, and slave all survived the traumas arising from their subordinate position and in time found ways to assert themselves, to pursue their own objectives, and to articulate new identities.

The typical nineteenth-century, post-enlightenment discourse on "freedom" and "unfreedom" is reproduced in much colonial writing and in subsequent historical accounts. The cultural specificities of these ideas have been highlighted effectively by David Davis, Gyan Prakash, and others.[1] The assumption by the modern state of responsibility for the policing of relationships between individuals, as advocated in Rousseau's *Social Contract,* inevitably called into question feudal forms of servitude while imposing new kinds of legal and contractual restraint. The inconsistencies of this approach were apparent, of course, even in the nineteenth century. Thus Marx wrote of the "veiled slavery" of wage earners in Europe, and contemporary authors defended the comparative liberties of chattel slavery in the southern United States.[2] Even so, the contrasting of freedom and unfreedom is characteristic of nineteenth-century debates on the abolition of slavery and has dominated the discourse of indenture.

All too many studies of subaltern migration cast recruiters in the role of villains acting at the behest of dark colonial forces to defraud ignorant and unwilling victims into overseas migration, the classic example being Hugh Tinker's monumental work *A New System of Slavery: the Export of Indian Labour Overseas, 1830–1920* (1974), which paints a portrait of evil *arkatis* (labor recruiters) kidnapping and drugging young children and women in terms reminiscent of nineteenth-century Anti-Slavery Society literature. This appraisal, of course, leaves little room for understandings of more complex relationships between returnee recruiters drawn from the ranks of ex-indentured laborers, who frequently returned to natal villages to bring their kin and family members into indentureship. Tinker's provocative title has spawned many recent imitators who begin from a blind acceptance of the notion that indenture was simply a "new form" of slavery. Such works seek to deconstruct the colonial discourse but fail to illuminate the actual mechanisms through which labor migrants from India spread throughout the Indian Ocean and beyond.

In the case of indentured migration, Michael Roberts has questioned "the appropriateness of such concepts as 'debt bondage' and 'unfree labor' in a context when the labor supply was marked by circular migration" and has warned against treating labor intermediaries such as the *kanganis* (and by extension the *arkatis* and returnee recruiters) as "a mere arm of the planters."[3] These individuals operated also as bargainers for the laborers and as crucial informants. Roberts calls upon scholars "to decipher the bargaining power, such as it was, of these migrant laborers by unpacking details pertaining to labor relations . . . studies of this subject must be more attentive to the experiential aspect of plantation labor life."[4]

If the identity of Indians—both ascribed and offered—was complex, so too was their perception of their role and rationale in migrating. Indians are too easily viewed as victims both in traditional and more recent historical accounts, but a re-examination of the sources can reveal a very different story. Interviews with laborers reproduced in Commissions of Enquiry can be particularly enlightening in this regard. They can reveal, for example, that subaltern migratory networks did not necessarily compete with the recruitment agencies hired by European planters, but that they often worked side by side.

Within these networks of official, unofficial, paid, and volunteer recruiters, the role of the *kangani* or *sirdar* (foreman/overseer) is the aspect of labor migration and workers' organizations perhaps most seriously in need of revision in the historiography of labor migration, both within India and abroad. Patrick Peebles' account of the role and history of the *kanganis* in Ceylon begins this process with a useful deconstruction of contemporary descriptions of their activities and of historians' generalizations about them.[5] Peebles' work thus reveals that even for key intermediary figures such as the *kanganis* of Ceylon, there is little known fact and much that is misleading written about such subaltern networks. He dismisses historians' notions of the *kangani* as a "patriarch" or as necessarily a man whose caste status gave him a position of authority with his workers—pointing out that cases occurred of low-caste *kanganis* with higher-caste laborers under them. He notes that recruiting *kanganis*, thousands of whom were sent by planters to recruit in India in the nineteenth century, did not always recruit their own kin, but that they sometimes bought coolies from other recruiters, or induced bonded laborers to desert. Peebles also discounts the usual demonization of the *kangani* as a physical abuser of coolies, pointing out that the evidence suggests "they relied more on moral influence than coercion" (37).

Peebles argues that contemporary accounts of *kanganis* "do not reflect actual conditions but rather planters' distaste for the independence and prosperity of the kanganies. . . . [P]lanters had little control over the kanganies" and insufficient knowledge about their recruits (37). Accounts from colonial sources of *kanganis* as patriarchal or as exploiters who defrauded laborers must therefore be treated with caution, as "there certainly is some truth in both accounts, but by themselves they carry little weight" (38). Peebles also points out "since one in eight plantation Tamils was a kangany, the possibility of becoming a kangany was a real one for labourers. Anyone who could re- turn to India and bring back labourers or who was chosen to supervise others became a kangany . . . and had a substantially higher income" (38).

A similarly measured account of the role of the *kangani* was made earlier by S. Arasaratnam, who wrote that a *kangani* is

> a person who was himself an immigrant working on the plantation as a foreman, or even as a labourer of some influence and standing. The em- ployer would send him to India provided with money, to go to his vil- lage and district and recruit labourers among his own people. . . . There was now scope for the migration of families rather than individuals. . . . When the kangany returned to Malaya with his group of labourers and delivered them to his employer, they were employed in that plantation, usually under the kangany who had recruited them. Thus there was a continuing connexion. . . . [T]he kangany had subtle means of keeping the labourer on a lead, attached to and dependent on him.[6]

In reappraising the role of the *kangani*, it should be recognized that the transformation of India into a source of cheap labor for the British Empire, and the increasing involvement of overseas capitalists in recruitment for plan- tation economies, resulted in competition both among colonial recruiters and between them and local employers.[7] The sourcing of recruiters from within the ranks of migrants became crucial to the effectiveness of labor mobiliza- tion, but in the process the increasing autonomy of these agents subtly altered the balance of power between laborer and employer, with far-reaching conse- quences for the plantation societies to which they resorted in large numbers.

Recruiting *sirdars,* men and sometimes women who had been overseas and could speak with firsthand experience of conditions in the colonies, emerged—both formally and informally (they did not always bear the title of *sirdar*)—as a "middleman" network between the subaltern and employer. This undoubtedly typified the involvement of *sirdars* in recruitment for industrial labor within India as much as abroad. For this reason their demonization and later disappearance from contemporary records post-1914 (noted by Chandarvarkar) should be taken with a grain of salt.[8] Their role was never quite what it seemed in the first place and is unlikely to have disappeared immediately once they lost either official sanction or their usefulness to employers.

Women migrants within the indenture system have been commonly considered the greatest "victims," "super-exploited," and subjected to patriarchal controls by a double layer of colonial and male oppression. A recent study that has sought to "recast" women labor by portraying the debate between imperial policy makers and Anti-Slavery Society reformers in terms of a battle that was "lost" by the latter merely takes the discussion into a different cul-de-sac.[9] The Anti-Slavery Society reformers, based in England, often had a less than firm grasp on conditions and events in the colonies. Their "insights" were frequently as wide of the mark as the more extravagant assertions of estate owners. Some of their wilder claims—for example, that family life was nonexistent on the colonial sugar plantations—have been taken up by historians and anthropologists and contributed to the persistence of absurdities such as Hugh Tinker's depiction of overseas Indian women as "sorry, broken creatures" and the notion common among anthropologists until recently that "caste" and community disappeared once Indians had embarked on a migrant ship. The reality was a far slower and complex transmutation of ideology, form, and substance.[10]

Research has increasingly demonstrated that the vast majority of women who migrated to the sugar colony of Mauritius sustained their family ties throughout the period of indenture.[11] Moreover, an analysis of individual life histories of indentured women reveals that the decision to migrate was usually made within a wider family context and that most women accompanied kin members or were summoned to rejoin family overseas.[12] If this has been established in the case of one Indian Ocean destination, then such may also have been the case in the migrations to Southeast Asia and the Caribbean too. New research by Veronique Bragard and others is leading in this direction, addressing the means Indian women found to survive and prosper in the Caribbean and in which they were able to assert themselves in social and cultural terms.[13]

The reappraisal of individual male and female migrants and family groups leads to the necessary recognition that if chain migrations existed for European laborers migrating to North America, it should be recognized that they also existed for migrants within India and the Indian Ocean region.

M. Kale depicts indenture as occupying "ambiguous space . . . in the dichotomising discourse on slavery and freedom" but fails to enlarge upon the part played by evidence of "family colonisation" or subaltern migration strategies.[14] These have increasingly placed Indian labor migrants on a par with Irish or Polish laborers, who are often seen to be engaged in "opportunity-maximising" movements while simultaneously "fleeing famine." Returnees, *sirdars,* and recruiters created out of indenture a dynamic that operated clearly outside the planter/administrator worldview, but Kale has little to say about this crucial area of subaltern agency in which the "coolie" ceased to be and the Indian overseas created his or her own world.

Discourse analysis creates its own victims and baddies in precisely the same way as the now discredited pro-planter or pro-laborer treatises. The uncritical appraisal of the white anti-indenture activists by Kale is a case in point.[15] Similarly, K. Ghosh portrays the *arkatis* as evil seducers of innocent labor in a direct borrowing from reform pamphlets of the period. The politics of discourse analysis may therefore be sound, but not always its methods and techniques.[16]

Many of the still current misconceptions about indenture can be traced back to the nationalist agitation of the early twentieth century. When it comes to the stigmatization of the Indian coolie laborer, it can reasonably be questioned which was worse: the planters with their bland commercial transactions in coolie "cargoes" or the supposed sympathizers of the overseas Indians' plight, such as C. F. Andrews, who reviled the "doe-eyed immorality" of the Indo-Fijian women, or Mahatma Gandhi, who claimed that "if the badge of inferiority is always to be worn by them, . . . any material advantage they will gain by emigrating can . . . be of no consideration."[17] One wonders, furthermore, what feelings were aroused among the formerly indentured populations in Guyana, Trinidad, Fiji, and Surinam when the Indian National Congress propounded that their very existence testified to the "international shame of the Indian." Studies of indenture have failed to deconstruct the nationalist discourse as thoroughly as they have critiqued that of the "colonialists."

Leaving aside the nationalist political dimension and concentrating on empirical data revealing of economic trends, several useful accounts of internal, rural migration evolving into longer-distance labor movements are worthy of further investigation. Often this began as contract labor at harvest time:

> In the Jubbulpore haveli there is an immigration of Chaitharas, or those who come in Chait (March–April) to cut the wheat crop. Year by

year . . . the Gond comes down from the Rewa hills to the Lodhi in the haveli; the same Gond to the same Lodhi and from father to son. Till the crop is ready to be cut, he occupies himself in roofing the house, building up the walls, and doing any other odd job that may be required. Then he assists in the reaping of the crop, and when it is threshed and harvested, he returns home, having received his food while he is there, and taking across his shoulders as much grain as he can get into a *kawar* load.[18]

Even as late as 1927, long past the heyday of the wheat trade, the total number of migrants flocking into the Narmada valley each year to assist in harvest operations was estimated at 120,000, and the scale of this seasonal migration must have been proportionately much greater in the 1880s, when wheat exports and acreages were 340 and 25 percent higher, respectively.[19] Estimates in 1931 based on a plateau district in the Central Provinces of India suggested that 4 percent of the total population was a fairly normal proportion of casual migrants, but migration could be greatly increased by warfare (there was a huge increase in indentured migration overseas following the uprising of 1857), famine, and land loss. Many of these migrants in central India were Gond tribals, or *adivasis,* known as "coolies" in eastern India:

The Gond appears unable to retain the good land in his possession and as soon as his holding begins to produce anything like valuable crops, he falls back into the position of a farm-laborer and his fields too often pass to others to whom he has become indebted. The bulk of the Gond population are labourers. . . . Till lately they were always paid in kind, but with the great rise which has lately taken place in the value of wheat, there is a tendency now for payments in kind to be commuted into cash. At the time of cutting of the wheat harvest, there is always a great movement among the labouring classes. Like the hop-pickers at home, whole families will travel long distances to places where plenty of harvesting is going on. . . . A considerable number . . . have emigrated.[20]

From this, systems of chain migration readily evolved, which took migrants away from agriculture altogether. Thus Anand Yang quotes a district officer who stated that Saran's inhabitants "having once acquired the habit of emigrating for wages, and having found that it is easy to save money in this way . . . now emigrate yearly as a matter of habit to supplement their incomes, whether agricultural conditions are prosperous or the reverse."[21] Another official wrote, "In districts where there are returned emigrants, emigration is popular. In districts where there are none, it is the reverse. Every coolie who emigrates, on his return becomes an apostle of it." Those who migrated far away were often described as following "some friend or relation."[22]

The involvement of friends and relatives is crucial, since from a perspective that emphasizes subaltern agency, historians must challenge the widely held notion that colonial societies, particularly those on the Indian Ocean littoral, with long traditions of Indian migration in its various guises, experienced—or exercised—such a level of control that the character it assumed in each case was entirely different. Nowhere, in any instance, did indenture operate simply as a European-sponsored importation of a non-white workforce. The control of trade and shipping was always at least partially in the hands of Indian merchants. Goods from India and the staple foodstuffs of immigrants could be purchased from them to supplement the estate diet—but at a price; time-expired immigrants could negotiate a passage between the littoral states and India with Gujarati or Tamil merchants. Through Indian merchants and landowners, a significant number of indentured laborers were eventually able to acquire credit and small plots of land and establish themselves as small-holders during the last quarter of the nineteenth century.

An understanding of why the achievements of overseas Indians have been comparatively neglected in the literature lies in the nationalist discourse that came to dominate appraisals of indenture in the early twentieth century and that, to this day, has not been critiqued effectively. A former indentured migrant turned recruiter, Peria Gengadu, provides a graphic account of the discriminatory treatment he received on returning to India, and one could argue that in this case the so-called exploiter has himself become the victimized:

> I was really astonished to see my close relations and intimate friends holding aloof. . . . The public believed all that was stated in the pamphlets. Rumours were afloat that some sirdars were killed. All these put me in great fear. I could not eat. I had no sleep. . . . In the meantime some 15 men who were negotiating with me privately to emigrate changed their minds and absconded at Ramapuram railway station. This made the situation worse. The villagers began to suspect me. The village magistrate put a guard on me. I was more or less a state prisoner. Seeing all these difficulties, I begged of my wife to go with me. . . . After a deliberate consideration she agreed. She also influenced 3 Indians.[23]

Gengadu's story shows nonetheless that even in the midst of a propaganda drive, it was still possible for close relatives to be persuaded to migrate.

Munusamy Naidu, an Indian labor migrant promoted to the position of *sirdar,* further expressed the real dichotomy of the indenture experience—that migrants who were viewed as desperate victims, and their recruiters as exploitative scum, often had a totally different image of themselves: "In India, everybody—young and old—did spit on sirdars. Sirdars are treated like pariah dogs—not as gentlemen. . . . I am not a young man to stand all abuses, to receive kicks and blows from the public. I belong to a respectable family."[24] It is this self-image that the historian must refract and assess, rather than merely the splintered fragments of opposing discourses of pro- and antimigration lobbies.

The difficulty of this enterprise is compounded by the types of sources historians have often employed. These are commonly less overtly political official accounts or inquiries that are concerned with the conditions or circumstances of migrants insofar as they related to the needs of legislation. This demand for legislation arose primarily, as Dipesh Chakrabarty has argued, from the needs of employers. Under the monopolistic conditions in many industrial and planting concerns in the nineteenth century, there was often little demand for legislation to regulate the conditions of Indian labor (on the model of the British Factory Acts of the 1820s) because of the abundance of labor supplied.[25] This abundance arose, particularly in the north and east of India, from the expropriation of *adivasis* and low-caste groups who are found in a majority among the workforce. In India therefore the administration gave full vent to its natural alliance with the predominantly European employers and completely ignored the conditions of labor. The motivation behind official accounts was initially the desire to demonstrate the lack of any need for legislative control of mining and industrial enterprises within India.

As competition increased, however, particularly that between the Indian and European capitalists, a growing voice began to be heard within colonial documents making a case, also motivated by the needs of capitalists, for an alternative approach: the intervention of government and the controls required by industry in order to equalize competition. This voice was heard particularly in the 1920s and 1930s but also at other times when declining prices or competition for labor put pressure on profits. The case then needed to be made for legislation, and evidence was then sought for a completely contrary interpretation: that all things were bad and there was a need for dramatic reform. By simply reproducing colonialist accounts either for or against systems of production, historians have all too easily fallen into the trap of becoming themselves crude advocates of one position or another, failing to notice that these accounts were produced for a purpose—usually that of justifying or rejecting a policy of legislative intervention by the colonialists themselves.[26] From this perspective one can argue that by critically examining colonial Government of India sources on migration, much more can be made of than has hitherto been the case. At the same time, greater use could be made of sources originating beyond the shores of India.

The Evidence

In the eighteenth century some of the earliest Indian migrants overseas were transported as slaves by the French.[27] Tens of thousands of Indian slaves were shipped to the Mascarene islands and South Africa over the course of the eighteenth century, while considerable numbers of Indian convicts were transported by the East India Company to penal settlements in Southeast Asia, such as Penang, Arakan, Malacca, Singapore, and the Tenasserim coast. Later, more were sent to Mauritius, the Port of Aden, and the Andaman Islands (a favorite destination for the mutineers of 1857), and a few to Australia. The total number of Indian convicts transported to Aden, Mauritius, and Southeast Asia totaled at least one hundred thousand.[28] They were an extremely important source of labor, providing an infrastructure and facilities at the very inception of these colonies.

Convict indents and slave registers reveal that there was a far wider and more diverse migration of Indians overseas than is commonly realized. The records of transportees from London to Australia, for example, included several Indian *lascars* (sailors) who had left ships and settled ashore in London and who subsequently committed an offense and were transported. One can deduce that there were many others more fortunate who, apart from fleeting references, remain invisible in the historical record, not least because British records in the eighteenth and early nineteenth centuries are almost completely oblivious to concepts of race. Racial profiling of offenders, in local government records and in census returns, does not become commonplace until the second half of the nineteenth century.

One example of many individuals who emerge from the records, and who crossed the categories from South Asian migrant to seaman to convict to new world settler, is Sheik Brom, a "dark-skinned" servant, aged twenty-two, originating from Surat, who was arrested and indicted for stealing in London on March 4, 1824. Details of his crime are to be found in the printed records of the London Old Bailey Sessions papers for 1824, which state that Sheik Brom stole from the dwelling house of Francis Robinson at All Saints, Poplar, in west London, a "provision-merchant" who ran a "depot for the reception of black men." (Most probably he was providing accommodation for "black men" as a commercial enterprise.) Sheik Brom was no petty thief, having taken three coats, two pairs of trousers, four waistcoats, a pair of breeches, two handkerchiefs (these were usually highly decorated silk and lace), a pair of gaiters, two pairs of stockings, a pair of shoes, a towel, five gloves, six shillings, and two sovereigns (each worth twenty shillings)—all the property of William Green, a clerk to Francis Robinson. Altogether, these were valued at a total of 101 shillings, equivalent to a minimum of 500 British pounds in modern terms, although almost certainly much more.

Sheik Brom was most probably a Muslim seaman out of Bombay who had left his ship and resided in the locality where he committed his crime. His mistake was that he had lived in the locality long enough to be known, yet did not move away to sell the stolen goods. He thus sold a waistcoat and breeches to a tobacconist from whom he regularly purchased snuff, other items he sold to another shopkeeper, and two coats he pawned to a pawnbroker (using the name Jack Brown), all of whom gave evidence against him in court. When arrested he had 17 shillings, 6 pence sewn in his trousers, but claimed that he had only 2 pence about his person. Sheik Brom was sentenced to death, but this was commuted to transportation to New South Wales (whence he traveled on the ship *Asia*) in that he was a foreigner for which he was "recommended to mercy." The resolution of his case was helpfully explained to him by an interpreter.[29]

A less charismatic character, but still clearer example, is Mahomed Balletti, five feet two inches tall, "Black," and thirty-two years of age, a literate Muslim from Bombay, who, it is stated, "can read and write in his own language." He was tried in the Central Criminal Court in London on May 9, 1842, for the crime, to which he confessed, of sodomizing a lascar on board a ship. Mahomed was sentenced to transportation "for life" to Van Diemen's Land (Tasmania), where he served for nine years in Wedge Bay, including four consecutive sentences of up to three months hard labor for disobedience or laziness. He was eventually given his ticket of leave (i.e., permission to work for a private employer under probation) in 1851 and was clearly reformed by his experiences, since he soon after married a rowdy young woman by the name of Martha (who herself got into trouble for drunkenness and talking in chapel). Likewise, Sheikh Brom was pardoned conditionally in 1854 and disappears from the records, having managed to avoid falling into trouble with the authorities thereafter.[30]

An interesting instance of mutiny, of sorts, is to be found in the case of Talicouty, a cook and groom from Trichinopoly. "Heathen" by religion (i.e., Hindu), he was tried in the Port Louis Assizes in Mauritius, December 7, 1843, and sentenced to ten years transportation to Van Diemen's Land for the crime of "murder by poisoned pudding of a ship's mate." Talicouty conspired in this crime with no less than three others: Osensa and her husband Samba, and Yacousal, a Muslim servant from Trichinopoly. All were sentenced to ten years transportation to Van Diemen's Land. Yacousal was given a ticket of leave in 1849 and his freedom in 1853, but Talicouty excelled at creating mayhem and was sentenced to additional hard labor or solitary confinement on no less than nineteen occasions, usually for disobedience, but also for gambling, insolence, absconding, or other absences from work. He was not given his freedom until after 1853, and subsequently fell foul of the law in Australia in 1868, and again in 1869 for "idle and disorderly conduct" and a "breach of the Police Act" for which he was returned to prison for a further month's hard labor.[31]

A surprising number of convicts are to be found who were literate, such as one "John Solomon" from Bombay, a Muslim cook and waiter who could read and write Gujarati. (In 1840, he was tried and sentenced in Sydney, Australia, for sodomy and transported to Van Diemen's Land.) Solomon had either migrated on his own or, most probably, had been in service on an East India ship that he abandoned in search of employment ashore in Australia. "Nowardin" (Nur Al-Din?), an Arab from Muscat, seems also to have served on an East India ship, being arrested and tried in February 1815 at the Middlesex assizes in London for the crime of stealing (with the aid of accomplices) one five-pound bank note, one three-shilling bank note, sixteen calico shirts, sixteen pairs of trousers, two brass pans, and a quantity of spices from the trunk of one Mahomet Cassam, or Sarane, of the East India ship *Forbes,* who was staying at the time in the East India barracks in London.[32]

If the gripping accounts of the criminal careers of Indian convicts demonstrate that they cannot easily be fitted into any category, so too do we find that the "coolie," the "servant," and the "sepoy" in history frequently step out of the categorizations neatly applied to them. The case of Sadayen from Alemparve near Pondicherry, who was recruited as a soldier but discovered he had been sold as a slave, illustrates the fragility of distinctions between such military recruits and the victims of slave *razzias* (warriors). Luckily for Sadayen, a chance meeting with a free Indian of his acquaintance from Pondicherry who worked for an officer in the artillery regiment at the Isle of France (Mauritius), and who was able to identify him, secured his release. The overlapping of categories of servant, sepoy, and slave is clearly evident and frequent when historians have the opportunity to follow individual case histories.[33]

Rengasamy Naicker, who went to Mauritius in the 1830s, was one of countless labor migrants who flitted between "categories":

I was formerly employed as a sepoy under the Danish Government of Tranquebar [in the Kaveri delta]. After the annexation of that settlement

to the company territories, I obtained a Vesharipoogarship in the Tranquebar talook. As my younger brother was living at Singapore and as I was
desirous of paying a visit to him, I resigned the Vesharipoogarship's post
and went there. After a lapse of one year, I returned to my native land and
was without employment. A native of Karrical of the Vellala caste was
acquainted with me. . . . He said he was going to Mauritius and desired
me to follow him. I consented to it, and went along with him.[34]

That discharged sepoys often became "coolie" migrants was articulated as
early as 1838 by the collector at Godavari, who noted that many of the recruits belonged to this category. Boodhoo Khan's story is illustrative of the
process through which a sepoy became a coolie before returning to India. His
evidence, given to a commission of enquiry into labor migration held in 1840,
was as follows:

I am a Pathan, and my home is at Gyah; I left my home in the month of
July (Assar) about two years ago; I left my home to seek service. I entered
into the service of the rajah of Morbaugh, as a sepahie, for 5 rupees per
month and food; I served him for a year, and received 15 rupees only in
cash, but I got altogether 9 cows, some worth 3 rupees, some 4. I sent the
cows to my home at Gyah. I have a brother in the Calcutta militia, named
Sheer Khan. . . . I quarrelled with the rajah's commissary about food,
and took my discharge; besides, there was no fighting, or I would have
remained. I met with a duffadar at Seersa, in the same district of Morbaugh. . . . He took me to Beehbhul; the duffadar told me I was to get
14 rupees wages. . . . When I arrived in Calcutta I learnt that I should
have to go on board a big ship, and that I was to engage for 5 years. . . .
My brother who is employed as a sepoy at Alipur heard this and came to
me and said, "Why should you go? If you are in debt, I will pay for you.
This is to go on board ship. . . ." I told him, "Be it as it may, I came for
service, and I must go; this is the Company's service, and why should I
refuse it?" I did not know how far the island was, or what time would be
expended in the passage until at sea, when the mate of the ship asked me
if I knew how long I should be; I said no; he then told me I should be four
months. I did not mind; I am a man, not a woman, and I am a Pathan's
son; I had given my word, and I did not care if it were 8 months; I would
have gone if they had told me in Calcutta that I should be four months.[35]

While it may be argued that Boodhoo Khan was confused about the nature of the "Company service" he was to undertake, the numbers of sepoys

migrating as coolies indicates that many were prepared to undertake agricultural labor. This was underscored by the emigration agent at Madras in 1879, when he presented his reasons for shipping ex-sepoys, noting "a laborer from the Madras presidency is a 'maid of all work.' A sepoy, or a peon, is taken from the plough and as easily returns to it. I have in my own employ coachmen and grooms, as good field laborers as could be found anywhere." He pointed out the case of Mooneesamy, then awaiting shipment as a coolie, who had formerly served "seven years as an orderly boy in a regiment, and five years as a sepoy, but since that he has worked as a carter, and a field laborer. I have had him tested in my garden, where he not only ploughed, but did a good day's work in digging and leveling."[36]

It is clear that after 1857 many ex-sepoys resorted to migration as indentured laborers. Unfortunately, no study to date has sought to investigate the remarkably high figures of out-migration in 1858–1860 and to provide reliable estimates of the number of sepoys who used indenture as an escape route from economic dislocation and political victimization. However, occasional British inspections of the Indians on colonial sugar estates offered a rare opportunity to weed out potential "rebels." Parushram, seen by inspectors on a Mauritius estate in 1872, was believed to have been a rebel on the grounds that he was an ex-sepoy from Ghazipur and had emigrated in 1859. Other ex-sepoys on the overseas sugar estates, like Sheik Abdoola, who had served in the 28th Bombay Native Infantry, had no need to be reticent about their former careers.[37] It has been argued that there was a direct relationship between the Rebellion of 1857–58 and the increase in numbers emigrating to the Caribbean, both because their districts of origin were those most affected by those events and because of the unemployment among ex-soldiers from disbanded native armies denied employment in the British Indian army, along with mutineers running from arrest.[38] Into the twentieth century, examples continue to be found of sepoys migrating overseas in search of work. In 1906 Harman Singh, formerly of the 96th Sikh Infantry Regiment, went to Mauritius as a passenger, hoping to find work there.[39]

It was stated clearly by one British colonial official who investigated migration in the late nineteenth century that recruiters of overseas labor were usually men who had already worked for colonizers in one capacity or another: "The class from which recruiters spring is that which supplies sepoys, chaprassis, and domestic servants. I found men who had previously been employed as bearers, khidmatgars, cavalry sowars, infantry and police sepoys, cutcherry chaprassis, and so on."[40] This was equally true of the migrants themselves. Many servants to Europeans also subsequently became indentured laborers. The examples are legion: examinations of returning migrants revealed that many had been employed as *syces* (horse keepers), gardeners, and domestic servants of one kind of another.[41] Women migrants were often specifically recruited as servants: Lakshmi, a widow, stated, "I heard that several of my caste people were about to embark for the Mauritius, men as laborers, and women as ayahs. I offered my service as an ayah."[42]

Dibbee Dheen, a "Bunneya" by caste, who spent five years in Mauritius and returned to Goruckpur with four hundred rupees in savings, had originally come to Calcutta for service as a *chuprassy* (messenger, servant). He was now armed with a certificate from his employer, Mr. Barlow, and a general order to Colville, Gilmore & Co as a recruiter:

> Dear Sirs,
>
> The bearer of this, Dhibby Deen, is a man of good character, who returns to his native country with a sum of money. His intention being to come back to the Mauritius, we authorise you, should he apply to you for the cost of his passage, to pay the same at a rate not exceeding Co. Rs. 30 besides the cost of food, as well as to any able-bodied men who may wish to accompany him, not exceeding 50 in number, forwarding us their receipt in duplicate for the sum paid. The present authority to remain in force until 31 Dec 1840. We request the favour of an early advice, should you make this advance for us.
>
> Chapman Barclay (addressed to Colville, Gilmore & Co, Calcutta).[43]

As the above certificate carried by Dibbee Dheen shows, subalterns made use of village networks to structure their journey into indentureship, a characteristic not necessarily incompatible with the role of European agencies at the port towns, who generally worked in close cooperation with local and returnee recruiters.

The following statements made by returning laborers at Calcutta revealed that *dhangurs* (tribal laborers) were not invariably tricked by recruiters.

> Juggurnath a dhanga used to cultivate land in Chota Nagpore has saved 294 rupees, "I could never save any money from my old trade as cultivator." Went with Roghoonath, and took his wife and 4 children, all have returned, and he now has two more. His wife earnt 2 rupees for 1 year and 3 rupees for 2 years, and then stopped work having a large family to look after. Karmie, his adopted child, also with them, married Bulram.
>
> Burgee, a Dhangur of Chotanagpur had married his wife in Mauritius, daughter of one of the coolies, he had paid 20 rupees for the marriage.[44]

This group of *dhangurs* went with friends and family and were recruited by another *dhangur,* called Roghoonuth. Clearly there has been a large voluntary element in this process, notwithstanding the straitened economic circumstances from which the migration first arose. Other examples abound that illustrate a process of chain migration, such as in the following comments added to the statement of a returning laborer in Calcutta:

> Moshurruf, a barber by caste, and a cultivator had been living with his brother, a barber, in Cooliz Bazaar and was unemployed. His relative, Peer Bussh has been 14 years in Mauritius, a barber by profession there he is well off.[45]

Ghosh quotes the experience of disgruntled tribal migrants to demonstrate the helplessness of these subalterns in the face of colonial labor mobilization, but he omits to mention that the same source also records the existence of a sophisticated network of tribal recruiters, already operational in the 1830s, which provided information from migrants located in Calcutta to the tribal heartland of Chota Nagpur and elsewhere.[46]

The networks of information that fueled migration did not necessarily always work in the interests of the plantation owners. When wage rates fell in Mauritius in the 1860s, the recruiting networks were soon drawing laborers to more remunerative opportunities in other colonial destinations. Agitation fomented by Gandhi in South Africa in the early twentieth century also filtered down to would-be migrants through subaltern networks, showing that disaffected returnees could effectively spike chain migration. Their information could quickly spread rumors about adverse events in the colony, demonstrating the effectiveness of coolie information networks. Muthusamy, a *sirdar* recruiter, ruefully reported that he had managed to collect only seven Indians:

> I would have done better, if one Venkatachalam had not arrived in my village in the meantime from Natal. He was drawing there 4s. a month. He returned about two months ago. He told the villagers [about] the present agitation in Natal. He warned the villagers to take care of their children chiefly young women. He made the people believe that some sirdars are purposely come to India to take away from their kith and kin, some young women of fair complexion to get rich husbands in Natal, and thereby get some large amount. This was a talk all over.[47]

Munusamy Naidu, a *sirdar* from Natal, recruiting in 1911 at the height of nationalist anti-indentured agitation, still found that simple word of mouth, the evidence of known individuals—that greatest propeller of chain migration—was sufficient to procure a band of recruits from his village:

> My master's advice was not to speak untruth, not to exaggerate Natal and its advantages, not to force Indians to emigrate, etc. I spoke to my own people. I told them the whole truth. I secured in April last some Indians and sent them to my master. I patiently waited in my village. All the time I was treated by the villagers very respectably. They knew that I was one of the sirdars. They also understood that I was not influencing by false statements and pretences any Indian to emigrate. Of course, Tamil notices, printed, warning the public not to emigrate to Natal were freely distributed in my village. These notices did not interfere with my work. I must admit that these notices contained some true statements. . . . When time came for my departure to Natal my people about 4 quite willingly started with me. No one in the village raised any sort of objection. I got a name for myself and my estate.[48]

Subho Basu's recent study of factory workers in Calcutta, *Does Class Matter?*, offers similar evidence of migratory networks and quotes Foley's report on the sources of labor supply in Bengal:

> The rates and conditions of work in the Calcutta industries are well known in the (Saran) district. . . . The people from Saran . . . are well aware of the benefits to be derived from employment in the industrial centres, and a larger number than from any other district seek employment in those centres spontaneously.[49]

Basu goes on to provide a useful critique of historians who have depicted the workers as in the grip of conservative *sirdars,* such as Dipesh Chakrabarty, who has written that "in the jute worker's mind itself, the incipient awareness of belonging to a class remained prisoner of pre-capitalist culture; the class identity of worker could never be distilled out of the pre-capitalist identities that arose from the relationships he had been born into."[50]

Similarly, Tanika Sarkar has argued that

> the very oppression which the sardars embodied was not only far more personalised, but was also deeply familiar to the worker. With his patronage functions, his caste and kinship connections, with his ownership of land and bustees and his control over the caste panch, the sardar and the system based on his control in several significant ways

replicated the village authority structure within Bengali industrial sub-
urbs while, at the same time, subtly modifying the known aspects,
through the additional new functions that were tied to the factory floor
[and] urban slum control.[51]

By contrast, Subho Basu provides numerous examples of subaltern networks (i.e., family members finding jobs for relatives in jute mills) and shows
that considerable care and effort was often made by people to reach labor
centers:

> Myna Khandayet, a worker from Puri district, stated that he borrowed
> money to pay his train fare from Puri to Calcutta. Narsama also bor-
> rowed money to come to Calcutta.[52]

> Behari Rai, a worker in the Angus mill, told the Royal Commission that
> he had been recommended by returning migrants to go to Angus be-
> cause it was known to be free from accidents.[53]

The extraordinary degree of effort some migrants, particularly returnees,
were prepared to make to re-emigrate to a colony in which they had formerly
found service is further exemplified by the story of Cassiram Juggurnath.
Sent back from Mauritius with another nine men to recruit in Bombay, they
arrived with their wives and families there only to find that the depot had
been closed and emigration from that port suspended. The recruiters and
their bands remained for almost three months in Bombay waiting for a ship
that might be able to take them to Mauritius. During this time, one of the ten
recruiters died and another declined to continue. With no passage to the island forthcoming, the eight remaining recruiters resolved to travel to Calcutta on foot. They set out in November 1855, but after a quarrel broke out
amongst them at Nassick, Cassiram Juggurnath returned to Bombay. He was
eventually embarked on the *Futtay Mobarak* in 1856.[54]

The importance of relatives and returnee recruiters in encouraging further migration (although not always with the desired outcome) is clearly under-
lined in the depositions of indentured laborers themselves. Chummun was
one of a band of twenty who set out for Mauritius on the advice of "a relative
of mine who had just returned from that Colony." Moorzan had made several
trips home to Calcutta and with her brother had recruited numbers of her
countrymen and women. Jhurry declared that he was recruiting his villagers
on behalf of the plantation owners where he had worked for ten years to repay
their kindness to him. However, his brother, who had left Arrah to join him,

had been "enticed away by an Arkotty who took him to the Trinidad Depot. I endeavoured to communicate with my brother, but was prevented by the Arkotty who had charge of him. I have heard that my brother has been sent away to Trinidad."[55]

Overseas Indian migrants not infrequently made use of both family networks and the new relationships forged with employers to achieve substantial upward mobility in both economic and social terms. The case of Telucksing, a former indentured laborer who became a shopkeeper in Durban, Natal, is instructive:

> I have been in Natal between twenty-four and twenty-five years. I came to the Colony indentured. I first worked for Mr. Walford, and two months after I was transferred to Mr. Palmer with all the other coolies. I remained ten years working, and then became a storekeeper, working on my own account in West Street, Durban. I sell rice, dholl, ghee, and different kinds of clothing, in fact everything that is required for the Indian trade. I am trading on my own account and not as an agent. I generally buy goods here, but I sometimes get goods from India. I generally deal with the white merchants here for the articles which I resell in my shop. During the last two years I have been dealing with white merchants only; I think I get my goods cheaper from them; they include rice, which I buy from Messieurs Arbuckle, Dunn and Rennie. I do not consider that the white merchant is able to compete with the Indian, because the expenses of the white merchant are far in excess of those of the Indians. I manage my business with the assistance of a relative and one kaffir. White planters purchase coolie rations from me, especially fish. All those Indians who are respectable and look after their own interests, and do not eat and drink to excess, or incur large household expenses, are able to save money.
>
> All the Indians here are comfortably placed, and it chiefly depends upon their own behaviour whether they are happy or not. . . . If an Indian conducts himself properly and works, he is better off here than in his own country. At the termination of his period of indenture, the ambition of the Indian is to become a landed proprietor, and, after amassing a considerable amount of money, to go back to his own country.[56]

Telucksing's account helps to give the lie to another enduring stereotype about the Indian labor migrant—that the "coolie" itinerary necessarily differed greatly from that of the merchant. In practice, capital acquisition was a frequent outcome of indentured recruitment, and furthermore, the coolie overseas, or far from home, did not necessarily lose touch with his natal village, as so much of the literature implies.

Despite the distance and the often lengthy periods of separation, Indians working overseas made frequent attempts through remittances, returnees, and written correspondence to maintain contacts with their families back home. It was common for migrants to transmit money or news via other returnees or relatives, and such means generally constituted effective ways of reaching family members outside the more cumbersome official channels. And the letters that have been preserved in various archival collections include a surprising number written by the migrants themselves, particularly from the 1880s onward, as in this example:

> The Honourable Protector of Immigrant
> Sir,
> I most humbly and respectfully beg to inform your kindful honour that as my qualifications are in English up to the 2d class and in Hindi up to the 1st class and in urdoo tolerably—petitioner beg to say and further that I am a poor man of Basti District but now come to your honour therefore I hope that you will be kind enough to give me a good post as I have been in the police force for sometime and also works in an hospital and lately been a teacher.
> I am yours most obedient servant
> Debi Sanker Singh of Basti, newly arrived immigrant[57]

The South Asian diaspora is central to an understanding of the evolution of Indian Ocean societies—the routes of the trader, the slave, the convict, and the coolie have all been separately explored in innumerable studies of the East African littoral, of Southeast Asia, South Africa, and the Mascarene islands. The roots and shoots of this extraordinary dissemination of ideas, skills, faiths, and labor power, however, have rarely been explored in a single context—perhaps the *Sea of Poppies,* and its successor volumes by Amitav Ghosh, will provide a literary inspiration in this regard. Surely one reason is the comparative neglect of the Indian Ocean in comparison with the "Atlantic route." This study has attempted to offer some insight into the peculiarities and richness of the notion of diaspora in the Indian Ocean context—one where the colonial South Asian figures of slave, convict, servant, coolie, and merchant could frequently occupy several of these diasporic "spaces" in one lifetime.

The hollowness of the category of labor in colonial archives has made it all too easy for historians to be ensnared in debates of the time. In this chapter we have endeavored in part to read the colonial past backwards from the present in an attempt to explain the clear disjuncture apparent between the latter-day success of many diasporic South Asian communities and the previous misfortune that not only initiated, but is said to characterize, much of the migration experience. This requires an emphasis on sources and an approach that enables us to read across the discourses of the time. This includes the statistical, a determined juxtaposing of contexts and archival sources, the personal correspondence of migrants themselves, and finally (although omitted from this chapter) an analysis of the figurative and artistic representations of the "coolie" as seen in Victorian sketches and photographs, and particularly in the stylized postcards beloved of the early tourist—images in which perceptions are, for the most part, divorced from their immediate, practical utility. By such means, the experiences of migrants might be understood in ways independent of their representation by outsiders. Above all, by looking at what migrants have in common rather than what separates them, South Asian migrants may be permitted a dynamic and an agency, of which they are otherwise deprived in conventional colonial and nationalist tales of misery and exploitation.

The aim is to resituate the migrant laborer and thereby disrupt the reified, fixed category of the "coolie," which is so often found in the literature on migration, both past and present. This does not require that we deny the constraints and exploitative character of field, factory, and plantation work in the colonial period. Indeed, it is the very coherence of colonial systems of labor control that created competition in labor recruitment and the space in which Indian itinerant laborers could seek out alternative opportunities for employment on a global scale. However, in studying these diverse forms of employment at home and abroad, we must avoid victimizing the victims of unequal labor relations and endeavor to establish instead an "emic" perspective on the choices exercised by migrants, which analyzes and emphasizes the agency and ambitions of the Indian laborers themselves.

While this chapter locates the problematic of colonial labels and colonial lives within the context of the colonial South Asian labor diaspora, it is intended that the issues raised will be of service to scholars of diaspora more broadly, as well as to historians grappling with issues of slaves' cultural autonomy, familial ties, and personal lives. By highlighting in particular the potentialities for agency, too often subsumed within essentializing categories of analysis, we wish to highlight a central epistemological problem facing scholars engaged in studying the great variety of displaced peoples across time and space that have come to characterize the globalized "modernity" of the twentieth and twenty-first centuries, the unpicking of which may reveal more blossoms amidst the sea of human suffering than has hitherto been assumed to be the case.

NOTES

1. David Brion Davis, *The Problem of Slavery in Western Culture* (Ithaca, N.Y.: Cornell University Press, 1966); Gyan Prakash, "Terms of Servitude: The Colonial Discourse on Slavery and Bondage in India," in *Breaking the Chains: Slavery, Bondage, and Emancipation in Modern Africa and Asia,* ed. M. A. Klein (Madison: University of Wisconsin Press, 1993). There are many other ways in which arguments about slavery have been dominated by the historiography of the early modern Atlantic, such that slavery for Indians came always to be imagined as involving manual labor, coercion, and migration overseas, rather than something that could be found closer to home. See Indrani Chatterjee, *Gender, Slavery and Law in Colonial India* (Oxford: Oxford University Press, 1999).

2. See Marcus Cunliffe, *Chattel Slavery and Wage Slavery: The Anglo-American Context* (Athens: University of Georgia Press, 1979).

3. Michael Roberts, review of *Indian Immigrant Plantation Workers in Sri Lanka: A Historical Perspective, 1880–1910* by Dharmapriya Wesumperuma, *Indian Economic & Social History Review* 26, no. 3 (September 1989): 380–85.

4. Ibid.

5. Patrick Peebles, *Plantation Tamils of Ceylon* (Leicester: University of Leicester Press, 2001), 34–38. Parenthetical page references are to this edition.

6. S. Arasaratnam, *Indians in Malaysia and Singapore* (Oxford: Oxford University Press, 1970), 16.

7. Crispin Bates and Marina Carter, "Tribal and Indentured Migrants in Colonial India: Modes of Recruitment and Forms of Incorporation," in *Dalit Movements and the Meanings of Labour in India,* ed. P. Robb, 159–85 (New Delhi: Oxford University Press, 1993).

8. Rajnarayan Chandavarkar, *The Origins of Industrial Capitalism in India* (Cambridge, UK: Cambridge University Press, 1994).

9. Madhavi Kale, *Fragments of Empire: Capital, Slavery, and Indian Indentured Labor Migration in the British Caribbean* (Philadelphia: University of Pennsylvania Press, 1998).

10. Hugh Tinker, *A New System of Slavery: The Export of Indian Labour Overseas, 1830–1920* (London: Oxford University Press, 1974); Crispin Bates, ed., *Community, Empire and Migration: South Asians in Diaspora* (London: Palgrave, 2001).

11. Marina Carter, *Servants, Sirdars and Settlers: Indians in Mauritius, 1834–1874* (Oxford: Oxford University Press, 1995).

12. Marina Carter, *Voices from Indenture: Experiences of Indian Migrants in the British Empire* (Leicester: Leicester University Press, 1996).

13. Veronique Bragard, "Gendered Voyages into Coolitude: The Shaping of the Indo-Caribbean Woman's Literary Consciousness," *Kunapipi: Journal of Post-Colonial Writing* 20, no. 1 (1998): 99–111.

14. Kale, *Fragments of Empire,* 173.

15. Kale, *Fragments of Empire.*

16. Kaushik Ghosh, "A Market for Aboriginality: Primitivism and Race Classification in the Indentured Labour Market of Colonial India," in *Subaltern Studies* X, ed. G. Bhadra, G. Prakash and S. Tharu, 8–48 (Delhi: Oxford University Press, 1999).

17. Mohandas Karamchand Gandhi, *The Indian Review,* September 1917, in the *Collected Works of Mahatma Gandhi* [CWMG] (Electronic Book) 16 (September, 1, 1917–April 23, 1918), 3, http://www.gandhiserve.org/cwmg/VOL016.PDF.

18. India Census Commissioner, *Census of India,* 1901 XIII (Bombay: Government Central Press), 215. See Crispin Bates, "Regional Dependence and Rural Development in Central India: The Pivotal Role of Migrant Labour," in *Agricultural Production and Indian History,* ed. David Ludden, 354–68 (New Delhi: Oxford University Press, 1995).

19. *Royal Commission on Agriculture in India,* vol. VI, *Evidence Taken in the Central Provinces and Berar* (Calcutta: Government of India Central Publication Branch, 1927), 5.

20. R. V. Russell, ed., *Central Provinces District Gazetteers: Seoni District Gazetteer,* vol. A: Descriptive (Allahabad, India: Pioneer Press, 1907), 113–14.

21. Anand Yang, "Peasants on the Move: A Study of Internal Migration in India," *Journal of Interdisciplinary History* X, no. 1 (1979): 54–55.

22. L. S. S. O'Malley, *Memorandum on Material Condition of the People of Bengal and Bihar and Orissa, in the Year 1902–03 to 1911–12* (Darjeeling: Darjeeling Branch Press, 1912); G. A. Grierson, *Report on Colonial Emigration from the Bombay Presidency,* Calcutta, 1883; and J. A. Bourdillon, "District Report to Commissioner," July 8–10, 1890, in *Bengal General (Misc.) Proceedings* December, 1890: 402.

23. Surendra Bhana and Bridglal Pachai, *A Documentary History of Indian South Africans* (Cape Town: David Philip, 1984), 28.

24. Marina Carter and Khal Torabully, *Coolitude: An Anthology of Indian Labour Diaspora* (London: Anthem Press, 2002), 33.

25. Dipesh Chakrabarty, *Rethinking Working-Class History: Bengal 1890–1940* (Princeton, N.J.: Princeton University Press, 1989), 93.

26. Bates and Carter, "Tribal and Indentured Migrants."

27. J. Anthony Barker, *Slavery and Anti-Slavery in Mauritius, 1810–33: The Conflict between Economic Expansion and Humanitarian Reform under British Rule* (London: Macmillan, 1996); W. G. Clarence-Smith, ed., "The Economics of the Indian Ocean Slave Trade in the Nineteenth Century," *Slavery and Abolition* 9, no. 3 (1988); Moses D. E. Nwulia, *The History of Slavery in Mauritius and the Seychelles, 1810–1875* (Rutherford, N.J.: Fairleigh Dickinson University Press/Associated University Presses, 1981); and others.

28. Hargrave Lee Adam, *The Indian Criminal* (London: J. Milne, 1909); Clare Anderson, "Unfree Labour and its Discontents: Transportation from Mauritius to Australia, 1820–1850," *Australian Studies* 13, no. 1 (1998): 116–33; and Clare Anderson, *Convicts in the Indian Ocean: Transportation from South Asia to Mauritius, 1815–53* (Basingstoke, UK: Macmillan, 2000); and others.

29. *Sheik Brom,* State Archives of New South Wales [AONSW], R.2662, ICS 1823–6, *per* "Asia," arr. ex England April 29, 1825. Copies of these indents and relevant court

cases (where available) have been passed on to us by Dr. Ian Duffield, University of Edinburgh. We gratefully acknowledge his permission to reproduce them.

30. *Mahomed Balletti,* 549, Con. /33/32, *per* "Moffat" (3), November, 28 1842. Van Diemen's Lands (VDL) transportee.

31. *Yacousal,* 277, Con. 37/1, *per* "Ocean Queen," 1844; *Talicouty,* 278, Con. 37/1, *per* "Ocean Queen," 1844. VDL transportees.

32. *John Solomon,* Con. 37/1, Dec. 1840–June 1840, *per* "Waterloo" 1842; *Nowardin,* AONSW, COD/141, ICS, July 1814–Jan. 1816, *per* "Fanny," arr. ex England January 18, 1816.

33. M. Jumeer, "Les Affranchis et les Indiens Libres à l'Ile de France au XVIIIe Siècle" [Freedmen and free Indians to the Isle of France in the eighteenth century, 1721–1803] (doctoral thesis, third round, University of Poitiers, 1984), 223–24.

34. Carter and Torabully, *Coolitude,* 28.

35. Parliamentary Papers (PP) 1841[427], Commission of Enquiry, exhibits 14 and 15.

36. Mauritius Archives (MA) PL 41 EA Madras to PI, June 3, 1879.

37. *Royal Commissioners' Report,* 1875, Appendix B, Visit to Trianon estate, July 11, 1872.

38. Walton Look Lai, *Indentured Labor, Caribbean Sugar* (Baltimore, Md.: Johns Hopkins University Press, 1993), 27.

39. MA PL 11B Col Secy to Receiver General, June 25, 1908.

40. Major D. G. Pitcher, Judge, Small Cause Court, Lucknow to Sec. to Govt. NWP and Oudh, June 17, 1882, p. 9.

41. PP 1841 (43), examination of 14 laborers returned from the Mauritius in the *Ceylon,* April 6, 1841, at the Calcutta Police Office.

42. India Office Records, Indian Public Proceedings (IPP) 186/75, Deposition of Lakshmi, August 8, 1842.

43. PP 1840, p. 58 ff.

44. Ibid.

45. Ibid.

46. Ghosh, "A Market for Aboriginality."

47. Bhana and Pachai, *Documentary History,* 27.

48. Carter and Torabully, *Coolitude,* 33.

49. B. Foley, *Report on Labour in Bengal* (Calcutta, 1906), paragraph 83, cited in Subho Basu, *Does Class Matter? Colonial Capital and Workers' Resistance in Bengal, 1890–1937* (New Delhi: Oxford University Press, 2004).

50. Chakrabarty, *Rethinking Working-Class History,* 218.

51. Tanika Sarkar, *Bengal, 1928–1934: The Politics of Protest* (New Delhi: Oxford University Press, 1987), 65–66.

52. *Royal Commission on Labour in India* (RCLI), XI (1929), 360–62.

53. Ibid., 355.

54. MA RA Series (Immigration) RA 1361, Report of Bombay Committee of Enquiry, April 13, 1856.

55. MA B1A, Beyts Report on Immigration, 1861.

56. "Report of the Indian Immigrants Commission, 1885–7," in *Documents of Indentured Labour: Natal 1851–1917,* ed. Y. S. Meer (Durban, South Africa: Institute of Black Research, 1980), 388–89.

57. MA PA 62, Dabi Sanker Singh, May 6, 1884.

PART 2
MAPS OF INTIMACY

CHAPTER FOUR

Empire, Anglo-India, and the Alimentary Canal

PARAMA ROY

Introduction: Making Sense of Mutiny

In a century that was, in the words of one critic, "[militarily], . . . perhaps the busiest period in British history," the event popularly known as the Indian Mutiny of 1857–58 stands out both for the challenge it posed to colonial notions of race, rule, and hierarchy and for the impact it had upon a metropolitan and Anglo-Indian imagination.[1] Begun as an anti-British mutiny by disaffected Muslim and high-caste Hindu sepoys (soldiers of the Native Infantry regiments of the British Indian army), the uprising soon turned into a full-scale though uncoordinated rebellion in northern India. The proximate cause of mutiny has conventionally been understood to be the introduction of greased cartridges for the new Enfield rifles, cartridges greased with beef and pork fat that had to be bitten off before being inserted into the rifles and that therefore were obnoxious to both Hindu and Muslim sepoys. These greased cartridges, combined with rumors of contaminated food supplies—deliberately contaminated by the state with bone dust and the blood of cows and pigs, it was said—and a mysterious circulation of chapatis among north Indian villages that apparently served as a signal to mobilization, have generally served as the mise-en-scène of the events of 1857–58. They have been glossed by many colonial commentators and historians (as well as by some postcolonial Indian ones) as symptoms of a deeply reactionary, feudal, and outmoded social order struggling against the doctrines of social equality and material progress embedded in the reformist impulses of the East India Company in mid-century. Time and again, these details have been read in terms of a clash of civilizations that finds its most expressive form in the institution of caste, the most striking and non-negotiable sign of a Hindu/Indian difference from that of the subcontinent's colonial rulers.[2]

While the greased cartridge has most often been presented as the trigger for the mutiny, other causes have been adumbrated by some nineteenth-century commentators and by twentieth-century historians. They point to the egregiously expansionist policy of Lord Dalhousie in the 1840s and 1850s, which led to the forcible annexation of several Indian kingdoms that were bound by treaty to the East India Company. The most flagrant and deeply resented of these was the annexation of Oudh in 1856, a state from which many sepoys were recruited. Related to this were changes in land revenue policy that stripped *talukdars* (traditional landholding elites) of their property, overassessments of property for tax purposes, and widespread unemployment in the region as a result of the dissolution of the Nawab of Oudh's court and army. The sepoys themselves had seen their conditions of employment deteriorate, with low pay, minimal prospects for promotion, the reduction of special allowances, mandatory foreign service, and contemptuous treatment by British officers as the leading causes of discontent.

The mutiny was launched on March 29, 1857, at Barrackpore by the sepoy Mangal Pandey of the 34th Bengal Native Infantry regiment, acting, it was said, under the influence of opium and bhang (a cannabis product).[3] (Mutineers would come to be known as "pandies" in British mutiny lore.) Launched in a state of intoxication, the mutiny apparently began early, ahead of an agreed-upon date for a widespread uprising—to coincide, some Anglo-Indian commentators suggested, with the centennial in June of the battle of Plassey that had marked the first major military triumph of the Company in the subcontinent. In the weeks after Mangal Pandey's mistimed rebellion, at least two of the regiments that had refused to receive the cartridges were disbanded, and eighty-five troopers were put in irons and hauled off to prison in a display of public humiliation. On May 10, 1857, sepoys from three regiments of the Bengal army in Meerut rose in mutiny against their European officers, killing several of them along with their families and setting fire to their houses and opening up the prisons. After disposing of their European officers at Meerut, the sepoys marched to Delhi, where they hailed the titular Mughal ruler Bahadur Shah II as emperor of Hindustan and compelled him to lend his authority to the revolt. In the following weeks mutiny spread among other regiments (until roughly half of all the sepoys and *sowars* [cavalrymen] in the Bengal army joined ranks with the mutineers). These weeks also saw a spate of uprisings in which Indian rulers of princely kingdoms, peasants, petty criminals, whores, itinerant marauding groups, fakirs, religious leaders, and landowners in northern India, especially in Oudh, all played a part. Among the princes and aristocrats who rose against the colonial order were those who had been dispossessed of their kingdoms or pensions by the Company's refusal to recognize rights of adoption; the best-known of these were Rani Lakshmibai of Jhansi and Nana Saheb of Bithur, near Cawnpore. It should be noted that there were multiple uprisings rather than a single one, and that in some cases the wrath of the insurgents was directed against moneylenders (whose existing power was strengthened by the consequences of the colonial state's land revenue policy), allies of the colonial state (such as Bengalis), and the propertied as much as against Company and Anglo-Indian interests. The latter were sorely beset and had to endure long sieges at Delhi, Cawnpore, and Lucknow. Cawnpore in particular came to have a great resonance in mutiny lore, since it was the scene of three massacres, of which two were particularly notable. In one case, Anglo-Indian men and women, who had surrendered to Nana Saheb on condition of safe passage out of Cawnpore, were fired upon and killed in large numbers as they were boarding boats at the Satichaura Ghat on the Ganges; in the second case, Anglo-Indian women and children who were prisoners of Nana Saheb and survivors of the first massacre were slaughtered and their bodies cast into a well. It was the second of the massacres, involving the killing of Anglo-Indian ladies and children, that was to make Cawnpore an almost mythic symbol in the British and Anglo-Indian imagination of Indian depravity. Rumors also circulated among Anglo-Indians and metropolitan Britons of the widespread rape, torture, and sexual humiliation of white women and girls, including those held captive in Cawnpore, even though there was no documentary evidence of systematic rape, as official records themselves noted. These served as a rationalization post facto of the brutality of British armies. Even though General Neill's "Bloody Assizes" predated the violence at Cawnpore, Anglo-Indian and British writers claimed it was the massacres in that city that led to a ferocious policy of counterinsurgency that included military battles, the sacking of cities, the burning of villages, and wholesale hangings, bayonetings, and shootings of sepoys, peasants, and other Indians, whether combatant or civilian, unfortunate enough to find themselves in the vicinity of the Company's troops. The subcontinent was substantially subdued by mid-1858, and the East India Company's rule replaced by that of the British Crown.

For metropolitan Britons and for Anglo-Indians, the mutiny was both a manifestation of the utter irrationality and depravity of their Indian subjects *and* a sign of their own divinely appointed right to rule. A favored explanation for Indian actions was, as already noted, the institution of caste, an ensemble of permissions and prohibitions mind-boggling in their archaic, inhumane, and irrational character. Thus the mutiny was sometimes viewed as a Brahmin conspiracy, at other times as a result of the Company's indulgence about the caste requirements of high-caste sepoys.[4] Often it was explained in terms of a widespread Indian panic about a plot to convert everyone to Christianity through widespread alimentary pollutions. Such a panic encompassed Muslims and Hindus, and indeed Muslims were indicted as frequently as Hindus for their purported fanaticism and exclusiveness. The power of such an analytic of purity and pollution rendered Indian antagonists mysterious and repugnant, but nonetheless scrutable; it was a way of managing the greatest threat to the British paramountcy in the nineteenth century, one that had taken Britons and Anglo-Indians by surprise and had made clear the fragility of their power. Such a schematization of racial-civilizational difference helped produce what most scholars of the mutiny and its aftermath have defined as a crucial turning point in the racial logics of belonging and alienation.[5] Nonetheless, an attentive reading of the texts that delineate the Anglo-Indian experience of the mutiny suggests that such a rendition might overlook certain shared idioms and tropes that bound Anglo-India and India in cognate experiences of appetites, aversions, and intimacy. Indeed, I will suggest that the metropolitan and Anglo-Indian historian or writer's focus on the mutiny as a peculiar problem of caste embodiment and caste anxiety exists in a complex and productive relationship with Anglo-Indian experiences of bodily purity and bodily violation during the mutiny. Their accounts make vividly clear that on both sides of the colonial divide, colonial politics was a visceral politics, whose traumas were experienced in the mouth and in which the stomach served as a kind of somatic political unconscious where the phantasmagoria of colonialism came to be embodied. Bread, grease, bazaar gossip, and rumor form important constituent parts of an alimentary habitus that was the banal, yet crisis-ridden, theater for staging questions central to encounter and rule—questions of proximity, cathexis, consumption, incorporation, digestion, commensality, and purgation. This is true, I suggest, not just of the Hindus, Muslims, and other Indians who experienced alimentary incorporations and prohibitions as the quotidian facts of colonial rule, but of Anglo-Indians as well. For Indians and Anglo-Indians alike, the experience of the mutiny was routed through some fundamental questions of somatic and affective integrity: what did it mean to eat? What was food? And what were the dangerous supplements that threatened to metabolize it? What constituted an "eating well" in which one could not but eat the other?[6]

For Anglo-Indians, the mutiny was a stunning reminder of their status as fragile and vulnerable bodies in the subcontinent, subject in entirely unexpected ways to experiences of violence, decay, deprivation, disease, and exhaustion. Their texts of the mutiny provide both an extraordinarily literal sense of the shock of bodily encounter and a highly charged metaphorics of bodily contamination and dissolution. Their sense of outrage was profoundly tied to the rough handling their hitherto inviolable bodies received at the hands of mutinous Indians bent upon the complete extermination of the colonial order and of all whites and Christians. The pedagogy of the alimentary canal enacted by these texts suggests that palate, sinew, and gut were central to the self-fashioning of dominator *and* dominated in a colonial order. The proliferation of literal and vulgar details—of hunger, stenches, drunkenness, flux, and wounding, in addition to cartridges and chapatis—serves to underline the often overlooked social and embodied grammars of that process that has been described as soul making.[7] Reading mutiny texts in relation to midcentury discourses (indigenous and Anglo-Indian) of ingestion, commensality, pollution, and purgation lays bare certain insistent somatic tropes, tropes that are metaphorical indices of widely shared cultural fantasies and panics about rule and rebellion, purity and pollution. What this reading will suggest is that the event generated an enormous gestural repertoire of intimacy and pollution that encompassed Anglo-Indians and Indians within a shared affective and corporeal circuit, and that their dietary and sexual permissions and prohibitions were braided together rather than disjunct.[8]

A familiar historical event, seen from the seemingly anomalous perspective of the mouth or, more broadly speaking, of alimentation, confirms on a surprisingly corporeal register what we know of the severe retreat of Anglo-India from intimacy with Indian bodies and modes of life following the mutiny. But why might this have happened? Some of the texts of the events of 1857 might give us some semblance of an answer, and I will examine some of them to that end. Some of the gastropolitical tracts I read here are the familiar ones: Hindu and Muslim texts of unwonted and abominated caste intimacies. This is a set of texts altogether familiar to us from the anthropological literature on the subcontinent, which has tended to emphasize a thematics of purity and pollution. But some of the others are less familiar but equally somaticized texts in which Anglo-Indians reveal themselves to be somewhat like secret sharers of "irrational" Hindu and Muslim fears, archaic interdictions, and ritual outrage. The racial, ethnic, and religious gap that presumably divides the Anglo from the Indian into two mutually antagonistic and distanced forces under conditions of normality breaks down under the crisis precipitated by insurgency. In its aftermath we see Anglo-Indians reassert the boundaries of their breached, fragile subjecthood by processes of abjection and self-purification that, perhaps surprisingly, draw their inspiration from the caste-bound other. What we have in the moment of mutiny is not so much the well-rehearsed face-off of caste and modernity as an encounter between caste anxiety and something that we can denominate as "caste envy."[9] This renders a new twist to the meanings of the hyphen that separates but also conjoins the "Anglo" and the "Indian" at the level of the phenomenological body and at the level of ritual and of moral and cosmological ordering. To understand this more fully, we have to turn to the cultivation of the hyphen.

The Rule of the Hyphen: Anglo-Indians and Diaspora

In the first chapter of *The Wretched of the Earth,* Frantz Fanon has a well-known description of the Manichaean geography of the European colony:

> The colonial world is a world cut in two. The dividing line, the frontiers are shown by barracks and police stations. In the colonies it is the policeman and the soldier who are the official, instituted go-betweens, the spokesman of the settler and his rule of oppression. . . . The zone where the natives live is not complementary to the zone inhabited by the settlers. The two zones are opposed, but not in the service of a higher unity. Obedient to the rules of pure Aristotelian logic, they both follow the principle of reciprocal exclusivity.[10]

While Fanon is describing the spatial contours of an early- to mid-twentieth century colonial city, the fact is that these spatial and racial limits had come to assume a conceptual and material reality from at least the 1820s onward, at least in a colony like India. While the new East India Company rulers had adopted large elements of the lifestyle of Indian elites in the eighteenth century, maintaining Indian-style retinues and spatial arrangements in their households, adopting Indian garb and culinary habits at home, cohabiting with free and slave Indian women (though only rarely marrying them in Christian ceremony), sometimes in polygamous arrangements, and providing for their mixed-race children either through education in Britain or through appointments in civil and military departments in the subcontinent, by the last decade of the century the contours of this diasporic population had begun to change at the level of policy and official recognition.[11]

It is worth noting that even before formal shifts in policy the Anglo-Indian nabob, with his parvenu ambition and taint of Asiatic corruption, had been a figure of both derision and moral opprobrium in Britain, and the colony, with its corruptions of place, was seen as debilitating to dignity, virility, and moral welfare. The Company began in the 1790s—a decade of reforms introduced by the governor-general Lord Cornwallis—to discourage marriages and liaisons between Indian women and Englishmen in the upper echelons of civil and military service, to promote the entry of white women from Britain, to bar mixed-blood sons from the services (and to dismiss those who were already ensconced in them), to prohibit the payment of educational and other stipends from pension and charitable funds to the orphaned children of European fathers, and to proscribe the dispatch of mixed-race children to Britain.[12] Reacting aversively to the possibility of the emergence of a significant creole population in the subcontinent—perhaps, as Sudipta Sen and others have suggested, in response to rebellions in the creolized Spanish Americas—the Company took decisive steps to demarcate racial and civilizational distinctions of constitution and entitlement between communities now more decisively marked as native *or* expatriate/diasporic, but not both.[13] Indeed, a major distinction between the first and second European empires in Asia and Africa was the the maintenance of control through "demographically lighter colonization of company, army, and administration rather than a settler population" in the latter case.[14] Practice did not necessarily accord with policy, especially at the lower ranks, as the presence of a sizeable Eurasian community attested, even when interracial cohabitation and racially blended familial arrangements enjoyed a much reduced legitimacy and official recognition.[15] While some prominent Englishmen "living on the frontiers" continued, as Durba Ghosh has shown, to maintain relationships with Indian women and to produce mixed-race children into the 1830s without damage to their careers, even they were critically concerned about upholding the Britishness of the children that they publicly acknowledged as their own.[16]

Indeed, there seems to have been a strenuous effort from this point on to unthink the possibility of India as a creole or even as a settler colony and to maintain an Anglo-Indian identity as an avowedly exilic or diasporic one. It is worthwhile to pay some attention to this European diaspora, if only as an act of historical attentiveness to the racially variegated character of diasporic voyaging and settlement. As Radhika Mohanram notes, the nineteenth century saw significant movements of Europeans to the colonies in the 1820–1914 period, yet diaspora studies concerns itself primarily with subjects of color rather than with white subjects.[17] Anglo-Indians themselves in later decades would assert an Anglo-Indian identity not entirely reducible to that of metropolitan Britons (but cognate with theirs nonetheless).[18] Many took pride in an Anglo-Indian ancestry that had bound their families to official service in India through many generations, and that came to be embodied in Anglo-Indian cemeteries in the subcontinent; Kipling was to memorialize these generational continuities in "The Tomb of His Ancestors."[19] Nonetheless, the possibility of India as a settler colony, or of a colonial diaspora as anything but temporally finite, was inconceivable to most Anglo-Indians, including writers. Of the latter, only Kipling—and only in *Kim*—was willing to imagine this eventuality, and quite emphatically as one best suited for the "country born," rather than those born and raised in the British Isles.

Under these circumstances it is perhaps no surprise that for the better part of a century Anglo-Indians had a profoundly vexing and contingent relationship with the question of their own legitimacy and autochthony in a colony far from a place denominated as home. In India, they saw themselves as heirs both of the Roman Empire and of the Mughal one, and despite the inconsistency and ambiguity of their relationship with the Mughal emperor—they were technically his feudatories but he was in fact by the early nineteenth century their pensioner—they were unwilling, before the events of 1857–58, to repudiate decisively the notion of a shadow legitimacy derived from their relationship with him.[20] This led to a continuous tension between the idioms of intimacy and distance that formed the grammar of their relationship to their place of rule and long, if sometimes reluctant, habitation. Such a tension can be said to enact the precarious dialectic between "roots" and "routes," rather than the stable rootedness, that James Clifford describes as characteristic of diasporic affect and experience (and that the editors emphasize in the introduction to this volume).[21]

What Eric Stokes has denominated as the transformation "from nabob to sahib in India" had been, by 1857, the strenuous endeavor of several decades.[22] This transformation was marked by an intensely somaticized logic and by certain orificial obsessions. If the Indian male was characterized by improper appetites (a predilection for opium and bhang and, during 1857–58, by an overwhelming and murderous lust for white women), improper aversion (the failure to eat meat, or some kinds of meat, and the failure of commensality), and improper evacuation (the failure to manage bodily waste in accordance with the dictates of civilization), the nineteenth-century Anglo-Indian sought to distinguish his civilizational status through the "clean and proper" modes of managing food, commensality, and bodily waste.[23] In this he was analogous to the secular upper-class European so vividly described in Norbert Elias' *The Civilizing Process* as the end product of the management over several centuries of such mundane bodily practices as eating at table, expectoration, farting, urination, and defecation. Elias details the ways in which changes in the management of sexual life and of the alimentary canal—how, where, and in whose presence one ate, belched, farted, urinated, defecated, or had sex (or not)—were transformative of affective structure and response.[24] This historically contingent and socially constructed second nature or habitus was at the same time part of a differential system, designed to separate modern from primitive, civilized from uncivilized. Elias suggests that it is an emerging vocabulary of social distinction in the Renaissance that governs the micrologic of bodily and intimate practice (and leads to the emergence of what is designated the "private" today), rather than considerations of the medical or hygienic values of cleanliness or changing technologies of waste management.[25]

These transformations of mundane bodily practice, affective life, interpersonal relations, and technologies of waste removal occurred slowly and unevenly in Europe, though the diacritical character of this "civilizing process" was never in doubt. By the nineteenth century, as the work of Peter Stallybrass and Allon White (among many others) on sanitary reform in Britain has shown us, a middle-class interest in slums and sewers and their products and inhabitants—pigs, rats, bodily wastes, and impoverished populations scarcely distinguishable from them—was the sign of a "reformation of the senses" that established "new thresholds of shame, embarrassment, and disgust."[26] A process of transcoding linked these avatars of the low to the "lower bodily stratum" and to uncovenanted sexual behaviors that retained their fascination despite or perhaps because of their relegation to a social and moral periphery.

The marked sanitary preoccupations and reforms of nineteenth-century London and Paris undoubtedly form one of the contexts for the organization of Anglo-Indian living space in a distant colony (though, as we shall see, caste is inseparable from the thinking of social class formation for Anglo-Indians). Described by Florence Nightingale as a "focus of epidemics," a land of "domestic filth," and as a place where plague and pestilence were "the ordinary state of things," India came to be identified by its unremitting filth and stenches.[27] Europeans, as unprotected newcomers in this alien and dangerous landscape, were thought to be susceptible to a variety of fevers, fluxes, and liver diseases to which the natives were largely immune. With the passage of time, however, the susceptibility of Occidentals came to be explained less through the logic of their lack of acclimation than through the pathologization of the bodies of the Indians they encountered. Long before germ theory gained ground among European and (much later) Anglo-Indian epidemiologists, theories of contagion emphasized atmospheric and moral vulnerability. Contagionists believed that cholera was spread by contact with infected people, food, and objects, while subscribers to the miasmic theory insisted that it rose from the noxious effluvia of slums, which were marked by accumulations of dirt and decayed matter.[28] As in Britain, cholera and many of the other diseases of the subcontinent— plague, dysentery, malaria, and enteric fever (typhoid)—were associated with the foul odors of contaminated food, drink, and sewage, disseminated among Anglo-Indian populations by contaminated native bodies themselves immunized against infection by long familiarity with filth.[29] This provoked demands for greater physical and social distances between the Indians and Europeans over the course of the century. Thus Anglo-Indians in the nineteenth century came to reside at a marked distance from the miasmas and disease of crowded Indian bazaars and mosquito-ridden tanks. A public health policy that would involve cleaning up Indian towns was expensive and politically chancy. So European settlements—cantonments and civil stations—were what Dane Kennedy has described as "islands of white," built at a safe distance upwind from the stenches and clamor of the "black town."[30] Servants' quarters were situated far away from the bungalow, at the outer limits of the compound, and vigorous efforts were often made to police the bodily and sartorial cleanliness of the servants, from cooks and bearers to the *Dai* whose breast milk nourished fragile Anglo-Indian infants.[31] As in high-caste Hindu households, the untouchable figure of the sweeper was regarded with particular suspicion and was often barred from every place but the latrine.[32] "Hill stations" were developed in the foothills of the Himalayas and in the southern mountain ranges to provide sanatoria for troops, schools for the European children who could not be sent to Britain for their education, and as a refuge, especially for women and children, from the heat, dust, and disease of the plains. With houses and gardens on the English rural model, and significant restrictions on the entry of plains-dwelling Indians (except for servants, porters, and shopkeepers), these hill stations came to be seen as islands of Britishness in an insalubrious land.[33] Unlike their forebears of the preceding century, Anglo-Indians wore clothing (flannel underwear, suits, evening dress for dinner, and hooped skirts) that made few concessions to the temperatures of the subcontinent (though the Indian practice of daily bathing was readily adopted). Though curries, chutneys, kedgeree, and mulligatawny soup were incorporated into the Anglo-Indian diet, a concerted effort was made in the official community to procure and serve European foodstuffs, especially on official occasions, with canned foods of dubious quality often substituting for fresh Indian vegetables.[34] It should be noted that these endeavors to eschew tactile, oral, and olfactory contact with Indian bodies were characteristic primarily of the members of the covenanted civil service, the so-called "heaven born," the Brahmins of the Anglo-Indian community, and of military officers, second to them in the protocols of precedence. At the lower reaches of this hierarchy there was a not inconsiderable traffic, primarily sexual, with Indian bodies, as the frequent alarms about the British soldier's health indicated.

Patho-logics

The voluminous Anglo-Indian and metropolitan record of the mutiny rehearses certain alimentary tropes that define the conditions of mutiny from the Indian perspective—namely, the greased cartridge, the bondage of salt, bazaar rumors of contaminated foods, and the mysterious and itinerant chapati. Indeed, Homi Bhabha has described cartridge and chapati as the "totemic foods" of the mutiny, which must be ingested before any accounting of the events of 1857–58 can be produced. What we do not as easily remember perhaps is the degree to which these tropes also dominated and even structured the Anglo-Indian investment in rule and rebellion. It is worth noting, for instance, that notwithstanding the dismissal of bazaar rumors of contamination and force-feeding as forms of illicit speech, the predictable emanations of a native bazaar that trafficked in fraudulent commodities, especially fraudulent information, the Anglo-Indian experience of the mutiny was itself powerfully undergirded by rumors, whether by rumors of the sexual subjugation of white women or rumors of chapatis that traveled with preternatural speed across the landscape of rebellion. Whatever the initial confusion caused by the chapatis, the recounting of the trauma of 1857 came quickly to be gothicized in the sahib imagination, and this hallucinatory bread became, along with dreams, portents, prophecies, and unspeakable terrors, part of the phantasmagoria of the event itself. "The organizing principle of the *sign* of the chapati is constituted," Homi Bhabha suggests, "in the transmission of fear and anxiety, projection and panic in a form of circulation *in-between* the colonizer and the colonized. Could the agency of peasant rebellion be constituted through the 'partial incorporation' of the fantasy and fear of the Master?"[35]

A like transactional logic marks the Anglo-Indian attitude to the "bondage of the Salt" that supposedly tied sepoys to the Company's service in terms that exceeded wages and contracts. Salt was to serve in 1857 as a brilliantly condensed and extraordinarily visceral sign of the tensions of colonial rule. In northern and eastern India, salt had long been invested with a host of symbolic and non-utilitarian associations, connoting loyalty, hospitality, patronage, and trust. At the same time, under the Company's rule, it had entered a new regime of commodification, being taxed at an extremely high rate that caused profound popular discontent. In a context where salt was semiotically inflected in these ways, the rumors of its contamination—and that of other staples such as sugar, flour, and water—indexed the most fundamental of betrayals. It suggested that the very salt that was the symbol of sepoy dependence and sepoy loyalty could be deliberately, maliciously, and duplicitously turned into an instrument of complete subjugation through pollution and conversion. What is worthy of note for our purposes is the degree to which such beliefs accorded with the affective premises of British rule, which harped obsessively upon a calculatedly archaized "fidelity to one's salt" as the single measure of Indian worthiness in all accounts of the mutiny.[36] Thus the shock of the mutiny was its enactment of "disloyalty" and "ingratitude"; popular and official accounts are replete with tales of British officers who, beguiled by long residence in India and too unheeding an intimacy with natives, were massacred by sepoys whose fidelity to their salt they had taken as given.

As in the case of rebellious Indians, account after Anglo-Indian account of the sieges at Cawnpore and Lucknow (two of the three centers of the mutiny) stresses a metaphorics of bodily defilement and disintegration, as epidermal and orificial limits were repeatedly ruptured or violated. For vulnerable and cosseted Anglo-Indians suddenly thrust into a world of unwonted uncertainties and panics, the outrageousness of the mutiny lay not only in the betrayals and ingratitude it enacted; it lay also in the violence and degradation it visited upon hitherto sacrosanct Anglo-Indian bodies, as they came to be exposed to bodily labor, dearth, filth, overcrowding, and captivity, and in the contact with vermin, corpses, bodily waste, and strange foods (or nonfoods). One of the earliest intimations that something was out of joint in the relations of Anglo-Indians and natives manifested itself in the experience of a Mrs. Elizabeth Sneyd, traveling through Cawnpore in March 1857. When she stopped at the Old Cawnpore Hotel, the only suitable commercial lodging for a European lady, she learned, disturbingly for her, that the best rooms had been booked by a group of "native princes & chiefs" and their numerous armed retainers. A recent popular account of the mutiny speculates that these native princes might have been Nana Saheb and Azimullah Khan, though we cannot be sure of this. Given two shabby little rooms normally occupied by the head clerk (possibly an Indian), she was dismayed to find that the sepoys outside her rooms laughed and pointed at her rather than showing the deference to which she was accustomed. What was worse yet, when she finally received her meal, it was "only a small quantity of the stale remnants of the natives' dinner." At this point she fled the hotel to continue on her journey.[37]

The episode has something of a nightmare quality, being marked by an escalating set of encroachments, pollutions, and humiliations: the usurpation of the best rooms by natives, the assignment of rooms normally occupied by native bodies and therefore "dirty and comfortless," the threatening proximity and insolence of armed men, the belated production of leftovers from native tables, and the flight into the Indian night. At each step the trespasses, proceeding from the spatial to the alimentary, become more intimate and threatening. It is apt perhaps that the tipping point comes for her with the (belated) arrival of the "stale remnants." How, one wonders, did these come to be identified as "stale remnants" rather than the food proper to an English lady? Their late arrival? Their meager quantity? The fact that this was probably Indian rather than Anglo-Indian food? Was Mrs. Sneyd indeed served half-eaten remains of others' food? The narrative does not clarify this, only her dissatisfaction at the leavings that were, like the room, contaminated by Indian usage. It is instructive to read this through the lens of a Hindu caste-based gastropolitics—one with which Anglo-Indians were thoroughly familiar—especially through the concept of *jootha/uchhishta*. The concept of *jootha/uchhishta*, encompassing anything that has come into contact with saliva, is central to an understanding of caste norms of purity, pollution, and ritually enforced degradation. In normal interactions every effort is made to avoid consuming food or water left over from another's plate or table, especially those of equal or inferior rank, though younger children are often fed from a parent's, usually a mother's, plate. This is because, as Charles Malamoud reminds us, "leftover food is not only the remains of *some thing,* it is the remains of *some one;* and as such, the more vile and impure the person who might have eaten or touched it, the more impure the leftover" (emphasis added).[38] Consuming cooked food from another's table or plate is consequently an acknowledgment of one's ritual inferiority and may be undertaken or mandated to give concrete form to such inferiority. Thus wives will eat off their husbands' plates, disciples will consume the leftovers of their guru, and everyone partakes of food offered to the gods (*naivedyam*), which returns to devotees as *prasad,* or divine leftovers. Even more significantly, such leftovers were and are routinely given to untouchables; this receipt of leftovers becomes one of the most explicit reminders of their degraded status. In light of this, we see that the word *jootha* is immensely recalcitrant to translation into English, in which it is often rendered as "leftovers" or, occasionally and more accurately but still imperfectly, as "garbage."[39] In a context in which the consumption of high-caste *jootha* is one of the definitional axes of ritual degradation, the English lady's encounter with the Nana's *jootha* constitutes for Mrs. Sneyd a portent of apocalypse.[40] In an insurgent context marked by the undermining of the prestige of dominant figures and classes through verbal and ritual insults and the forceful inversion of the terms of mastery and subordination, this may indeed have been the import of Mrs. Sneyd's reception at the Old Cawnpore Hotel. Many sepoys did commence their commitment to mutiny by throwing off deference to their white officers.[41] Certainly, as an Anglo-Indian steeped in the caste-based habitus of spatial and alimentary deference and degradation, she seems to have read it in these terms.

Once the outbreak was under way, mutineers' alimentary offenses, and Anglo-Indian alimentary sufferings, took a variety of forms, some of them quite sensational. Alexander Duff for one declared that "in [a] well-authenticated case, *the European servant* of a mess was seized and slowly *cut up into small pieces, and portions of his flesh forced down the throats of his children,* before they were themselves cruelly destroyed!" (emphasis in original).[42] This became an insistent trope, appearing in accounts of rebel atrocities committed at Delhi, Meerut, and Allahabad, and even featured in the *London Times.* (It features prominently in Edward Leckey's account of the "fictions connected with the Indian outbreak of 1857.") This was perhaps unsurprising for a nineteenth-century European imaginary fascinated with cannibalism as an exemplary instance of the waning or absence of civilization, or for a centuries-long Christian literary and visual tradition of seeing hell as a giant mouth or kitchen, and chewing, digestion, and regurgitation as its punishments for the damned.[43] In a macabre echo of indigenous fantasies of force-feeding, Indians did not turn cannibal themselves but compelled white children to devour their own parents. In other tales, mothers were fed upon children. Occasionally the cannibal fantasy teetered on the edge of comic absurdity—this is perhaps inescapable in the cannibal tale—as in the story of twenty-eight white officers slaughtered in an Allahabad mess with their arms and legs cut off to be arranged in dishes like joints of beef.[44]

There were also more banal but no less consequential instances of alimentary privation. In fact, a significant experience of the mutiny for Anglo-Indian women and men involved living in conditions of alimentary dearth, hygienic deprivation, and overcrowding that were entirely unwonted for them, and a number of the accounts of survivors describe the distresses of diminishing rations and unequal distribution in contexts where social hierarchies continued to flourish despite the scope of the crisis. For those living in the beleaguered entrenchment at Cawnpore, the early days of plenty (featuring champagne, rum, canned herrings and salmon, sweetmeats, and jam) soon gave way to meager rations of split peas and flour. Anglo-Indians unskilled in domestic labors complained of the high prices charged for cooking by the few remaining Indian servants. Even this diet of chapatis and dal (the food of the common folk on the subcontinent) had to be eked out with other anomalous, primitive, and even forbidden forms of nutriment. "Food, which in happier times would have been turned from with disgust, was seized with avidity and devoured with relish," says John William Kaye in his *History of the Sepoy War in India* (1870). "To the flesh-pots of the besieged no carrion was unwelcome. A stray dog was turned into soup. An old horse, fit only for the knackers, was converted into savoury meat. And when glorious good fortune brought a Brahmani bull within the fire of our people, and with difficulty the carcase of the animal was hauled into the intrenchments, there was rejoicing as if a victory had been gained."[45] While this picture of the Anglo-Indian turned eater of carrion is not without a sense of irony and even of gusto—though we are also told that some members of the entrenchment were too consumed with disgust to partake of horse flesh and dog soup—what was unequivocally troublesome was the lack of water, the well inside the entrenchment being particularly vulnerable to enemy fire. Drawing water was thus a hazardous task and performed (after the death of the Indian water carriers) by volunteers from the European regiments, who sometimes charged high prices for their services, delegated the task to Indian servants, and on other occasions threatened the water supplies of weaker members of the entrenchment. When water could be procured it was sometimes contaminated by fallen mortar and by human and animal blood.

Those in the Residency at Lucknow were much better provisioned, though many of the *memsahibs* (married, white, upperclass women) possessed the most rudimentary domestic skills and were hard put to cook meals and wash clothes and keep themselves cool without the usual contingent of Indian servants. Notwithstanding the crisis under which all inhabitants of the Residency labored, some civilians had access to a stock of gastronomic delicacies, which could be augmented by purchases at auctions of the supplies of the dead. Women and sepoys received less food than did white soldiers, and camp followers even less. The experience of subsisting on unfamiliar, nutritionally unsuitable, monotonous, and sometimes meager rations was exacerbated in both Cawnpore and Lucknow by the health and sanitary conditions that prevailed in the heat and rain. In Cawnpore water was obtained with difficulty and was available only for drinking, not for ablutions; before long the stench in the barracks drove many families to the open air of the trenches. In Lucknow there were no sweepers to empty the latrines, which were soon filled to overflowing. To the stench of these was added the stench of rotting corpses and animal carcasses. There were vermin of all kinds, and a high and often fatal incidence of diarrhea, cholera, typhoid, malaria, typhus, hepatitis, scurvy, and dysentery. In the Residency hospital, patients were surrounded by and sometimes covered in blood, vomit, pus, excreta, vermin, and amputated limbs; gangrene and blood poisoning were common.

This experience of bodily deprivation and penetrability and this adjacency to dirt to bodily waste and human remains served in a fashion as a form of Indianization, as hitherto pristine and invulnerable Anglo-Indian bodies became malodorous, pulpy, suppurating containers of blood, excrement, and sweat. In a reversal of the usual relationship of white body (or half-white) body to cleanliness, when W. J. Shepherd, a Eurasian member of Wheeler's entrenchment in Cawnpore, went into the city in Indian guise, he was almost immediately recognized as one of the English party because he was markedly smelly and greasy (and because he was drunk on rum).[46] And Mowbray Thomson, seeking to quell rumors of the rape of the ladies at the Bibighar, provided a grossly corporeal reason for their having been spared such violation: "Such was the loathsome condition into which, from long destitution and exposure, the fairest and youngest of our women had sunk that not a sepoy would have polluted himself with their touch."[47]

This dissolution of bodily boundaries was exacerbated in conditions of captivity. George Otto Trevelyan, the author of *Cawnpore* (1865), a classic mutiny narrative, speaks at length of the numerous bodily indignities visited upon the Anglo-Indian women and children who were the captives of Nana Saheb at the Bibighar. Notwithstanding the considerable privations suffered during the three weeks at Wheeler's entrenchment—weeks marked, as has been noted, by dirt, disease, and a diet of pariah dog and horse soup—Trevelyan stresses the delicacy and privileged status of the victims: "Here, during a fortnight of the Eastern summer, were penned two hundred and six persons of European extraction: for the most part women and children of gentle birth." Their privations included overcrowded lodgings meant for servants, matting in place of bedding, heat, manual labor such as the washing of one's own linen and the grinding of corn, "coarse Indian food" of lentils and chapatis, and trips to the verandah rather than the rides on horseback to which they had been accustomed. These deprivations are properly glossed, he intimates, not according to any commonplace understanding of privation or punishment but according to the sensibility of the victims: "If the various degrees of wretchedness are to be estimated by the faculty for suffering contained in the victim, then were these ladies of all women the most miserable."[48]

Like Kaye, J. W. Sherer, W. H. Russell, Mowbray Thomson, and other contemporary historians, writers, and eyewitnesses, Trevelyan repudiates the stories of the rape of white women at Cawnpore: "if we except a single case of abduction, it is absolutely certain that our ladies died without mention, and, we may confidently hope without apprehension of dishonour."[49] Nonetheless the expulsion of the Indian rapist from the scene of incarceration and suffering does not do away altogether with other kinds of unseemly and quasi-sexualized proximity. Seventy-five paces from the Bibighar, we are told, was a hotel favored by Nana Saheb. Here he lived "in a perpetual round of sensuality" in the company of "priests, pandars, ministers, and minions" and his favorite courtesan "Oula or Adala." His rooms were the site of nightly entertainments of feasting, music, dance, pantomime, and other all-too-obvious debaucheries. "The noise of this unhallowed revelry was plainly audible to the captives in the adjoining house," says Trevelyan.[50] More than this auditory link connected the scene of the Nana's noisy, libidinal revelries and the ladies' prison, however; the "Begum," the woman who was the ladies' warden, was a member of the entourage of "Oula or Adala." For Trevelyan, there is little question that this was a deeply gendered insult, standing in to some degree by the logic of contiguity for the sexual trespasses that he is compelled overtly to disavow.[51]

In the grotesque sensorium that was the Nana's prison every sense came under assault—sight (of jeering sepoys), sound (of the Nana's debaucheries), smell (in cramped and insalubrious quarters), touch, and taste. The "nauseous and unwonted food" served up to the captives was an additional part of the Nana's visceral assault. "They fed sparely on cakes of unleavened dough, and lentil-porridge dished up in earthen pans without spoon or plate. There was some talk of meat on Sundays, but it never came to anything. Once the children got a little milk."[52] Compounding this outrage was that the ladies were served their food by sweepers (outcaste menials who were usually assigned the cleaning of latrines) rather than by high-caste attendants, a detail that Trevelyan sees as a significant component of the English ladies' degradation: "The attendance of such debased menials was in itself the most ignominious affront which Oriental malice could invent: and even these were provided exclusively for the humiliation of our countrywomen, and might do nothing for their comfort."[53] The revulsion caused by having to eat the same food as the Indians is inseparable here from that caused by being served by handlers of excrement; indeed, Trevelyan's narrative suggests that to the delicate-stomached English lady, Indian food, bodily waste, and low-caste Indian bodies are scarcely distinguishable from each other. Here eating, digestion, and being served are far from being self-contained; mouth, nose, epidermis, and stomach function as conduits rather into an infinitely vermiculated series of distinctions and maneuvers. Eating in this narrative functions as a trope for other dangerous interminglings and metabolizations, but it is also risky in the most irreducibly somatic terms. For the ladies it had the expected apocalyptic results. Within eight days, Trevelyan tells us, these bodily torments had claimed—notwithstanding the ministrations of an Indian doctor—twenty-five European lives through dysentery and cholera, an annihilation effected through offenses against nourishment, hygiene, leisure, and habitation that anticipated the greater massacre to come. In the weeks and months to come, avenging British troops would register their sense of these Cawnpore outrages though the digestive troping of their own violent actions; to give a mutinous sepoy (or indeed any Indian) a "Cawnpore dinner" was to assault him with six inches of steel in the gut.[54]

The Well of the English

The imagination of atrocity came most often to rest in the environs of the Bibighar in Cawnpore, where Anglo-Indian women and children had been imprisoned by Nana Saheb, and in the well into which their dead and dying bodies were cast. It was no accident that Trevelyan's celebrated account of the mutiny was entitled *Cawnpore,* or that it read the events of 1857–58 in terms of developments in that city: General Hugh Wheeler's entrenchment, the attack at the ghats, and the slaughter of the women. Patrick Brantlinger notes the ways in which mutiny texts return obsessively to the "well of horror." It is an architectural landmark that tropes in these texts reflect the breach signified by the mutiny: "the well becomes a widening chasm dividing the forces of absolute righteousness from the demonic armies of the night."[55] The well came to be productive of an immense train of associations, recalling the Black Hole of Calcutta of a hundred years earlier, the polluted wells of Indian rumor, and the besieged wells—one serving as a source of water, another as a makeshift sepulchre—of the entrenchment at Cawnpore. It also opened up, as in the case of the rumors of rape, a semipornographic portal to an imagined world of raced and sexualized atrocity.[56] It does not take too much imagination to read the well as a giant gullet or as a cloacal opening, drawing unsuspecting British innocents into the unsavory depths of an all-devouring subcontinent (much as Morrowbie Jukes is engulfed into a village of the polluted Indian undead in Kipling's story). While it does not focus on the Bibighar as such, the description of the entrenchment and its environs by the *Times* journalist W. H. Russell affords a vivid sense of an encounter with the colonial bowels:

> It was a horrible spot! Inside the shattered rooms, which had been the scene of such devotion and suffering, are heaps of filth and rubbish. The entrenchment is used as a *cloaca maxima* by the natives, camp-followers, coolies, and others who bivouac in the sandy plains around it. The smells are revolting. Rows of gorged vultures sit with outspread wings on the mouldering parapets, or perch in clusters on the two or three leafless trees at the angle of the works by which we enter. I shot one with my revolver; and as the revolting creature disgorged his meal, twisting its bare black snake-like neck to and fro, I made a vow I would never incur such a disgusting sight again.[57]

Rooms, trenches, and wells here are sewers rather than the monumentalized *lieux de memoire* they were to become in other mutiny texts.[58] In an interestingly de-idealizing move, Russell does not—unlike many of his contemporaries—expend too much energy, in the diary at least, on the pathos of helpless and doomed ladies and children and unsuspecting British officers proceeding all unwittingly to their massacre.[59] He can take as given his readers' familiarity with the "devotion and suffering" enacted on this spot. More than anything else, this encounter with one of the scenes of mutiny atrocity is an intense experience of almost gothicized architectural and natural decay (moldering parapets, leafless trees) and of bodily grossness. The latter is represented by all the most disgusting operations of an alimentary canal open at both ends: gorging, vomiting, and excreting. Human remains and human waste—among the most potent of polluting substances—are powerfully conjoined here.[60] What renders the conjoining most disturbing is that the former (human remains) has been converted to the latter (human waste). What remains here of slaughter and suffering is a great stench and "filth and rubbish" generated by natives indifferent to, perhaps even deliberately contemptuous of, sanctity of place. Excreta and rubbish have both a material and a figural character here. As we have seen already, scatology is powerfully tied to the representation of backwardness or underdevelopment, and olfactory and especially excremental vigilance functions as a marker of civilization.[61] The natives in Russell's account are no longer mutinous or murderous; but odor, of all senses the most akin to animality and mortality, and the one which most threatens to engulf us, is the form in which the native body assaults him.[62] And it induces in him a moment of marked cultural and somatic panic, attended by a discharge unusual in a text marked in many respects by its deliberative and restrained character. Written in February 1858, well after General Neill's capture of Cawnpore and his widespread slaughter of the local population, the work of cleansing/vengeance is presumably complete and yet, judging from the excretory activities of masses of natives, not quite done. The paragraph moves from excreting native to gorged and revolting vulture in a fashion that cannot but establish the slide as allegorically marked; the repletion of the vultures, who function simultaneously as birds and snakes, exceeds the norms of empirical depiction. Still gorged (presumably upon white flesh, given the affective drift of this tableau) several months after the deaths and massacres of their former Anglo-Indian and Eurasian inhabitants, they call for an Englishman's violent vengeance, a vengeance that must be withheld (but only barely) from the human objects of disgust.

The revenge that Russell deflected to the vultures was to be carried out by Frederick Cooper, deputy commissioner of Amritsar, who slaughtered nearly five hundred unarmed and famished sepoys of the 26th Native Infantry regiment. The sepoys had surrendered to him, after killing two of their officers, upon being assured that they would face a court-martial rather than more summary punishment. Thus he was able to conclude: "There is a well at Cawnpoor; but there is also one at Ujnalla."[63]

The real and imagined atrocities of the mutiny were avenged with a ferocity of which even metropolitan and Anglo-Indian commentators took note. What is worth noting about the counterinsurgency is the way it fully and inventively incorporated indigenous ideas about ingestion and contamination; its tactics may have seemed therefore to Indians to have borne out the logic of profanation and force-feeding in the bone-dust and cartridge stories. A common punishment for mutineers was to blow them to bits from the mouths of cannons, a punishment that made burial or cremation impossible. In the case of those dispatched by hanging, shooting, or bayoneting, the corpses were in most instances not released to their next of kin, but left deliberately to feed jackals and wolves. Captives were frequently made to eat beef and pork before being dispatched to their doom. In some cases Muslim corpses were sewn in pigskin or burned and Hindu bodies buried in a reversal of customary funerary practice—acts of desecration that encompassed living kin in their punishments.[64] In a particularly noteworthy instance, Indians captured in Cawnpore, who were automatically held culpable in the deaths of women and children at Bibighar, were forced to lick clean a square foot of the blood-soaked floor before being taken to the gallows.[65] General Neill, who ordered these measures, made it clear that more was at stake than punishment for crimes committed and that he was as much invested in the gastro-logic of pollution as those he was punishing: "To touch blood is most abhorrent to the high caste natives; they think by doing so they doom their souls to perdition. Let them think so."[66] Russell reprobated these "excesses" even as he suggested that the tortures practiced by the English avengers were neither English nor Christian but part of a peculiarly Indian contagion: "all these kinds of vindictive, unchristian, Indian torture, such as sewing Mohammedans in pig-skins, smearing them with pork-fat before execution, and forcing Hindus to defile themselves, are disgraceful, and ultimately recoil on themselves."[67]

What is fascinating here about Anglo-Indian affect and practice is the appropriation of caste against the caste-bound, in a deadly combat in which the servants' tools are used to dismantle the servants' house.[68] The Anglo-Indian borrowing of structures of somatic response suggests, resists, and manages ideas of acculturation and intimacy. As we know, conquest and war in the colonial context produce in their wake anxieties of counterinvasion and reverse colonization; counterinsurgency therefore becomes a way of generating prophylactics against the threat of contamination.[69] We have seen from a reading of the Anglo-Indian texts of mutiny that these affects have powerful bodily manifestations. What these texts also underline is the way in which the conquerors' identification with their subjects is most inexorable, ironically enough, during the crisis of counterinsurgency. After all, when the enemy has perfected the art of ritual degradation to such an extraordinary degree, what better instructor can one hope to find? One might characterize this peculiar process of identification as a certain caste envy on the part of those who would always be found wanting, despite their long history of imperial conquest and notwithstanding their most sanguinary fantasies, in the endeavor to best or even to match such a richly baroque and remarkably durable apparatus of abjection as caste appeared to be.

Such forms of caste emulation and caste envy could not be practiced, needless to say, without a certain degree of ambivalence. Thus the spectacular and archaic grossness of bloody, ritually degrading punishments sits uneasily, undigested, in the colonial texts. While details of Indian atrocities are described in thorough and often stomach-churning detail, there is greater decorousness about English ones in *Cawnpore*. "Of what did take place the less said is the better," says Trevelyan about the vengeance visited upon Cawnpore. "Reckless as men . . . half-starved, and more than half-intoxicated, . . . they enacted a scene into the details of which an Englishman at least will not care to inquire."[70] As the author's terse summary intimates, the availability of enormous quantities of alcohol made drunkenness among tommies—always regarded as a physical and moral liability because of their uncontrolled appetites—and occasionally among Sikh soldiers a significant trial for officers and chroniclers. On occasion drunken troops disobeyed their officers and on others widespread intoxication made military advances impossible. In several cases stores of alcohol had to be destroyed to ensure a minimal degree of sobriety among the ranks of the noncommissioned. Sometimes the wanton looting of Indian cities and indiscriminate slaughter of Indians were also—as in this instance—attributed to the influence of alcohol. Such excesses of appetite and expression made it enormously difficult for Anglo-Indian officers to maintain the discipline that supposedly separated white troops from opium- and bhang-stupefied mutineers and fanatics.[71]

Episodes such as these are awkward and unsettled moments in the narrative of mutiny, turning the gastro-logic of colonialism on its head and producing white bodies as embodiments of drives, decay, and delirium. The imperative to obliterate these fraught carnalities—carnalities that, as I have suggested, showcased the unexpected and uncanny alimentary and sexual intimacies of Indian and Anglo-Indian—might account at least in part for certain obsessive forms of purification, purgation, and memorialization that followed the conclusion of the mutiny. If the tenuous hyphen separating and conjoining "Anglo" from/with "India" collapses, or at least teeters, in the course of the mutiny, post-mutiny recovery is an endeavor to overcome self-estrangement and restore decorum to an Anglo-Indianness beside itself.

Bernard Cohn for one has described the way the fetish of the mutiny pilgrimage—to mutiny sites in Delhi, Cawnpore, and Lucknow—became a routine part of English travel to India.[72] This was as much a memorialization of the martyrdom and the eventual triumphs that characterized British rule in the subcontinent as it was an elaboration of the estrangement of the sahib's body from its place of habitation. In a curious way this simultaneously configured India as part of a sacred diasporic geography, with Anglo-Indians distinguished as the salt of that alien earth. Ian Baucom puts it aptly: "In thus discovering the Mutiny as the pretext for a narrative of imperial belonging, the colonists rendered a visit to the Mutiny sites an act of Ruskinian remembrance and anticipation in which the present and future are subordinated to a privileged past, and memory emerges as the angel of history and the god of the everyday."[73] Note, for instance, Trevelyan's meditations (from 1865) on the afterlife of the well at Cawnpore, now cleansed and architecturally remade: "It is interesting to observe the neat garden that strives to beguile away the associations which haunt the well of evil fame, and to peruse the inscription indited by a vice-regal hand. It may gratify some minds, beneath the roof of a memorial church that is now building, to listen while Christian worship is performed above a spot which once resounded with ineffectual prayers and vain ejaculations addressed to quite other ears. . . . For that is the very place itself where the act was accomplished."[74] The well at Cawnpore is, less than a decade after the mutiny, a bucolic spot, purged of all signs of corpses and bodily wastes, and presided over by Marochetti's beautiful marble angel.[75] What makes this picture of innocence possible is the exclusion of all non-Christian Indians from the site. (They were barred from it until the end of British rule in 1947.) This angel—not quite a Benjaminian angel of history!—works as an apt figure of a reformed and etherealized Anglo-Indian body, freed finally of the appetites, emissions, and injuries of an all-too-corporeal diasporic embodiment.

NOTES

A revised version of this essay appears as chapter 1 in Parama Roy, Alimentary Tracts: Appetites, Aversions, and the Postcolonial *(Durham, N.C.: Duke University Press, 2010).*

1. Gautam Chakravarty, *The Indian Mutiny and the British Imagination* (Cambridge, UK: Cambridge University Press, 2005), 1. Since my focus in this essay is on the Anglo-Indian experience and representation of the events of 1857–58, I have retained specifically colonial designations and names such as "mutiny" (not "rebellion" or "war of independence"), "Oudh" (not Awadh), and "Cawnpore" (not Kanpur).

2. Ron Inden, *Imagining India* (Oxford: Basil Blackwell, 1990).

3. While a medicalized lexicon of drug addiction was some decades away even in Britain, and opinions about the recreational and medicinal use of opium and bhang far from unanimous from Anglo-Indian medical personnel, these substances were sometimes seen to fuel the fury demonstrated in 1857 by the antagonists of the Company's rule. James Mills suggests that it was not until the 1870s that opium usage came to be regarded with alarm; it was then, he suggests, that it came to be tied much more firmly with various forms of political violence, including that of 1857 (*Madness, Cannabis, and Colonialism* [New York: St. Martin's Press, 2000]).

4. Seema Alavi takes note of the way the Company's recruiting practices actively "sanskritized" the military, that is, nurtured upper-caste rituals and practices (*The Sepoys and the Company: Tradition and Transition in Northern India, 1770–1830* [Delhi: Oxford University Press, 1995], 76).

5. Thomas Metcalf argues for the mutiny's transformative character in the relationship of Anglo-India to India (*The Aftermath of Revolt: India, 1857–1870* [Princeton, N.J.: Princeton University Press, 1964]). One need not agree *in toto* with this diagnosis to concede that the mutiny, generating as it did a novel vocabulary of loyalty and betrayal, did inaugurate a significant insistence on racial distance as a matter of policy and as part of an Anglo-Indian psychic landscape.

6. Jacques Derrida, " 'Eating Well,' or the Calculation of the Subject: An Interview with Jacques Derrida," in *Who Comes After the Subject?*, ed. Eduardo Cadava, Peter Connor, and Jean-Luc Nancy, 96–119 (New York: Routledge, 1991).

7. For soul making under colonialism, see Gayatri C. Spivak, "Three Women's Texts and a Critique of Imperialism," in *"Race," Writing, and Difference,* ed. Henry Louis Gates, Jr. (Chicago: University of Chicago Press, 1986).

8. I maintain a certain looseness of appellation in my use of terms such as *Anglo-Indian, Briton, English, sahib,* and even *Indian* that is not entirely accidental. The community of whites of British origin resident in India used a variety of designations for itself, a variety that marks its ambivalent sense of belonging and legitimacy in the subcontinent. Occasionally these subjects were identified as Indians (though distinct from the "natives" of the subcontinent) in metropolitan writing. Kipling, for one, delighted in calling himself a Punjabi. During the mutiny years the community of whites in India was augmented significantly by military personnel requisitioned from Britain.

9. My thanks to Sandhya Shetty for suggesting this term.

10. Frantz Fanon, *The Wretched of the Earth,* trans. Constance Farrington (New York: Grove Weidenfeld, 1963), 38–39.

11. In the seventeenth and eighteenth centuries, soldiers' liaisons and marriages with local women were encouraged by the Company as a cost-saving device, though the children of such liaisons were their mothers' charges and not necessarily provided for by their fathers. See Percival Spear, *The Nabobs* (London: Curzon Press, 1963).

12. See Spear, *The Nabobs;* and Kenneth Ballhatchet, *Race, Sex, and Class Under the Raj* (New York: St. Martin's, 1980).

13. Sudipta Sen, *Distant Sovereignty: National Imperialism and the Origins of British India* (New York: Routledge, 2002), 134.

14. Engseng Ho, "Empire Through Diasporic Eyes: A View From the Other Boat," *Comparative Studies in Society and History* 46, no. 2 (2004): 226.

15. C. J. Hawes, *Poor Relations: The Making of a Eurasian Community in British India, 1773–1833* (Richmond, UK: Curzon Press, 1996). Also see Betty Joseph, "The Politics of Settlement," in *Reading the East India Company, 1720–1840: Colonial Currencies of Gender* (Chicago: University of Chicago Press, 2004), 92–122. The work of Anglo-Indian writers of the late nineteenth century such as Kipling and Steel suggests that concubinage did not disappear despite official disapproval. Eurasians were the targets of the mutineers in 1857, along with Britons and native Christians.

16. Durba Ghosh, "Colonial Families Across the British Empire in the Eighteenth Century," paper presented at the Berkshire Conference of Women Historians, Scripps College, June 2005.

17. Radhika Mohanram, *Imperial White: Race, Diaspora, and the British Empire* (Minneapolis: University of Minnesota Press, 2007), xxi.

18. See Bart Moore-Gilbert, *Kipling and "Orientalism"* (London: Croom Helm, 1986), for a study of Anglo-Indian assertions (sometimes defensive) of distinctiveness from metropolitan Britons. This is distinct from Ho's sense that "the British . . . became *a people* as they became *an empire*: Britannia ruled the waves" ("Empire Through Diasporic Eyes," 214).

19. Rudyard Kipling, "The Tomb of His Ancestors," in *The Day's Work,* ed. Constance Phipps (1898; Harmondsworth, UK: Penguin Books, 1988).

20. Sudipta Sen suggests that sovereignty was "ill defined and jealously guarded in the new regime established in India by the East India Company" (*Distant Sovereignty,* xiii). Nicholas Dirks notes that the Company struggled with the question of sovereignty over several decades and with respect to more than one state entity, since its rights and privileges had to be defined not only in relation to the Mughal empire but also in relation to a British Parliament that sought periodically to regulate its proceedings and to manage its unsound finances. "The Company continued in many respects as a rogue state," Dirks says, "in its relation both to the Mughal empire and the British Crown" (*The Scandal of Empire: India and the Creation of Imperial Britain* [Cambridge, Mass.: Harvard University Press, 2006], 182).

21. James Clifford, "Diasporas," *Cultural Anthropology* 9, no. 3 (1994): 302–38.

22. Eric Stokes, *The English Utilitarians and India* (Oxford: Clarendon Press, 1959), xiii; also see E. M. Collingham, *Imperial Bodies: The Physical Experience of the Raj, c. 1800–1947* (Cambridge, UK: Polity Press, 2001), 6–7 and 50–92.

23. Julia Kristeva, *Powers of Horror: An Essay on Abjection,* trans. Leon S. Roudiez (New York: Columbia University Press, 1982).

24. Dominique Laporte notes the Renaissance rediscovery of and admiration for Roman sanitation, including the institution of the *cloaca maxima* (*History of Shit,* trans. Nadia Benabid and Rodolphe el-Khoury [Cambridge, Mass.: MIT Press, 2000], 14).

25. Norbert Elias, *The Civilizing Process: Sociogenetic and Psychogenetic Investigations,* rev. ed., trans. Edmund Jephcott and ed. Eric Dunning, Johan Goudsbloum, and Stephen Mennell (1939; Oxford: Blackwell Publishers, 2000). Also see Pierre Bourdieu, *Distinction: A Social Critique of the Judgment of Taste,* trans. Richard Nice (1979; Cambridge, Mass.: Harvard University Press, 1987).

26. Peter Stallybrass and Allon White, *The Politics and Poetics of Transgression* (Ithaca, N.Y.: Cornell University Press, 1986), 148.

27. Quoted by David Arnold, *Colonizing the Body: State Medicine and Epidemic Disease in Nineteenth-Century India* (Berkeley: University of California Press, 1993), 98.

28. Erin O' Connor, *Raw Material: Producing Pathology in Victorian Culture* (Durham, N.C.: Duke University Press, 2000), 226–27.

29. Arnold, *Colonizing the Body,* 89–90.

30. Dane Kennedy, *Islands of White: Settler Society and Culture in Kenya and Southern Rhodesia, 1890–1939* (Durham, N.C.: Duke University Press, 1987).

31. On the development of the bungalow as a model dwelling for Anglo-Indian rulers, see Anthony D. King, *The Bungalow: The Production of a Global Culture* (London: Routledge & Kegan Paul, 1984).

32. Collingham, *Imperial Bodies,* 171.

33. See Dane Kennedy, *The Magic Mountains: Hill Stations and the British Raj* (Delhi: Oxford University Press, 1996).

34. Collingham, *Imperial Bodies,* 156–59. Writing in the next century, Forster provides an acerbic summary of the menu at an Anglo-Indian dinner party: "Julienne soup full of bullety bottled peas, pseudo-cottage bread, fish full of branching bones, pretending to be plaice, more bottled peas with the cutlets, trifles, sardines on toast: the menu of Anglo-India. A dish might be added or subtracted as one rose or fell in the official scale, the peas might rattle less or more, the sardines and the vermouth be imported by a different firm, but the tradition remained; the food of exiles, cooked by servants who did not understand it" (*A Passage to India* [1924; San Diego: Harcourt Brace, 1984], 48–49).

35. Homi Bhabha, "By Bread Alone," in *The Location of Culture* (London: Routledge, 1994), 206. Bhabha's emphasis on the vertiginous possibilities of this sign differs somewhat from Ranajit Guha's reading of the chapati as that which comes to be transformed from being a token of the management of epidemic—it belonged to a time-honored mode (called *chalawa*) of using a ritually consecrated animal or object to act as the carrier of an epidemic (cholera in this case) and bear it outside a designated territory—to being a preliterate, subaltern mode of rebel transmission. See his *Elementary Aspects of Peasant Insurgency in Colonial India* (Delhi: Oxford University Press, 1983), 226ff.

36. Edward Thompson, *The Other Side of the Medal* (London: Hogarth Press, 1925), 117–19. Also see Ian Baucom, "The Path from War to Friendship: E. M. Forster's Mutiny Pilgrimage," in *Out of Place: Englishness, Empire, and the Locations of Identity* (Princeton, N.J.: Princeton University Press, 1999), ch. 3.

37. Cited by Saul David, *The Indian Mutiny, 1857* (London: Viking, 2002), 67–68.

38. Charles Malamoud, *Cooking the World: Ritual and Thought in Ancient India,* trans. David White (Delhi: Oxford University Press, 1996), 8.

39. McKim Marriott, "Caste Ranking and Food Transactions: A Matrix Analysis," in *Structure and Change in Indian Society,* ed. Milton Singer and Bernard Cohn, 142 (Chicago: Aldine, 1968).

40. In general, high-caste Hindus in mid-nineteenth century India did not dine with casteless Europeans, nor did respectable Muslims, who were concerned about the presence of pork and alcohol on the sahib's table. Anglo-Indians often complained of this; their own racially exclusionary practices in dining and entertainment were generally explained in terms of the local practices that treated Christians as polluting because of their failure to abide by dietary restrictions.

41. Rudrangshu Mukherjee, *Spectre of Violence: The 1857 Kanpur Massacres* (New Delhi: Viking, 1998), 60–62; and *Awadh in Revolt, 1857–1858* (Wimbledon: Anthem Press, 2002), ix–x. Anglo-Indians were not the only ones to be subjected to these practices of inversion. The mutineers were high-handed and coercive even with those traditional leaders—Bahadur Shah, Nana Saheb, the Rani of Jhansi—whom they had chosen as the leaders of their uprising.

42. Alexander Duff, *The Indian Rebellion: Its Causes and Results* (New York: Robert Carter & Brothers, 1858), 63.

43. Marina Warner, "Fee fie fo fum: the child in the jaws of the story," in *Cannibalism and the Colonial World,* ed. Francis Barker, Peter Hulme, and Margaret Iversen, 158–82 (Cambridge, UK: Cambridge University Press, 1998).

44. Christopher Hibbert, *The Great Mutiny, India 1857* (Harmondsworth, UK: Penguin Books, 1978), 213.

45. John William Kaye, *A History of the Sepoy War in India, 1857–1858,* vol. 2 (London: W. H. Allen and Co., 1870), 331.

46. W. J. Shepherd, *A Personal Narrative of the Outbreak and Massacre at Cawnpore,* 2nd ed. (London: R. Craven, 1879), 64.

47. Mowbray Thomson, *The Story of Cawnpore* (London, 1859).

48. George Otto Trevelyan, *Cawnpore* (1865; London: Macmillan, 1886), 278.

49. Ibid., 284. J. W. Sherer, *Daily Life During the Indian Mutiny: Personal Experiences of 1857* (London, 1898; Allahabad: Legend Publications, 1974 [reprint]).

50. Trevelyan, *Cawnpore,* 281.

51. Ibid., 278–79.

52. Ibid., 277–84. Shepherd, on the other hand, subscribes to the notion that the Nana's interest in his captives was irreducibly sexual and that they were supplied with clean clothes and with superior victuals (beer, wines, rum, milk, and meat) so as to facilitate their sexual surrender to him (*A Personal Narrative,* 94–95).

53. Trevelyan, *Cawnpore,* 280.

54. Vivian Dering Majendie, *Up Among the Pandies: A Year's Service in India* (London: Routledge, Warne, and Routledge, 1859), 223.

55. Patrick Brantlinger, "The Well at Cawnpore: Literary Representations of the Indian Mutiny of 1857," in *Rule of Darkness: British Literature and Imperialism, 1830–1914* (Ithaca, N.Y.: Cornell University Press, 1988), 204.

56. On the Black Hole's status as "founding trauma" for the East India Company in the eighteenth century, see Betty Joseph's "Archival Fictions: Memories of Violence in the Age of Sensibility," in *Reading the East India Company, 1720–1840: Colonial Currencies of Gender* (Chicago: University of Chicago Press, 2004), 61–91.

57. W. H. Russell, *My Indian Mutiny Diary* (London: Cassell, 1957), 34. My thanks to Catherine Robson for raising the question of the well in the mutiny's gastropoetics.

58. Pierre Nora, "Between History and Memory: Les Lieux de Mémoire," *Representations* 26 (Spring 1989): 7–25.

59. I have not read the reports that Russell wrote for the *Times*.

60. We might recall that for Kristeva the two are linked in terms of their operations and affect: "The corpse (or cadaver: *cadere,* to fall), that which has irremediably come a cropper, is cesspool, and death; . . . refuse and corpses *show me* what I permanently thrust aside in order to live" (*Powers of Horror,* 3).

61. See Warwick A. Anderson, "Excremental Colonialism: Public Health and the Poetics of Pollution," *Critical Inquiry* 21 (Spring 1995): 640–69; and Joshua Esty, "Excremental Postcolonialism," *Contemporary Literature* 40, no. 1 (Spring 1999): 22–59, on the metaphoric slide between improper modes of defecation and the racially marked primitive subject.

62. Sigmund Freud, *Civilization and Its Discontent,* trans. James Strachey (New York: W. W. Norton & Co., 1961); William Ian Miller, *The Anatomy of Disgust* (Cambridge, Mass.: Harvard University Press, 1997), 66–79.

63. Frederick Cooper, *The Crisis in the Punjab,* quoted by Thompson, *The Other Side of the Medal,* 66.

64. Mukherjee, *Spectre of Violence,* 32–34.

65. Michael Edwardes, *Red Year: The Indian Rebellion of 1857* (London: Hamish Hamilton, 1973), 87–88.

66. Mukherjee, *Spectre of Violence,* 32.

67. Russell, *My Indian Mutiny Diary,* 161.

68. I am indebted to Sandhya Shetty for this turn of phrase.

69. For a fine elaboration of reverse colonization, see Stephen Arata, "The Occidental Tourist: Bram Stoker's *Dracula* and the Anxiety of Reverse Colonization," *Victorian Studies* 33, no. 1 (Summer 1990): 621–45.

70. Trevelyan, *Cawnpore,* 332.

71. Flora Steel, *On the Face of the Waters* (Rahway, N.J.: Mershon, 1896); Kaye, *A History of the Sepoy War in India,* vol. 1.

72. Bernard Cohn, "Representing Authority in Victorian India," in *The Invention of Tradition,* ed. Eric Hobsbawm and Terence Ranger, 179 (Cambridge, UK: Cambridge University Press, 1983, 1992). Pilgrimages or tours to mutiny sites continue to be offered by British outfits with an interest in military history.

73. Ian Baucom, *Out of Place: Englishness, Empire, and the Locations of Identity* (Princeton, N.J.: Princeton University Press, 1999), 112.

74. Trevelyan, *Cawnpore,* 190–91.

75. A beautiful carved marble figure placed over the Bibighar well head in February 1863, the statue was commissioned by Viceroy and Lady Canning and carved by Baron Carlo Marochetti (P. J. O. Taylor, *A Companion to the "Indian Mutiny" of 1857* [Delhi: Oxford University Press, 1996], 210).

CHAPTER FIVE

Domestic Internationalisms, Imperial Nationalisms
Civil Rights, Immigration, and Conjugal Military Policy

RACHEL IDA BUFF

Introduction

How do denizens of a nation come to imagine our imperial relations? How do we in the United States envision denizens of our far-flung territories, even as they are engaged in such intimate activities as manufacturing our clothing and pleasuring our soldiers abroad and crossing our borders to wash our clothes, raise our children, and serve our food? What avenues exist to create an oppositional political discourse that speaks the name of empire?

The discourse of diaspora implicitly contests the hegemony of the nation and its claims on social identities and cultural politics. For this reason, the heterodox diasporan imaginary is often obscured by discourse of nation and empire and needs to be retrieved by archival and analytical searching.

In foreign policy discourse in the United States, terms such as "making the world safe for democracy" and "the global war on terror" bear a seemingly incontestable weight. Repressing continuity with earlier practices of empire, these terms convey an urgency that wants to defy analysis. What reasonable person is against democracy, in favor of terror? Imperialism is thus naturalized. To speak of U.S. foreign policy for what it is—*the policy, practice, or advocacy of extending the power and dominion of a nation especially by direct territorial acquisitions or by gaining indirect control over the political or economic life of other areas; broadly: the extension or imposition of power, authority, or influence*—invites suspicion.[1] When I was traveling back from San Francisco in early 2002, I had my wallet with all my IDs stolen. Thinking that traveling this way, so close to

9/11, would be difficult enough, I left my new copy of Hardt and Negri's *Empire* with friends, who sent it to me later.[2]

Historical continuity is not all that is repressed as empire is naturalized. In the 1940s and 1950s, African American activists made connections between civil rights and decolonization struggles, working in terms of human rights. They imagined continuities between the freedom struggle taking place in the American South and those in places such as India, Trinidad, and Ghana. They imagined a diasporan, counterhegemonic map. As historian Carol Anderson demonstrates, Cold War pressure on these groups to limit their work to enfranchising African Americans as citizens severely limited the extent of coalition and change possible even on a national basis.[3] The business of maintaining an empire included curtailing transnational constructions of identity.

Currently, we witness the denial of both human rights and national citizenship at Guantanamo. Invoking national security, the Patriot Act redefines citizens as terrorists and threats from within. And so in Seattle, African American Muslim activist James Ujaama was indefinitely detained on charges of aiding and abetting the Taliban and Al Qaeda in London.[4] As Don Pease has magisterially put it, "The category of citizen is constructed through spectral subjectivity of the deported."[5] By their ghostly presence, the names of the deported create the possibility of national citizenship itself. But citizens don't know where the deported wind up—in detention centers held without bail or phone calls, on a military base outside our borders, in the far reaches of the empire, or beyond. And citizens like Ujaama, who call empire by its name, are suspect for that act itself. The possibilities of national citizenship are limited by the spectrality of the deported, because along with them, the transnational basis for justice and civil rights disappears.

Empire is, then, both crucial and obscured. This leaves standing the question of an imperial imaginary: how denizens of a nation that has an empire imagine the territories beyond. An official imperial imaginary incorporates the hard masculinity of national security policy with a more nurturing imperative: the international export of our democracy. National security takes on an incontestable toughness in public discourse; protecting the homeland is a rational calculus of force. In this post-9/11 epoch, the Immigration and Naturalization Service is absorbed into the Department of Homeland Security; every undocumented worker is a potential terrorist—much as the long-standing practice of buttressing fascist counterinsurgency in the hemisphere is newly dubbed "counterterrorism" in Plan Columbia. But the relations between people in the United States and those abroad is figured as softer and more feminine, whether in terms of foreign aid for schools and families; the importation of refugees stranded on our shores by imperial policy; or the collateral damage unfortunately, and always accidentally, engendered by the bombings of wedding celebrations in the Afghan hinterland. In this official imperial imaginary, the export of democracy abroad reinforces the hegemony of the nation and the invisibility of empire; denizens of the territories, too, are citizens of a nation like ours, but distinct from it.

But any narrative creates the possibility for opposition. Any discourse of democracy is freighted with multiple meanings of the term: as a civilizing mission, as grounds for just treatment, as an opening for insurgency. These inherent contradictions are often expressed in discourses of immigration and, in particular, in discourses connecting immigration to gender and sexuality. Just as, economically, immigration policy connects the feminization of the labor force in the United States with sexualized labor on military bases abroad, the congressional debates and popular images of immigrants that inform these policies map the "moral geographies," to use Melani McAlister's rich phrase, in which denizens of the center of an empire imagine our relations to denizens of the periphery, both in their far-flung homes and as they draw nearer to us.[6]

Immigration by its nature connects disparate territories and identities. The notion of democratic inclusion, of integrating immigrants into a national family, opens up possibilities for creating resistant identities as well as a geography of exclusion and inequality. As the empire "comes home," denizens of the territories arrive in the metropole. Their demands for justice open up democratic constructions of citizens long foreclosed.

A moral geography of empire maps not only the territories of center and periphery, but the routes of transport between them. "Young GIs," innocents abroad in service of the empire, encountered "native peaches" and, increasingly in the post-1945 period, brought them home as wives. The U.S. military and the Immigration and Naturalization Service took it upon themselves to scrutinize these matches and then to help transport these women back to the United States. They did this at the same exact moment that state laws and accepted local practices foreclosed the possibilities of interracial sex and marriage back home.

My research looks at divergent imaginings of early Cold War geopolitics. I draw on congressional debates over immigration policy, as well as the ways military officials and service people at imperial outposts attempted to understand the implications of immigration policy, particularly that concerning war brides, for their everyday lives.

This chapter traces the construction of an imperial imaginary structuring immigration policy at the outset of "the American century," after World War II. Changes in immigration policy in this period, while pitched in a dual language of Cold War and antiracialist imperatives, linked much more directly to the exigencies of an emergent imperial world system. Gender and sexuality, both of which received particular scrutiny and transformation in the new immigration policy, were crucial to imagining and regulating this world system. Discourses of immigration in this period were central to the construction of an imperial imaginary that denied the existence of empire. At the same time, immigration offers a social imaginary that illuminates the geography of empire and the implications of this geography for citizenship and identity.

Geography

This chapter is crucially concerned with the architecture of empire apposite to post-1945 United States imperial formations in Asia. This foundational architecture might be envisioned as a bridge bolstered in the East by the long U.S. presence in the Philippines and by the Eighth Army's occupation of Japan. This bridge has been built by a correspondence and then a silence between Ho Chi Minh and Harry Truman, a slow but steady flow of advisors and aid to "friendly" regimes in the region. The wide span east to California is braced by pylons resting on the Northern Mariana Islands, on Guam, Howland Island, Kingman Reef, and the territory of Hawaii. It finally reaches the Pacific coast of California and heads east to the imperial urban centers.

Even to argue that this bridge represents an imperial formation causes controversy in some quarters. After all, the post–World War II period represents a key moment of decolonization and nation building in former European imperial spheres. But events in Asia indicate the entwined nature of liberty and imperial reach during the twentieth century. Philippine independence in 1934 coexisted with the ongoing American occupation of the islands during and after the war and with restrictions on Filipino American immigration and civil rights. Declaring Guam an "unincorporated territory" in 1950, Congress in the Organic Act conferred the ambivalent benefits of U.S. nuclear citizenship on all denizens thereof, as did the incorporation of Hawaii as the fiftieth state. The occupation of Japan after Hiroshima-Nagasaki provided a bulkhead for a police action in Korea, eventually installing American bases there on a permanent basis. Two years later, Asian immigrants became eligible for citizenship for the first time in U.S. history, at the same time that the McCarran-Walter Immigration Act set tiny quotas of immigrants to be allowed into the country from an imaginary "Asia-Pacific Triangle." And Ho Chi Minh's literary appeal to Jefferson, that architect of the republic, in 1945 summoned military sanction rather than cultural recognition. Postwar imperial formations, then, entwined the development of national and colonial identities. The architecture of empire was a conduit for the reshaping of identities in both periphery and center.

In 1952 Congress overrode Truman's presidential veto to pass McCarran-Walter. This act reinstated race-based national origins quotas at the same time it ended the long-standing ban on the naturalization of Asians. It also implemented a distinction, still on the books and very much central to our understanding of immigration and refugee politics to this day, between "economic" and "political" refugees: essentially, those fleeing regimes more or less friendly to the United States. It has been true since that time, almost without exception, that lighter-skinned immigrants turn out to be more eligible for consideration as "political" refugees deserving asylum, while darker ones are deemed "economic" and undeserving, even if they are fleeing national economies shuddering from the ravages of U.S.-backed World Bank economic policy. This has been true in the widely divergent treatment of Haitian and Cuban refugees, to cite one of many examples.[7]

That McCarran-Walter was racially restrictive legislation that at the same time ended the long-standing ban on the naturalization of Asian immigrants has presented an interesting paradox for historians. Was this a part of a broader civil rights moment represented by the historic *Brown vs. Board of Education* decision? The law set tiny quotas for immigrants from Asia and newly decolonized nations in Africa and mobilized potent distinctions between deserving and undeserving refugees. We can resolve this seeming paradox by thinking globally rather than nationally. It's key that Asian exclusion ended at a time of escalating U.S. military involvement in Asia. Also, McCarran-Walter, while reasserting national origins as an important way of screening new immigrants, institutionalized the war brides programs of World War II and the Korean War as a permanent feature of immigration law. The wives of GIs were seen as particularly desirable, tractable immigrants, and the necessity of bringing these women in would be a permanent feature of a militarized postwar order. In general, immigrants—the great majority of whom would be women in the postwar period—entered the nation as feminized partners, subject to wifely transformation to become a member of the family. Immigration and foreign policy mediated the boundaries of the Cold War imperial order.

With McCarran-Walter, the move away from national origins quotas, then, did not necessarily mean a move away from a racialized immigration policy. Rather, the shift was from a eugenic model to a genealogical one, in which a heteronormative family model was to engender good American citizens.[8] As Siobhan Somerville suggests, both birthright citizenship and naturalization rely on heterosexual ideas of the reproduction of citizenship.[9]

As a result of the centrality of discourses of citizenship to the Cold War project as well as to emancipatory projects such as civil rights in this period, citizenship became a contested terrain, a culture war, in historian Nikhil

Singh's term.[10] At the same time that federal policy makers set out to create a safe way of filtering the addition of internal and external aliens into the national body, subaltern groups organized to press for inclusion on their own terms.

Citizenship holds the possibility for not only enfranchisement, but for coercion, for loss. As proffered by postwar public policy, citizenship represented a narrowing of identity for many people. People whose complex cultural loyalties challenged a political identity predicated on a narrow, national model came in for scrutiny and transformation into manageable citizen-subjects, compliant wives of the Cold War order. Because it was so crucial to Cold War policy to divide and map the world into First, Third, and New World constituencies, these new citizens were asked to choose and publicly ratify their alliances. This historic moment has clear parallels with our own, in which those with complex political, cultural, or national loyalties are subject to scrutiny, incarceration, deportation, and other forms of coercion. And as our current conditions so sharply remind us, such narrowing of citizenship and loyalty is rarely liberating.

Competing Internationalisms and the Struggle for Immigration Policy

The passage of the McCarran-Walter Immigration Act was highly contested, taking place as it did in a national atmosphere charged with questions about race and rights. As historian Carol Anderson has argued, Cold War politics forestalled attempts within the African American freedom struggle to articulate black claims in context of global human rights, instead imposing a restricted, national framework.[11] But domestic minority groups were very much aware of the international context in which their claims for expanded citizenship rights were made, including decolonization and the realignments of the Cold War moment. Conflicting internationalisms characterized the debate over immigration restriction in this period.

African American and Asian American groups, in particular, were compelled to recognize the parallels between international affairs and their struggles for citizenship and immigrant rights within the nation. It is important that the aspirations of these groups, some of which were blocked by the domestic policies of Cold War hegemony, represented a common cause during this key period for civil rights between different subaltern groups. Such solidarity was invoked at international gatherings such as the Afro-Asian Conference at Bandung in 1955. Domestic struggles, in turn, were influenced by what Nikhil Singh and Andrew Jones characterize as "the expansive hopes for popular democracy unleashed by decolonization."[12]

A coalition of civil rights, ethnic, and religious groups, including African and Asian American groups, opposed the restrictionism inherent in the new immigration legislation: its tendency to "ancestor hunt," in the words of Harry S. Truman; the tiny quotas set for newly decolonized nations, which, along with restrictions on immigration from colonies still existent, provided for the virtual exclusion of West Indians, Vietnamese, and Asian-Indian immigrants; and the way the law shut the door on large parts of a war-torn Europe that World War II had supposedly been fought to liberate. Catholic and Jewish groups were active in pressing for larger quotas for refugees and immigrants from Europe to allow the entry of those fleeing the ravages of the post–World War II context. An assortment of northern and western Democrats in Congress, as well as both presidents Truman and Eisenhower, supported these initiatives.

Catholic and Jewish activism around immigration questions in some ways referenced the diasporic connections, or "special sorrows," to borrow historian Matthew Frye Jacobson's phrase, of these groups.[13] But in the immediate postwar period, the Catholic and Jewish ethnic groups lobbying for expanded immigration were also experiencing historically unprecedented access to white privilege, predominantly through the racially selective benefits bestowed by the Veterans Administration and postwar housing policy. While these groups lobbied for the expansion of immigration and refugee quotas, they tended to rely on a rubric of equal rights and ethnic assimilation to do so. In testimony before Congress in 1952, for example, Senator O'Mahoney invoked a list of sports stars of European extraction—this at a time when the integration of baseball was just beginning—to demonstrate the patriotic utility of expanded immigration from Europe.[14] Appealing jointly to Congress, representatives of the Jewish Community Center of Detroit, the International Institute, the Archdiocese of Detroit, and the Detroit Council of Churches asserted that "further restriction of the quota system would seriously impair the influx of highly desirable persons whose ancestors in the past have and who would now contribute greatly to the integration and further expansion of our democratic way of life in business, industry, commerce, and intellectual pursuits at home and abroad."[15]

Typically, arguments like these invoked a particular reading of American history, in which masculinized, productive, and predominantly white ethnics had come together to build a nation. In this melting-pot interpretation, immigration restriction erred in not extending the benefits of American democracy to more Europeans, particularly those currently suffering behind the Iron Curtain. These arguments did not explicitly exclude nonwhites from the successful melting-pot past, and sometimes extended to include a liberal reading of civil rights for all. They also included in the national past southern and eastern Europeans, who had been targeted by previous restrictive legislation as undesirable influences on the national character.

But, in a historical moment characterized by Jim Crow at home and the transformation of long-standing empires abroad, there is little mention of non-white people anywhere. There is an internationalism here, one consistent with evolving Cold War ideas of the role of the United States in the world. As President Truman expressed it in his farewell address, this internationalism was characterized by a global "conflict between those who love freedom and those who would lead the world back into slavery and darkness." The question for immigration policy, then, was how best to maintain national democracy while extending the benefit of freedom and American citizenship to those dwelling abroad, presumably in Europe, and presumably bereft of such enlightenment.

In contrast, African American and Asian American political organizing in this period reflected an intense awareness of the ways that impaired access to full citizenship rights at home related to the international politics of the immigration question. This awareness compelled an international analysis that differed substantially from the "freedom and slavery" Manichaeism of Truman's dominant Cold War narrative. In black and Asian American political thought, the world was in conflict, but along different axes than those conceived of by representatives of the national security bureaucracy. Speaking on the proposed legislation, Representative Adam Clayton Powell, Jr., drew a map that differed sharply from the one presented by Truman and his national security advisors:

> This bill sets up a Cape Town–Washington, D.C. axis. . . . This bill makes this no longer a land of the free, but a place only for Anglo-Saxons. . . . Do not think that what you do here is not going to be heard over the world. It is going to be heard in the Caribbean, it is going to be heard where there are people of the dark races.[16]

Like Truman, Powell and African American groups such as the National Association for the Advancement of Colored People (NAACP) saw national immigration policy as one of the sites where the United States could promote international democratic freedom. But for Powell, the threat to this freedom came not so much from the long shadow of the Soviet Union, with its own presumed internationalism, as from the continuous history of colonialism, now recast as the international isolation of new nation-states in Africa, the Caribbean, and Asia. Powell's words echo W. E. B. Du Bois' famous assertion that the problem of the twentieth century is the problem of the color line—

quite a different diagnosis than the opposition posed by President Truman between freedom and slavery. As cultural critic Melani McAlister points out, Truman's familiar Cold War binary required some rigorous historical silencing in order to suppress the still very much present legacy of the enslavement of African Americans in this country, and refer instead to the crimes of Soviet totalitarianism.[17]

Powell's reference to a "Cape Town–Washington D.C. axis," at a time when segregation in the nation's capital was so intense that the United Nations had to be located in New York City for fear that nonwhite diplomats would be denied lodging, clearly refuses this silencing, instead arguing that the threat to international freedom was the continued and present racialism of slavery and colonialism and their reinscription into the postwar political regime. Echoing this logic, Senator Hubert Humphrey disputed the limits placed on immigration from the West Indies, arguing that such restrictions created a "new kind of de facto discrimination against Negroes" and laid fertile ground for the "anti-American agitation" of communists in these decolonizing areas.

The African American critique of Cold War immigration policy was based on diminished black access to citizenship rights and an awareness of a world being transformed by decolonization. In contrast to white ethnic agitation for more inclusive immigration policy, activists like Adam Clayton Powell, Jr., based their critique of the restrictive quota system on their awareness of the possibilities inherent in decolonization for domestic struggles. This internationalism proposed alternative concepts of citizenship and rights. In the immediate postwar period, many African American political thinkers were influenced by the immanence of decolonization. It is legendary, for example, that Martin Luther King's concept of nonviolence was influenced by the Gandhian concept of *satyagraha,* but far less widely known is that this influence came from the close involvement of black American intellectuals with the transnational politics of decolonization. Such transnational connections make clear that the aspirations of much of the civil rights movement were toward international human rights, a direction that was subsequently foreclosed by the force of Cold War international and domestic security policy.

Like African American groups, Asian American political organizations recognized the salience of immigration politics to their national standing, as well as to the international position of Asian nations in this charged moment of decolonization and global reorganization. Because of the legacy of exclusion, however, Asian Americans were in a different position from African Americans. Both groups recognized the possibilities for the transformation of their impaired citizenship status in the postwar period, but they confronted differing obstacles in claiming full rights.

As historian Mae Ngai has pointed out, the postwar period represented a limited rehabilitation of citizenship for Japanese and Chinese Americans. With the dispersal of Japanese internees from the camps and their resettlement into cities, groups like the Japanese-American Citizens League (JACL), deeply influenced by the experience of internment, saw it as in their best interests to accept a coercive and limited assimilation. At the same time, under the federal loyalty programs, Chinese Americans were offered the opportunity to "come clean" about the historical legitimacy of their immigration status and political ties, purging themselves as they testified to the veracity of their claims to Cold War citizenship.[18] Asian Americans, then, had to prove their eligibility for citizenship in this period. While their histories in this country often ran parallel, in terms of struggles with immigration policy and segregated living conditions, and while non–Asian Americans often mistook Asians of different groups for one and other, different Asian American groups were separated by language, community, and by divergent U.S. foreign and immigration policy toward them. Unlike African Americans, then, Asian Americans were not a united political constituency in this period.

The postwar period saw the lifting of long-standing bans against immigration from Asia. The McCarran-Walter Act itself repealed the ban on naturalization of "aliens ineligible to citizenship" prevailing in federal law since 1790 and applied most significantly to immigrants of Asian origin. From the Page Act of 1875 on, these racialized restrictions had operated through gendered and sexualized exclusions, in which all Asian women were suspected of prostitution and only those who could prove they were the wives or servants of merchants were allowed into the country. At the same time, the proposed changes in immigration law contained provisions reinforcing the status of Asian immigrants as racially other. Consonant with a Cold War genealogy of empire, McCarran-Walter created the "Asiatic-Pacific Triangle." Under this geographic trope, each nation in a triangular-shaped region ranging from Afghanistan to Micronesia was assigned an annual quota of 100. China and Japan were exceptions, with quotas of 205 and 185, respectively. But Asian racial identity was not solely defined by geography; the law envisioned a world mapped by a specific genealogy of empire and race. Individuals whose ancestry could be traced back to this particularly marked place merited particular scrutiny in immigration law, regardless of their current nationality. And though the bans against immigration from Asia per se were lifted, the quotas for immigration from Asian nations were tiny, while the restrictions on immigration from colonies and dependencies effectively excluded those from other territories, such as Vietnam.

Thus the proposed immigration legislation was an ambivalent proposition for Asian Americans. One the one hand, this legislation opened naturalization to Asian immigrants for the first time in American history. On the other, the law operated on racialized exclusions, subjecting all people of Asian origins to the same tiny quotas, small limitations, and racial scrutiny, regardless of nationality.

Many Chinese, Japanese, and Filipino American groups testified before Congress in support of McCarran-Walter. The JACL, in particular, actively lobbied for the law's passage. Such advocacy reflected a strategic awareness of the limited opening for citizenship offered to Asian Americans at this time. Mike Masaoka, national legislative director for the JACL, emphasized the importance of the bill's "extension of naturalization rights to all loyal resident aliens" and asserted that the repeal of exclusion would "abolish a needless barrier to understanding between our Government and the peoples of the Far East."[19] Robert Sugishita, the Nisei president of the San Mateo JACL, pinpointed the historic ambivalence of citizenship for Asian Americans by illuminating the ways imperial genealogy limited Asian American civic inheritance and connection:

> While we who were born here are American citizens, our citizenship is a matter of fortunate accident, since our parents are Japanese. We acquired our citizenship as a birthright, and as much as we cherish our birthright, we cannot but feel that our own status as citizens is clouded by the official slur which is cast on our parents.[20]

Other Asian American groups, such as the Chinese-American Citizens Alliance, the Korean National Association, and the Filipino Federation of America, joined the Japanese-American Citizens League in supporting the limited civil rights represented in McCarran-Walter legislation.

But many Asian American groups opposed the restrictive immigration policy as well. Several Chinese American groups, while compelled to echo the anticommunist rhetoric of the bill, argued about its effects on both the civil rights of Asian Americans and on the strength of U.S. alliances in Asia. "Please remember," chided the National Chinese Seamen's Union, "that some 7,000 people of Chinese ancestry gave their lives to the allied cause while serving on allied merchant vessels during the past war."[21] As with the African American "Double V" campaign for victory against fascism abroad and racism at home, this statement implies that if subaltern groups are good enough to defend democracy, they ought to enjoy its rewards on returning home.

Like many politicians on both sides of the immigration issue, the Lun Yee association invoked foreign policy concerns to critique the limitations on Asian immigration. "We as persons who are loyal to the United States and believe in the American form of government think that the United States Government will lose friends in Asia and make it easier for communism to push its way to the forefront in that continent if the McCarran Bill become the law."[22]

Asian American politics on immigration, then, represented an alternative internationalism. As with both dominant and African American interpretations, this internationalism connected the politics of immigration to global issues of alignment and decolonization. It also reflected an intense awareness of both the necessity and depredations of citizenship for Asian Americans.

In the postwar period, divergent constructions of internationalism clashed over the regulation of national homeostasis through immigration. The passage of the McCarran-Walter Act in 1952 represented the victory of a binary vision: a world rent not by "capitalism and slavery" in the words of Eric Williams, the first prime minister of Trinidad, but by socialism and democracy. The hegemony of this vision drew on a gendered imagining of national and international order and had important consequences for immigration policy well into the post-1965 period. In the next section and in the final section, I want to circle back and talk about the ways the politics of immigration and internationalism are connected to constructions of gender and empire.

"When Young GI Meets Native Peach"

The architecture of imperial reach brought young American men in contact with the "native peaches" of my heading, a line swiped from the musical *South Pacific*, first produced for the stage in 1949. Just as fruits ripe for the picking loomed large in erotic European fantasies of the Americas during the Age of Discovery, the fruits of twentieth-century empire included the annexation of lands, lucrative trade, and fantasies and practices of contact with native women. In the post-1945 period, Asian women became immigrants and laborers, military brides and sex workers, their availability as the "peaches" of the imperial South imagined in narratives of mail-order readiness, model minority assimilation, and domestic consumption.

As scholars of colonialism have firmly established, reshaping identity in the metropole and the colonies entailed redefining notions of gender and domesticity throughout empires. The regulation of patriarchal domesticity is a key constituent of an imperial order. Just as in previous periods, imperial formations in the post-1945 period dealt not only with the international balance of power and national concerns for economic development, but with the regulation of sexuality across racial and geopolitical boundaries.

Just as appropriate conduct for middle-class white women in Europe and the Americas was framed in the eighteenth and nineteenth centuries in reference to the real and imagined transgressive sexual activities among native workers in the colonies and immigrants at home, an ideology of a return to domesticity evolved in the postwar period that referenced both the chaos experienced by Europe refugees and the increased imperial presence in Asia. Immigrants and refugees were welcomed in terms of their suitability for postwar family life.[23] The national press celebrated the appropriate domesticity of white European refugees fleeing godless communism, although, as Franca Iacovetta's research documents, the reality of domestic relations among the much celebrated white Eastern Europeans fleeing communism required careful mediation by social workers.[24] As imperial interests turned to Asia in the postwar period, the question of Asian immigration and civil rights gradually refigured a national romance previously focused on the assimilation of Europeans.

In Asia, the U.S. military attempted to import notions of appropriate gender conduct and domestic relations. Occupying Korea and recently liberated from Japanese occupation, the American military government's Office of Public Information sought to support indigenous Korean culture by sponsoring dance performances and publishing, in its English-language *Chukan Digest,* English-Korean folklore that featured prominently tragic, but loyal, queens and children whose heroism distinguished them in service to the nation. Indigenous Korean culture was figured as essentially democratic, having survived Japanese occupation. The Office of Public Information set about "purifying" the Korean language of Japanese phrases. The *Chukan Digest* and other Office of Public Information organs often pictured women in costume. In addition, the *Digest* offered a pedagogy of domesticity through its cooking and housekeeping tips. The military clearly intended to impress the value of American domesticity on denizens overseas, as was perhaps best expressed by the official explanation for bread rationing in 1946: "The American people are sharing what they have with the Korean people. Perhaps it is not exactly what the Korean people would like, but it is some of the best which the United States has."[25]

Just as the military attempted to impress appropriate domesticity on Asians within the empire, there was great concern for the regulation of sexual conduct by American troops overseas. As Brenda Plummer has pointed out, relations between African American GIs and European women had been a special problem during World War II; liaisons between black GIs and local women did not receive the kind of official sanction and support that evolved in the case of white GIs romancing and marrying local women.[26] Because the occupations of Japan and Korea, in particular, were conducted at a pivotal moment in domestic civil rights, the troops were partially integrated. The conduct of black soldiers abroad came in for special scrutiny, whether in the approved sexualized zones of camp towns or the potential for unwelcome advances outside of them. The culture of the Jim Crow South found resonance in military police assumptions that black soldiers were more likely to commit sexual assaults on Asian women.[27]

The military also screened, sometimes with vexed confusion, the issue of racial intermarriage between GIs and Asian women. Until they were included in the McCarran-Walter Act as the spouses of U.S. military personnel in 1952, Asian women were "aliens ineligible to naturalize." Negotiations regarding the appropriateness of military wives took longer for Asian women; even Chinese women who married Chinese American GIs were sometimes subject to deportation if the loyalty or immigration status of their American-born husbands was brought into question. The immigration status of Japanese and Korean women as "aliens ineligible to naturalize" was debated during the occupations of Japan and Korea in the late 1940s and early 1950s. The newly integrated U.S. armed forces were nevertheless instructed and treated quite differently in the pedagogy of gender and sexuality concerning Asian women proffered by the military during this period.

This ambivalence was particularly dramatic in the case of Kowashi Hirai, a Hawaiian-born, bilingual Japanese American soldier who was denied permission to marry Japanese native Yachiyo Nagata in 1948. In a memo asking for reconsideration of his application for marriage, Hirai wrote:

> I believe that this handicap can be overcome because as stated in my prior application, I intend to repeatedly re-enlist in the Army or stay here in Japan as a civilian until such time as the law changes permitting me to return with my prospective wife and dependents to the United States or its possessions. . . . We are of the same racial background and I know that this marriage will be a success should permission to marry be granted.

While his commanding officer recommended the approval of the application, commending Hirai as "excellent" in character and efficiency, his application was turned down at a higher level.

This particular case illuminates many of the key issues informing immigration and imperial policy in this immediate postwar period. Hirai was a Japanese American citizen of what historians Beth Bailey and David Farber call "the first strange place" in the 1940s: the U.S. territory of Hawaii.[28] While the territory was placed under military rule after the bombing of Pearl Harbor in 1941, fewer Japanese Americans in Hawaii were interned during the war than those on the mainland. Nonetheless, racial tension ran high on the islands during wartime, and many Japanese Americans who most felt their community to be under suspicion volunteered to serve in the army. In fact, a larger proportion of Hawaiians of Japanese extraction volunteered for military service than any other ethnic group on the islands.[29] Such service, in both the European theater of World War II and in Korea, in turn became a component of the argument for Hawaiian statehood during the postwar period. Military service was one of the marks that Hawaii was no longer "Asian" and was unlikely to cause the kind of anticolonial upheavals brewing in other former colonies. At the same time, like African American participation in World War II, the military service of Asian Hawaiians pointed to the continued exclusion of nonwhites from full citizenship.[30]

Hirai's case points to the racialized complexities of citizenship for both Asians and Asian Americans, as the nationalistic construction of Asian exclusion was gradually being replaced by an immigration policy reflecting the neo-imperial Cold War order. As a bilingual Japanese Hawaiian, he may have been among those who most felt pressured during the 1940s to prove his loyalty to the United States through military service. He was petitioning to marry his Japanese fiancée at a high water mark for civil rights—Truman desegregated the military during the same year—so that the Korean War would be the first war fought by integrated U.S. troops. His optimism about his situation rings, even through the stilted language of military bureaucracy: "until such time as the law changes permitting me to return with my prospective wife and dependents to the United States or its possessions." At the same time, like others in his situation, Kowashi Hirai would not have legal grounds to bring Yachiyo Nagata home to Hawaii until 1952, when the McCarran-Walter Act simultaneously abolished all vestiges of Asian exclusion and affirmed the rights of all servicemen to import wives of whatever nationality they chose. Hawaiian statehood, of course, would be another seven years in the making.

The question of the status of Asian war brides was largely resolved by the McCarran-Walter Act. The law contains a great deal of legislation regarding alien spouses of citizens, children born to one alien and one citizen. It provides for the nonquota embrace of spouses and children of citizens employed by the military or the government overseas. Such imperial unions are one of the stipulations for eligibility to immigration.

The imperial imaginary required a transformation of immigration policy and, ultimately, a refiguring of demographics and culture. Asian immigrants, particularly Asian immigrant women, reshaped immigration policy from below.[31] Chinese women entering under the World War II war brides policy marked the largest cohort of Chinese women allowed into the country since the

1875 Page Act. As such, these women transformed social relations in China-towns across the country. Korean military brides have been responsible, directly and indirectly, for 40 to 50 percent of all Korean immigrants since 1965. Immigrants coming across the bridge of empire were both the subjects and the agents of a profound transformation of immigration and the imperial imaginary.

The politics of immigration and empire bring together concerns for global justice with the unequal distribution of citizenship rights, both domestically and in the far-flung territories. Denizens of both are linked by the architecture of empire and by our mutual need to subvert the official rhetoric in pursuit of democracy.

NOTES

1. *Merriam-Webster Online,* s.v. "imperialism," accessed 10/28/04, http://www.m-w .com/cgi-bin/dictionary?book=Dictionary&va=imperialism.

2. Michael Hardt and Antonio Negri, *Empire* (Cambridge, Mass.: Harvard University Press, 2000).

3. Carol Anderson, *Eyes off the Prize: The United Nations and the African American Struggle for Human Rights, 1944–1955* (Cambridge, UK: Cambridge University Press, 2003).

4. "From Community Activist to Alleged Terror Conspirator," *CNN.com/Law Center,* http://archives.cnn.com/2002/LAW/08/29/ujaama.background/index.html, accessed 9/27/07.

5. Donald E. Pease, "Global Futures of American Studies," roundtable discussion at the Globalizing American Studies conference, Northwestern University, Evanston, Ill., May 5, 2004.

6. Melani McAlister, *Epic Encounters: Culture, Media and U.S. Interests in the Middle East, 1945–2000* (Berkeley: University of California Press, 2001), 1–42.

7. In the Western hemisphere, this has also been true of the reception of refugees from Nicaragua, Guatemala, and El Salvador during their long, CIA-inspired civil wars.

8. As Ann Stoler and others have noticed, interracial marriage is one of the "internal frontiers" of colonization. Who will become a citizen, who loses citizenship in the metropole through this process? For example, in colonial Indochina, if a Vietnamese woman married a Frenchman, she and her offspring were considered French—as long as they conformed to certain cultural and social expectations. If a French woman married a Vietnamese man, she lost her French citizenship and the children were, at the very least, a problem for imperial administrators. See Ann Stoler, *Carnal Knowledge and Imperial Power: Race and the Intimate in Colonial Rule* (Berkeley: University of California Press, 2002), especially 79–112.

9. Siobhan Somerville, "Notes Toward a Queer History of Naturalization," *American Quarterly* 57, no. 3 (2005): 672.

10. Nikhil Singh, *Black Is a Country: Race and the Unfinished Struggle for Democracy* (Cambridge, Mass.: Harvard University Press, 2004).

11. Anderson, *Eyes off the Prize.*

12. Andrew F. Jones and Nikhil Pal Singh, "Guest Editor's Introduction," *positions: east asia cultures critique* 11, no. 1 (2003): 7.

13. Matthew Frye Jacobson, *Special Sorrows: The Diasporic Imagination of Jewish, Polish and Irish Immigrants in the United States* (Berkeley: University of California Press, 2002).

14. *Congressional Record* (*CR*), 1952: 5628

15. Ibid., 4251

16. Ibid., 4439

17. McAlister, *Epic Encounters.*

18. Mae Ngai, "Legacies of Exclusion: Illegal Chinese Immigration During the Cold War Years," *Journal of American History* 18, no. 1 (1998): 3–35.

19. *CR* 1952: 5092.

20. Ibid.

21. Ibid., 5791.

22. Ibid.

23. Wendy Kozol, *Life's America: Family and Nation in Postwar Photojournalism* (Philadelphia: Temple University Press, 1994).

24. Franca Iacovetta, presentation to History Department and Canadian Studies Program, University of Wisconsin–Milwaukee, March 2004.

25. *Chukan Digest* 51 (October 9, 1946).

26. Brenda Gayle Plummer, "Brown Babies: Race, Gender and Policy after WWII," in *Window on Freedom: Race, Civil Rights and Foreign Affairs, 1945–1988,* ed. Brenda Gayle Plummer (Chapel Hill: University of North Carolina Press, 2003).

27. Record Group #554, Stack Area 290, Row 51, Compartment 19, United States Army Forces in Korea. XXIV Corps, G-2, Historical Section. Records Regarding the Okinawa Campaign, US Military Government in Korea, US–USSR Relations in Korea and Korean Political Affairs, 1945–48.

28. Beth Bailey and David Farber, *The First Strange Place: The Alchemy of Race and Sex in World War II Hawaii* (New York: Free Press, 1992).

29. Roger Bell, *Last Among Equals: Hawaiian Statehood and American Politics* (Honolulu: University of Hawai'i Press, 1984), 76–82.

30. Ibid., 90–118.

31. See Ji-Yeon Yuh, *Beyond the Shadow of Camptown: Korean Military Brides in America* (New York: New York University Press, 2002); and Xiaolan Bao, "When Women Arrived: The Transformation of New York's Chinatown," in *Not June Cleaver: Women and Gender in Postwar America,* ed. Joanne Meyerowitz, 19–36 (Philadelphia: Temple University Press, 1994).

PART 3
NATION, NARRATIVE, DIASPORA

CHAPTER SIX

Serial Migration

Stories of Home and Belonging in Diaspora

LOK SIU

Growing up in Hong Kong and, later, Southern California, I had imagined the world to be much smaller than I know it to be now. It had to do with the way my parents talked about family and friends who were living in other parts of the world but whose thoughts and experiences were conveyed with such a sense of immediacy and proximity that I simply assumed they were "close by." Places with strange names were made familiar—and somehow physically near as well—with stories, stories about my grandfather who worked on a fishing boat in Australia or my aunt who moved to Singapore for love, or my uncle who lived in Nicaragua with his wife and seven children, and so on and so forth. Certainly, my family's long history of dispersal to different parts of the world has informed my understanding of diaspora and migration; it has made me more attuned to the messiness, unevenness, and meaningfulness of migration. So when I began my research with diasporic Chinese in Panama, I was not entirely surprised by how often migration emerged as a central theme in conversations. But what was striking was the way diasporic Chinese repeatedly situated their own migration routes within a longer history of family migrations. It was done almost without exception. Listening to their detailed accounts of unintended moves, not so voluntary relocations, and various attempts at family reunification, I came to recognize not just the significance of the actual migrations but also the role that these narratives played in articulating a distinct diasporic subjectivity. This essay, then, examines four migration stories in order to illustrate how migration, as both social experience and narrative trope, has shaped diasporic Chinese subject formation and their understandings of belonging in diaspora.

My focus on migration stories is inspired in part by Paul Gilroy's study of diaspora.[1] Using the metaphor of a moving ship to map the transatlantic and transcultural histories of the black diaspora, he effectively shifts diaspora studies' more conventional focus on homeland/diaspora dynamics to what James Clifford has called "the lateral connections" within the diaspora. Gilroy then de-centers the importance of the homeland and shifts our attention to the activities, interactions, and circulations taking place in the diaspora. What Gilroy locates in music—the reflections and conversations about diasporic (in his case black) identity—I encounter in migration stories. Through my interviews with diasporic Chinese in Panama, I discovered that migration stories not only provide a form of diasporic articulation but also embody the substance—the shared memories and experiences of migration—that informs diasporic Chinese consciousness. Indeed, narratives of migration provide a common framework through which diasporic Chinese describe and understand their experience of living in diaspora as well as their relationship to particular places and to one another. These narratives, then, constitute a living archive that brings into relief the multivalent significance of migration, not only in relation to places and routes but also as an aspect of contingent belonging. Taken collectively, they construct a shared experience of displacement as well as an emergent map of diasporic Chinese networks and communities. Through iteration, these narratives also help transmit a distinct affect and cultural knowledge that is simultaneously personal and collective, illustrative and pedagogical.

While each of the four narratives in this essay offers a distinct history and experience of migration, they reflect the larger pattern of "serial migration," by which I mean an open-ended, sometimes circuitous, process that entails crossing multiple national borders over an extended period of time. All four interviewees have migrated several times, and they all situate their experience along a trajectory of family migrations. They trace their ancestors' border crossings from China to different parts of the Americas and speak of their own experience of migration. Sometimes, they even include their children's and grandchildren's migrations. Often family members traverse the same places, though many initiate new paths. In a way, one can interpret these narratives to be "diasporic origin stories" of sorts. By reconstructing their diasporic genealogy through time and across space and connecting the dots between the different places where they, their ancestors, and their children have lived, these narratives create a spatial-temporal map of geographically dispersed but linked "homes" and, at the same time, affirm connection to those places via familial relations. By weaving together fragmented place-specific memories and attributing them to experiences of actual family members, these narratives give flesh, so to speak, to the skeletal network of places. And through these narratives, certain places accrue cultural significance and come to present themselves as important nodal points within the diaspora.[2] Cuba, Peru, and Jamaica, for instance, emerge powerfully as sites of out-migration at specific historical moments, while Nicaragua and Guyana—less documented sites of diasporic Chinese formation—are made visible through these narratives.

In addition to recovering a network of diasporic sites, this emergent cartography of home and community gives expression to the "lateral connections" among diasporic Chinese. The migration stories presented here—and those I collected in general—suggest continued circulation and interaction between China and Panama as well as between Panama and other parts of the Americas, especially the United States. Certainly the circular transpacific migrations of Chinese between China and their places of settlement in the Americas are widely recognized.[3] What is less known and now necessary to underscore are the transcontinental migrations that take place *within* the Americas. Indeed, as soon as the Chinese arrived in the Americas, as early as the 1600s, they began traveling and migrating throughout the New World. Some were indentured laborers who were sent from one country to another; some escaped from indentured servitude and migrated to other places; others were free men and women who sought better work opportunities and more welcoming environments.[4] One of the most striking features of these early migrants in Panama (and I suspect it is not unique to Panama) is that they came not just from Greater China, but also from different parts of the Caribbean and the Americas.[5] These migratory movements between Panama and Asia and within the New World were often circular and part of a series of migrations. And from these migratory movements emerged not only intricate webs of kinship and social networks that link diasporic Chinese to China and across the Americas but also a consciousness of being "diasporic Chinese" in the Americas.

Moreover, by situating one's multiple migrations within a longer family history of migration, these narratives give the impression that migration is an ever-present aspect of life. Migration, then, becomes less a monumental event and more a shared practice and a sort of family "tradition" that continues through the generations. Rendered as such, migration seems less anomalous and more like a series of occurrences that persist over time. In a way, the iteration of border crossings in these narratives helps normalize migration as an ordinary aspect of diasporic life, naturalizing it as a familiar and familial experience of contingent belonging. Through the narratives, we come to realize that serial migration, as both a socially significant practice and experience as well as a narrative device, is a dynamic process of self-realization and an attempt to locate, map, and make sense of the meaning of home and belonging in diaspora.

By highlighting the phenomenon of multiple migrations, serial migration explores the combined and/or cumulative effects these migrations have on diasporic subject formation. While migration scholars have used terms such as "step migration," "remigration," and "secondary" or "tertiary migration" to describe a singular act of border crossing and to underscore one specific segment within serial migration, the concept of serial migration allows one to examine the larger phenomenon of migrating multiple times.[6] It also opens up the possibility of thinking about the relationship between serial migration and diaspora. In some ways, serial migration is similar to a "transnational migrant circuit," a phrase used by Roger Rouse to describe the formation of a single community across a variety of geographic sites.[7] But rather than taking a synchronic analysis of this circuit, the concept of serial migration is concerned with how migration—as a historical process—both shapes diasporic subject formation (how people make sense of their experience of repeated displacement and how it informs one's understanding of self, home, and belonging) and maps a shifting cartography of community formation in diaspora.

While serial migration may resonate with James Clifford's notion of "travel itinerary," it differs in that it describes a more profound engagement with "dwelling" places.[8] If traveling connotes a transitory mode of moving across space, migration represents a more prolonged and meaningful interaction with place. Serial migration is also different from cosmopolitanism, which—despite recent attempts to make the term more inclusive—still evokes the kind of mobility that only a select group of worldly subjects can enjoy, a mobility that is facilitated primarily by class and gender privilege.[9] In fact, the category of cosmopolitan subjects has expanded only slightly to include the recent, more culturally diverse but equally privileged transnational migrants in the West.[10] Their inclusion in no way challenges the implicit privilege associated with cosmopolitanism, the privilege of exercising freedom of choice over when, to where, and how one migrates. Indeed, while cosmopolitanism may account for the experiences of some diasporic Chinese (for instance, Hong Kong Chinese elites as described by anthropologist Aihwa Ong), it does not represent the full range of Chinese migration, which also includes clandestine migrations involving human trafficking networks, escapes from political persecution, and migration in search of better working conditions, to name a few.[11] Still remaining largely absent from studies of cosmopolitanism is an examination of power and a consideration of structural constraints.

Serial migration, then, offers an alternative—and more expansive—framework to make visible the practice of multiple migrations taken up by a range of migrants and to examine the various modalities of migration within a complex web of social, economic, and political structures. It broadly describes the process of migrating more than once and engaging meaningfully with the various places of settlement; at the same time, it attends to the broad range of sociopolitical circumstances and shifting personal capacities that frame migration. Serial migration then challenges the notion that mobility across multiple national borders is exercised only by the privileged few and seeks to expand our understanding of different forms of mobility and types of migrants.

In many ways, my theorization of serial migration grows out of the desire to articulate a middle ground between two conceptual extremes in discussions of transnational migration: immobility (and the ultimate subaltern subject who is fixed in place) and cosmopolitanism (the privileged elite subject who is free to wander the world). It aims to address the common yet underacknowledged practice of multiple migrations exercised by diasporic subjects whose mobility is defined within a set of political, economic, and social parameters. By bringing to bear, for instance, the experiences of Ugandan Indians dispersed in Britain, Canada, and the United States; Korean Argentines living in Los Angeles; Japanese Peruvians working in Japan; and Chinese Cubans in New York and Miami; serial migration complicates our understanding of diaspora by showing the "layeredness" of diasporization.[12] These examples challenge Asian diaspora scholars to go beyond the conventional approach of studying homeland-diaspora relations and to begin paying attention to the circulations and interactions within these diasporas. In line with the editors of this volume, I agree that a focus on routes can enrich and deepen our current understanding of diaspora. It opens up the possibility of tracing less-expected transnational linkages and connections, of revising conventional cartographies of community, and of conjuring alternative imaginaries of belonging.

Several criteria guided my selection of narratives for this essay. Because the theme of serial migration emerged only in the process of conducting general interviews, I did not have a set of ready-made or neatly packaged migration stories from which to choose. So my first criterion was to pick interviews that offer the greatest amount of detail and richness on serial migration. Second, I intentionally avoided redundancy and chose narratives that complemented one another, with each extending and elaborating, in different directions, the theme of serial migration. Third, I tried to include a range of experiences that account for differences in race, gender, class, and generation.

My success in this area is limited by the kinds of people willing to be interviewed. Women often shied away, claiming that their life experience had little to offer. Recent and often less privileged migrants refused to expose their (presumably clandestine) method of migration. Gender and class, then, were the most prominent factors limiting a wider diversity of narratives. As with all ethnographic accounts, the narratives in this essay by no means represent the full spectrum of diasporic Chinese migration. It may also be worth remembering that they are all partial representations, both in the sense of being constructed subjectively and of being incomplete. What follows, then, are stories that attest to both the history and contemporary continuation of serial migration. They illustrate a range of circumstances, motivations, and effects of migration, and they map different places of significance within their respective imaginaries of home and belonging.

Fernando: Re-establishing Roots

I met Fernando through his son, a good friend of mine, who graciously helped set up the initial interview.[13] We met for the first time at his home in a quiet, middle-class neighborhood of Panama City. Being "part Chinese, part white, part black, and part indigenous," Fernando claims that he does not emphasize any one racial identity over the others. When asked, "How do you see yourself fitting into these different communities?" he responds, "Is there a category for mongrels? If so, that's the category I fit into." With brown skin and wavy black hair, he does not possess obvious Chinese features. Even his name, Fernando Jackson, gives no hint of his Chinese background. Despite his mixed racial identity and refusal to define his ethnic identity as exclusively Chinese, both his active participation in Chinese social networks and leadership in a prominent Chinese organization effectively demonstrate his affinity and identification with that community. Belonging in the Chinese diaspora, as demonstrated by Fernando, does not depend on essential definitions of race or ethnicity.[14] Rather, it is determined by self-identification and participation in diasporic activities. In other words, one belongs because one chooses to participate and take part in the community.

It may be important to note from the outset that one important difference between Asians in Latin America and those in the United States (with the exception of Hawaii) is the historically high rate of interracial unions and family formation.[15] Antimiscegenation laws did not exist in Panama (and Latin American more generally), as they did in certain parts of the United States at one time. On the contrary, the dominant ideology in most of Latin America of *mestizaje,* or racial and cultural mixing, encourages interracial unions.[16] Another factor in this cultural trend was the extreme imbalance in gender migration in the late nineteenth and early twentieth centuries. For many of the early Chinese bachelors, marrying or cohabiting with Panamanian women was the only available form of heterosexual relationship in Panama. Nevertheless, despite the prevalence of interracial relationships in Panama, discrimination persists on the part of Chinese and non-Chinese alike. Among the Chinese community, there is a bias against non-Chinese speakers and racially mixed Chinese. Meanwhile, in certain circles of non-Chinese Panamanians, being Chinese is not considered a positive characteristic. In a sense, it may be easier for racially mixed Chinese not to assert any particular identity. Fernando's identification as racially mixed reflects both the dominant ideology of *mestizaje* and his awareness of being more than just ethnically Chinese.

In the context of Latin America, Fernando's biography is not extraordinary in any way. What is particularly interesting is his prominence in Chinese social networks. In particular, he has been extremely active in the Panamanian Chinese organization Agrupación, or Agrupa, as many members call it, which promotes cultural and social events for Panamanian Chinese. His participation in this organization has less to do with his sense of being Chinese, however, than with his desire for social interaction:

> I have no trouble identifying with the Chinese community. However, it's not so much because of my Chinese heritage but that most of [the people in] my social circle [are] Chinese in varying degrees. Almost all the active members of Agrupa are my friends from years ago. Setting up the organization was merely a way of providing an occasion for all of us to get together. People bring their friends, and they bring their friends, and that's how we deal with our membership. Many of the people in Agrupa went to school with me in Colón [the main city on the Caribbean coast of Panama]. We basically grew up together. In fact, we all got married at around the same time, and our kids were born within years of each other.

Fernando walks into his library and returns with an old black-and-white, fourth-grade class photo in his hand. He begins naming all the faces on the picture, and sure enough, they are people I have met through Agrupa. Creating community, for Fernando, depends more on affiliation, a sense of connection based on social relations, than on filiation, a sense of connection based on kinship relations.[17] His practice of community and understanding of identity closely follow Stuart Hall's notion that identity is not a stable, essential self, but a positioning, a politics of identification.[18] As such, identity is a process and is created through memory, imagination, and narration. Fernando's migration story, as represented below, further illustrates how memory and experience generate diasporic identification. Our conversation about serial migration begins three generations back. "My paternal grandfather was Chinese and first immigrated to Jamaica before coming to Colón, Panama, in the late 1800s," Fernando explained. "He had owned a store in Jamaica, and it was there that he married my grandmother, who was a black Jamaican. After he married, he changed his surname from Cheng to Jackson in order to obtain a Jamaican passport. That's why my last name is Jackson, not Cheng."

The politics of naming is also noteworthy. For a Panamanian to have a surname like Jackson automatically indicates a connection to Anglophone Caribbean. Purchasing another person's documents and assuming his or her identity in order to immigrate was quite common in the nineteenth and twentieth centuries, and to a large extent it remains a common practice today. In fact, many of my interviewees have two different names: an official name on legal documents and a birth name. The combinations vary. Some have Anglo and Chinese names (e.g., Jackson/Lee, Wilson/Chan), while others have two Chinese names (e.g., Chu/Wang, Chen/Lee). Rarely have I encountered people who have used Hispanic names for immigration purposes. (Of course, this practice is not exclusive to Latin America, as the "paper son" phenomenon in the United States indicates.[19]) Fernando continued:

> I am not sure why [my grandparents] decided to move to Colón. That was common back then, because my other grandparents also moved to Colón from Guyana. My [maternal] grandfather was Portuguese, and he married my grandmother who was a mixture of different backgrounds, including Chinese and Caucasian. I don't have many memories of them. I only remember that my Chinese grandfather used to own a shop, and, from time to time, I could get a nickel from him. And my black grandmother, she was a nice fat lady who took care of us kids. My other grandmother was a good, caring person too, and my Portuguese grandfather . . . he left when I was very young. My father was born in Colón, and at a young age, he was sent to Jamaica for school. He didn't return until after high school, and when he did he worked in the shipping division of the United Fruit Company.

Fernando was born in Colón and attended the only private boys' school in the area. It was there that he met most of his lifelong friends. After the fifth grade, Fernando was sent to a boarding school in Jamaica that his father had attended, and after high school he went to Chicago for his university degree.

> At first I was attending a public school in Colón, but because I was getting into so many fights with other kids, my father decided to put me into a private school. From there, I went to Jamaica. My father wanted me to learn English well, so he sent me to Jamaica. I guess he knew that knowing English is important. Afterwards, I applied for college in the United States, and I was accepted. So, I left and spent the next four years in Chicago. So, in a sense, I spent much of my childhood and young adult life outside of Panama.

The practice of sending children, especially sons, to school abroad is popular among diasporic Chinese for accruing cultural capital, including language abilities and cultural values and practices. In Fernando's generation, many sent their children to China to get a "Chinese" education, while others like Fernando and his father were sent elsewhere in the Americas to learn English, a skill that would facilitate employment by American companies or the U.S. Canal Zone administration. Although this practice was an ideal for all diasporic Chinese, only those families of means could actually afford to pursue it.

When Fernando returned to Panama after college, he moved to Panama City instead of returning to Colón. He and his wife, who is also part Chinese, met through a social function sponsored by a Panamanian Chinese organization. When I asked why he had returned to Panama after graduating from the university rather than staying in the United States, Fernando sighed and said: "I was offered a job [in the United States] upon graduation, but after spending six years in boarding school and four years in college, I just did not feel like being away from home anymore. In reality my ties to home were not strong, because [in] four years of college I had been home just once. Nevertheless, I did not want to stay in the United States any longer. Perhaps there was an unconscious desire to re-establish roots in Panama." Fernando went on to tell a story about how he was perceived as a "colored" person in Chicago, which confused him at first because he had always considered himself to be racially and culturally Chinese. A friend's inadvertent comment about Fernando's "colored" identity, then, suddenly opened his eyes to people's understanding and treatment of him (for instance, not being a viable candidate to date white girls). His reflection suggests that U.S. racial ideology and his placement within it might have contributed to his decision to return to Panama.

Upon his return, Fernando became an English teacher in Canal Zone schools for "Latin American" communities, where the majority of students came from black families working in the Canal Zone. Fernando's return to Panama disrupts the dominant assumption in migration studies that people migrate unidirectionally from less-developed nations to more-developed ones, such as the United States, the countries of western Europe, and Canada. This perception is tied largely to our assumption that economic interests are the primary factors that motivate voluntary migrations. Fernando's return to Panama shows, rather, how affective ties to "home" also play a role in determining migration.

Clearly, the theme of serial migration is central to Fernando's narrative. Not only does he trace his migration from Panama to Jamaica to the United States and back to Panama, but he also includes his father's and grandparents' migration trajectories from China to British Guiana and Jamaica to Panama as part of his own history. Moreover, with a continual return to Panama, Fernando's migration story illustrates Panama's overriding significance for his whole family. Even as he traces their passage through different locations in the Americas, their returns mark Panama as "home" and their place of belonging.

A few months after our interview, Fernando became involved in his annual production of Neil Simon's play *The Odd Couple*. Since his retirement, he has been directing this same play every year, varying the script ever so slightly. It seems noteworthy that Fernando would choose to direct an American play, not a Panamanian one. While Panama may be "home," the United States, as a cultural force, clearly remains a significant part of his life.

Marco: Discovering Chineseness Abroad

In his mid-twenties, Marco is the youngest of four children and comes from a family that is quite well-established and respected in the Chinese-Panamanian community. As a fourth-generation Panamanian-born Chinese, he has an extensive family network in Panama. His father and all his siblings are in the medical field. Following in his mother's footsteps, Marco handles the financial and management aspects of the family business. Like most people of his social standing, Marco received his degree in the United States and speaks flawless English. He not only went to school in the United States but also studied Mandarin in Taiwan. In his extended family, he is the only one who is fluent in all three languages—Spanish, English, and Mandarin—and he is fascinated with Chinese culture and history.

I met Marco for the first time at the annual inauguration dinner of the Asociación de Profesionales Chino-Panameños (Chinese-Panamanian Professionals

Association), or APROCHIPA. His cousin, my good friend Laura, introduced us, and we immediately launched into a discussion of Chinese politics in Panama and the ins and outs of the Chinese community. Within minutes, we were like old friends who had known each other for years. A few months later, he invited me to join his family for Sunday dinner. I was honored, as I knew Sunday dinner was reserved for family, and I was grateful that he had reserved some time for me to speak with his father and maternal grandmother.

Marco Wong's family is considered one of the founding Chinese families in Panama City. His maternal great-grandfather immigrated to Panama in the 1890s and established both wholesale and retail businesses in Panama City's Chinatown. As proprietor of one of the three largest Chinese-owned operations of that time, he was one of the earliest and most successful Chinese entrepreneurs in Panama. In the 1910s, he married Marco's great-grandmother, a Chinese woman who had immigrated to Panama around that time. According to Marco's grandmother, this great-grandmother was called Maria Cheng. She laughed, explaining:

> Back then, almost all the ladies were called Maria. They each had different Chinese names, but their Spanish names were always Maria. What happened was that they had to use the same passport to come to Panama. Chinese immigration was not allowed then. So, to get the women here, they would use the same 'Maria Cheng' passport. The immigration officers couldn't tell who was who. So that's how they all ended up here and being called Maria.

As I mentioned earlier in discussing Fernando's narrative, it is not uncommon for diasporic Chinese to have two different names, and this seemingly mundane issue of naming actually reflects the complicated history of Chinese immigration to the Americas. Confronted with restrictive immigration policies, diasporic Chinese invented various strategies, such as the sharing of identification cards, to subvert practices of exclusion. As Marco's grandmother's account illustrates, it was not only men who had to adopt other names for immigration purposes.

On Marco's paternal side, his great-grandfather and two great-granduncles came to Panama around the 1850s. Marco recalled:

> They first landed in California in search of gold, but with little success; [then] they came to Panama to work on the railroads, and after the completion of the railroad, they migrated to Peru. My great-grandfather

eventually came back to Panama, and he started a shoe store in China-town. He married a Chinese woman and had seven children. I am not sure what happened with his brothers. Rumors suggest that I have lots of cousins in Peru. I haven't met any of them, but that's what people say. My grandfather was born in Panama City, and through an arranged marriage, he was sent to China to marry my grandmother. They came back to Panama together, had two sons, and were separated shortly afterwards. Is that right, Pa?

His father interjected:

Yes. My father remained in Panama City, but my mother took my brother and me to Colón. There, she opened a small *cantina* [bar] to get some income. My older brother was sent to China, as was common practice, and he was there until the 1950s. Needless to say, we didn't spend a lot of time together. I, on the other hand, grew up in Colón, and when I decided to study medicine, I first went to Panama City, but after a short time, I decided to go to Germany to study. Germany is a very different place. Once I finished school, I came right back to Panama.

Having been in Panama for more than four generations, Marco's family has an extensive kinship network. On his paternal side, Marco's great-grandfather had five children. On his maternal side, Marco's grandmother comes from a family of seven, and his grandfather came from a family of five. With each generation, his extended family grows exponentially. From what Marco tells me, the extended family gathers only on holidays and special occasions. Most of the time, they see one another only at association meetings and other com-munity activities.

Prompted by my interview, Marco set out to assemble a genealogy of his extended family in Panama, and once he had completed it, he decided to re-connect with relatives in Taiwan, Hong Kong, Peru, and the United States. Shortly after I left Panama, he and one of his brothers traveled to Taiwan and Hong Kong to visit a couple of their uncles there. On that same trip, they also visited Los Angeles, where another uncle and aunt reside. More than any other Panamanian Chinese I have met, Marco actively situates himself within a global diasporic family network. The fact that he is trilingual in Spanish, English, and Mandarin facilitates his efforts to maintain ties with family dispersed throughout the world.

In contrast to his peers of similar class and social background, Marco has been extremely enthusiastic about learning Chinese history, culture, and politics, and he is always equipped with the latest Taiwanese and Hong Kong CDs. I was thus surprised to learn that he has not always been this way. Ironically, he acquired his Chinese consciousness while living in the United States.

> As a teenager, I never liked the fact that I was Chinese. . . . But as I grew older, well, after I went to college in Miami and met some Chinese Americans, I came back to Panama with a new attitude. I wanted to learn Chinese and get in touch with my "Chinese side." I guess my Chinese American friends were so proud of their ancestry that they made me think about my own background. So, when I came back to Panama, I decided to go on this intensive language program sponsored by the Chinese Cultural Center. . . . I was determined to learn Mandarin. Living in Taiwan was the most amazing experience. It was tough in the beginning. I couldn't communicate with anyone, but that just made me work harder, and in a few months, I was talking to people and making friends. It was a great experience. I loved it . . . and I learned Mandarin.

Since returning to Panama, Marco has tried to keep up his Mandarin by listening to language tapes and Taiwanese-produced music CDs. And whenever he encounters other Mandarin speakers, he lights up and enthusiastically engages them in conversation.

Marco's narrative illustrates the many different locations he and his family have traversed. California, Peru, Miami, Germany, Taiwan, and Panama are only some of the places that make up a larger mapping of home and family. His narrative also conveys how serial migration has shaped his sense of identity and redrawn the boundaries of community. Much like the intellectuals in Gilroy's *Black Atlantic,* though in a more mundane fashion, Marco's migration to the United States and subsequent interaction with Chinese Americans helped raise his diasporic Chinese consciousness, leading him to go to Taiwan and later to reconnect with his globally dispersed family. For Marco, migration is as much about self-discovery as it is about remapping and extending the possibilities of home and belonging.[20] Indeed, it is through this process of serial migration that Marco firmly locates himself in the larger Chinese diaspora.

Pedro: Not Belonging Anywhere

After spending all morning wandering around Chinatown, I was ready to leave the area. But then my attention was caught by the Chinese character *Ko* on the exterior of a building. Ko is my mother's maiden name, and I suspected that the owner of the store must share that same surname.

Speaking in Cantonese, I asked the man behind the counter where I could find Mr. Ko, presumably the owner of the store. In response, the clerk asked for my name, then walked toward the back of the store. When he returned, he led me to a small office where a solemn-looking man was writing at his desk. As I entered, I extended my hand and greeted him in Cantonese: "How are you, Mr. Ko?" I quickly introduced myself as a doctoral student doing research on the Chinese in Panama and presented him with my business card. He examined the card, then asked in fluent English, "So, what can I do for you, Ms. Siu?"

When I began my research, I had naively expected that Panamanian Chinese would speak either Spanish or Cantonese. These two languages made logical sense, given that Spanish is the dominant and official language of Panama and Cantonese is the most common dialect spoken by diasporic Chinese in this region. Yet over and over again, my interviewees spoke fluent English. I quickly learned, through the process of interviewing, how profoundly the American presence in their country had influenced the Panamanian Chinese. Speaking English was no coincidence, but was a result of colonialism and a strategy for upward social mobility.

I proceeded to give Mr. Ko more details about my work. After we had covered the usual formalities of exchanging brief family histories, he warmly invited me back for a longer conversation and dinner with his family. Certainly the fact that my mother and he shared the same last name and that our families were from the same region of China helped establish an immediate sense of connection. Happily, I accepted his invitation.

Pedro Ko comes from another well-known Chinese family in Panama. His family's store has become something of a historical landmark in old Chinatown. His father's entrepreneurial success and his family's long-standing presence in Chinatown have made Ko a household name among the larger community. Moreover, the family also makes donations to various organizations and community events. Its name and logo can be found in pamphlets and posters. Pedro, who was in his late fifties at the time of the interview, appears serious and pensive. Although he seemed at first to be a man of few words, he was quite intent on telling his story.

> My father left China when he was sixteen years old. After the family rice fields in China were flooded in 1922, my father was sent to Latin America to help generate income for the family. He was originally on board a cargo ship heading toward Cuba. People in his village were raving about the opportunities on that island of abundance. But, en route to Cuba, he was detained at the quarantine station in Panama, where he

met a Chinese Panamanian who convinced him to stay.[21] In the beginning, my father worked at the public market, selling vegetables in carts.
Later he advanced to working in a shop across the street from the market. He worked hard and saved every penny, so that he eventually was
able to send for my uncles.

In the early 1930s, Pedro's father moved to the interior of Panama and
married his mother, a Panamanian-born Chinese. By the time Pedro and his
brothers were old enough for school, the family had relocated to Panama
City's Chinatown, now popularly known as Sal Si Puedes, which literally
means "leave if you can." (There are different stories about how Chinatown
acquired this unfortunate nickname. One version claims that the area is so
crowded with merchants and their outdoor stands that visitors can barely find
their way out once they have entered it. Another version suggests that Chinatown is so dangerous that visitors may not survive the sly Chinese merchants'
tricks and booby traps. These orientalist portrayals of Chinatown as an im-
moral, dangerous place resonate with portrayals of Chinatowns elsewhere in
the Americas.[22])

The old Chinatown in Panama City stretches no more than two city
blocks, and, as in other older neighborhoods, the streets are narrow and the
buildings are densely packed. During the day, the area is full of life. The fruit
and vegetable stands are crowded with shoppers. American and European
tourists busy themselves in the specialty stores, amused by the abundance of
exotic goods. All around them, Chinese old-timers hurry to get their errands
done. Despite its vibrant energy, however, the buildings in old Chinatown appear run-down, and the general area seems neglected. Of course, Chinatown
was not always like this. Nostalgically, Pedro commented:

> Sal Si Puedes was very nice before. It was clean, and it was a two-way
> street. Children played on the streets. It was safe, and everyone looked
> after one another. [My family] used to live right across from our restau-
> rant. My father started it when we moved to Panama City. It was one of
> the nicest restaurants back then. Presidents used to dine there . . . and
> the Chinese school was close to the sea. It offered classes in Canton-
> ese.[23] We were here until 1947. For some unknown reason, my father
> just decided to go back to China. We sold everything, and the entire
> family moved into a very exclusive area of Canton [Guangdong]. We
> started a textile company that made exercise outfits like T-shirts and
> sweats. Then, when the communists were approaching, our family sold
> everything again and came back to Panama. My oldest brother left first,

followed by my father and another brother. My mother and I were the last ones to leave in 1950. We came back to Chinatown and bought back our old house and restaurant. Business was good in the 1950s; we even had to expand the restaurant, adding two more floors.

Then the government decided to block the traffic around this area, and shacks began to appear. And by the late 1950s, most of the Chinese had moved away from Chinatown. Only some of the shops remained. We continued working at the restaurant until 1969, but the family started to go into the shrimping business. We invested in shrimp trawlers. At that time, shrimping was one of the biggest industries. . . .

From the late 1950s to mid-1960s, I went to school in Northern California and studied architecture. Three out of my four brothers went to California for college. I was in California from 1957 to 1966. After I graduated and worked for a little while in San Diego, I was called back home to help with the family business. By this time, my father had gone into business with another Chinese and had started building shrimp-processing plants in Guatemala and Mazatlán. In Panama, we would send the shrimp to a packing company and export it to the United States. In Guatemala, we had our own packing company. To make a long story short, a big storm in 1968 badly affected the conditions for shrimping in Guatemala. . . . We eventually came back to Panama in the late 1970s. When we returned, we came back to Chinatown again, and I started to look after the family store. . . . Well, I have been here ever since. I met my wife right here in Chinatown.

I asked, "You've lived in so many places, where do you feel most comfortable? Where do you feel you most belong?"

"Nowhere, really," he responded. "I don't feel like I belong anywhere, not even in Panama. Sometimes I get very sad about that. Well, anyway, what matters is that I have my family here in Panama. My children bring me happiness." For Pedro, home does not necessarily mean a sense of full belonging to a particular place; instead, Panama has become home because it is where his family lives. Belonging, for Pedro, is much more tied to family than to place.

Despite the prominence and visibility of his family name and business, Pedro almost never attends any community or social event. In contrast, Pedro's oldest brother is extremely active and visible in the Chinese community. In fact, his brother is on the board of the Chinese Association, and he and his wife attend almost all the activities sponsored by the different Chinese organizations. He is also—and this is an indication of how small and interconnected this community is—married to a distant aunt of Marco's.

Pedro's narrative elaborates a range of reasons for serial migration. For his father, immigrating to Panama was a way of sustaining his family in China, and once he had achieved a level of economic success there, he brought his brothers over as well. Pedro's own multiple migrations were determined by different factors. The family's return to China from Panama, I suspect, may have been part of the mass exodus of Chinese out of Panama when then-president Arnulfo Arias disenfranchised large numbers of Chinese immigrants and prohibited them from owning retail businesses. Many people I interviewed were faced with the same predicament of returning to China, immigrating to other parts of Latin America, or relocating to the Canal Zone. Many of the wealthier families, like Pedro's, left for China, only to migrate back to Panama when the communists took over. These back-and-forth migrations, then, were caused by political persecution. Finally, Pedro's migrations to the United States, Guatemala, and Nicaragua were efforts to accumulate cultural capital and to expand the family business.

Of the four narratives in this essay, Pedro's migration story most strongly resonates with Aihwa Ong's discussion of flexible citizenship, which she defines as "strategies and effects of [transnational elites] to both circumvent and benefit from different nation-state regimes by selecting different sites for investment, work, and family relocation."[24] In her study of Hong Kong elites in California, Ong argues that flexible citizenship is a response to globalization and that it is a strategy to minimize political danger while maximizing economic accumulation. To do this, Hong Kong elites send their families to the politically safe United States while the patriarch remains in Asia to mind the family business. Given the class status of Pedro's family, they were well-positioned to exercise this kind of flexible citizenship. Pedro and his brothers were sent to different parts of Central America to expand their family's shrimping business, for example, while the rest of the family remained in Panama. Yet Pedro's circular migrations between Panama and China were not financially motivated but were caused primarily by political unrest in these countries. Also, the family remained together as much as possible during these relocations. The notion of flexible citizenship, then, does not explain the full range of Pedro's migrations.

Thus far, the narratives have focused on middle-class, Panamanian-born men. This class and gender bias, not surprisingly, correlates to some extent with the phenomenon of serial migration, which specifically references multiple border crossings over time. Historically, migration among diasporic Chinese was primarily a male endeavor in that the majority of migrants were men and migration was encouraged, even expected, of men to fulfill their role as providers for the family and as the means to achieve upward social mobility.

This is not to say that women did not migrate; they did, but not to the same extent. Moreover, their migration did not have the same cultural connotations. They were not masculine adventurers seeking to build family fortunes; instead, they were often behind-the-scene caretakers responsible for the biological-cultural reproduction of the diaspora. During the early decades of the twentieth century, many of the women who migrated to Panama for marriage eventually returned to China. They often accompanied their children who went to China for education, but while many of the children returned to Panama once they reached adolescence, the women often remained in China. Since the 1960s, however, like their male counterparts, more and more women have been seeking a university education in the United States and other foreign countries.

While the gender ratio of migration has become more balanced, class bias remains strong. The fourth narrative offers a different example of both of these variables. As an immigrant woman whose family fled from political persecution in China and experienced downward social mobility after arriving in Panama, Victoria grew up in a household that struggled to make ends meet. Her narrative shows that while she has engaged in serial migration, her reasons for doing so were distinctly different from those of the others, and she went to Brazil rather than to the United States for her education.

Victoria: "I can do what a man can do"

Victoria and I met during the summer of 1994, when her close friend and colleague Roberto Tang introduced us at a dinner party. She has a warm personality and a great sense of humor, and she was immediately approachable and easy to engage. Within the first hour of our meeting, I had learned that she had migrated from China, grown up in Colón, studied medicine in Brazil, lived in the interior of Panama, and finally moved to Panama City.

Victoria does not consider herself a "typical" Chinese Panamanian woman. She made this very clear to me from the outset by stating that she is neither a member of any Chinese organization nor participates in the activities sponsored by the various Chinese Panamanian associations or "clubs," as she calls them. Essentially, she considers herself an outsider to these social networks. Since I had met most of my informants through such networks, I thought she could offer a distinctively different perspective on what it means to be Chinese in Panama.

Our time together was filled with food, stories, music, more stories, and always laughter. And despite her busy schedule, she was always generous with her time and energy. She shared memories and stories with me, introduced me to her family, and took me with her on weekend visits to her mother's house in La Chorrera.[25] As a doctor, Victoria made it clear that she treated our conversations as both interview and self-therapy: "I narrate my past in order to confront my own fears and, in a sense, to heal and remake myself." By explicitly stating her own agenda in this project, Victoria made certain that I was aware of her sense of complicity and control in the interviewing process.

Victoria's parents and brother fled China at the time of the communist revolution and arrived in Panama around 1949. Victoria and her sister were left behind in China for a few years. During that period, the girls went into hiding, while some of their close relatives looked after them as much as they could. Victoria's family had belonged to the landed class in China and was persecuted by the communists. She had watched her grandparents' execution at the town's center, and one of her aunts was imprisoned for almost two decades. Once released, this same aunt immigrated to Panama to reunite with her husband and family. I never had the chance to talk with this woman, and before the end of my field research in 1997, I learned that she had committed suicide. The suicide, one can suggest, exemplifies one extreme of how much the communist revolution affected people like Victoria and her family. Even after four decades, conversations about their lives in China brought tears to their eyes, and strong emotions of pain and rage kept resurfacing.

While most of the literature on diasporic Chinese has emphasized labor and economic reasons for migration, Victoria's story forcefully illustrates the salience of politics and political persecution in motivating migration. Fleeing China was not a choice for Victoria's family; it was the only way they could have survived. Most of the immigrants who fled China in the late 1940s came without any savings. They basically had to start over. Victoria's family was fortunate to have relatives already in Panama who were able to help them set up a small business. By the time Victoria (age nine) and her sister (age eleven) reached Panama, their parents had opened a small, simple cafeteria in Colón City, serving breakfast to workers in the Canal Zone and on the American military bases. The cafeteria opened at six in the morning and closed at noon. Victoria and her mother woke up at two or three in the morning to start preparing the tortillas, empanadas, and plantains for breakfast. After finishing her tasks at the cafeteria, Victoria would go to school, and by the time she returned home at four in the afternoon, the family would start preparations for the following day. "It was hard," Victoria remarked. "My brothers and father never did much to help. I was tired most of the time, [but] I never felt sad or depressed. . . . I guess I was just glad that at least I was here and not back in China."

The first time I visited Victoria's mother in Chorrera, I was struck by the decor of her home. From the outside, there was nothing remarkable about her house; it looked like any other Panamanian house in that area. But when I walked through the front door, I felt as though I had magically traveled thousands of miles and suddenly stepped into a home in a Chinese village. The interior of the house appeared almost identical to the homes I had visited in southern China. Colors of red and gold were all around the room, and an altar of the Chinese warrior saint Guan Gong sat by the entrance to the living room. Victoria's mother had been in Panama for more than four decades, but judging by the interior decoration of her home, she had never left China, or at least had never left it behind. Her house conveyed a powerful sense of diasporic nostalgia.

Nothing in their interaction with one another suggested that Victoria and her mother had been through difficult times. But during one of our trips, Victoria confessed that throughout high school, she had fought constantly with her parents, usually over issues of gender discrimination. She recognized that she and her sister were treated differently from her brothers, and she resented that her parents favored the boys.

> My mother and I used to get in fights all the time. Once, [my mother] beat me with a fish in her hand, and I was very, very angry. I screamed at her, "I never told you to bring me into this world." Now, I know it was very tough for her because she had to work, to care for us children. My father was drunk often, so she had to work alone, and she tried to get us to help her. . . . I was the only one who helped, and I couldn't understand why she never liked me. I tried to please her, but at the time, she was awful to me. . . . Many times when [our fights got out of hand], my father would shut me and my sister out of the house . . . the craziness of being immigrants. Well, right now, I can understand what happened psychologically. It was my mother projecting her devaluation onto us. From what she has told me about her life, I know she wasn't treated well as a child. Knowing that now helps me understand why she treated me the way she did, but at the time, when I was growing up, it was hard. My older brother was never around, and my father was often drunk. I remember he used to play records of Chinese operas, and he would just sit there listening, with tears flowing down his face. He was depressed a lot. I guess my mother was under a lot of pressure to keep everything together.

During the summer of my junior year in high school, my mother and I got into a fight, and my father told my sister and me to pack our suitcases. Then, he took us to the school where the nuns were and paid for our last year of high school. He just left us there, just like that. I promised myself then that I would not return anymore to my family. Instead, I studied a lot. I repressed my sadness, my fears, and my sense of powerlessness. I channeled all my energy into doing well in school, and I graduated first in my class.

After high school graduation, my sister and I lived with our [non-Chinese Panamanian] teachers. They are like family to me. The teachers have always been there for me. They have taken me in every time. They fed me, encouraged me, and gave me so much. To me, they are family. We were so poor then. My sister and I made money by crocheting and selling small items like doilies, baby socks, and clothes. And with the help of my teachers, I eventually won a scholarship to study at the University of Santa María Antigua [USMA]. But when I decided to study medicine, I had to transfer to the University of Panama.

Like many women who face hostility and rejection by their biological families, Victoria has redefined her understanding of family as relations based not on biology but on enduring ties and support.[26] Having been thrown out of the house by her father, Victoria clearly understands that biological ties do not automatically translate into familial support. Rather, she insists that because her teachers provided her with a home, gave her emotional and financial support, and have been there for her throughout the years, they are her family.

My goal was to be somebody. I was going to study . . . and this drive . . . the feeling of rage pushed me. It was the challenge to prove to [my parents] that even though I'm a woman, I can do what a man can do. . . . I started studying medicine in the University of Panama . . . but then, in 1968, the military had taken power, and it was a bad time in Panama and democracy was suspended, and the military government closed the university. At the time, my godmother was working at the Brazilian embassy, and she told me about the embassy's scholarship. So I applied, and I got the scholarship. It was the only way I could pursue medicine at that time. After three years of not seeing my father, I decided to go to Colón to ask my father for help. And he was very happy to see me. When it came to education, he was always extremely supportive. I remember one time when he was on his knees begging my older brother to finish high school. I think he has always been proud of me in that sense. He gave me $500 [to help with my education]. In 1969, it was plenty of money.

Brazil was a good period in my life. I got more autonomy, I met more people, and my professors appreciated me. I was the only Chinese in the class. Some of my patients would call me *japa*, thinking I was Japanese. Well, Brazil is different from Panama in that way. There are more Japanese there than Chinese. So, instead of calling [Asians] *china* or *chino*, they call us *japa*.

Chino and *china* are terms that non-Asian Panamanians (and others throughout most of Latin America) use to refer to anyone with an East Asian phenotype. More than a national identity, *chino/china* serves as a racial category that stands in for "Asian," a term that is more widely used in the United States. The racial category of "Asian," used in the United States to refer to the different ethnic groups in and from Asia, has no cultural currency in Latin America.[27]

While studying in Brazil, Victoria met her first husband, also from Panama, and as soon as she graduated from medical school, she remigrated back to Panama to join her husband in the interior. There, she did her internship and had her two children.

Those years were difficult. When my ex-husband came back to his hometown, he changed a lot. Things between him and me got worse and worse and worse. So I talked to my sister, who was married by then, and she lent me the money to move back to Panama City. I left my first husband and brought my children with me. It was such a crazy period then. I was still doing my internship at the hospital, and my children were so young. My daughter was about three years old, and my son was just a toddler. Again, my teachers came through for me. They took care of my children while I worked at the hospital.

Victoria and her sister Ana have maintained a very close relationship. They've always supported one another. Ana married a Panamanian Chinese whose family has been in Panama for several generations. With her husband's business and family networks, Ana's family actively participates in Chinese community activities. In fact, I frequently see Ana and her family at the Chinese banquets and functions. Victoria, on the other hand, is less inclined to participate in these activities. Part of her hesitation has to do with her sense of nonbelonging in the community and her sense of nonacceptance by it. "I don't participate in these Chinese activities because, well, I didn't marry a Chinese man, and my children are racially mixed and don't speak Chinese. The old Chinese can't accept that, so I don't go to these activities very often. Once in a while, I will attend a dinner banquet sponsored by my village association. But I don't go to them regularly."

Her statement highlights the community's intense bias against exogamy. Yet unlike Fernando, who is racially mixed but nonetheless actively partakes in community activities, Victoria, who married a non-Chinese, has chosen not to participate at all. Fernando's long-standing ties with fellow Panamanian Chinese and his gender role as patriarch enable him to assert belonging with confidence. As a single mother, Victoria has been faced with extraordinary demands and has had little leisure time to socialize. Moreover, being a divorced, single mother (once married to a non-Chinese) carries tremendous social stigma. These factors contribute to her sense of nonbelonging to the Panamanian Chinese community.

Moving from one place to another has never been a matter of "choice" for Victoria, at least not in the sense that she had other comparable alternatives. The communist revolution forced her to emigrate from China to Panama. The military government's shuttering of the university compelled her to move from Panama to Brazil. And her migrations within Panama were consequences of gender discrimination. Also, in contrast to the other three interviewees, Victoria went to Brazil instead of to the United States for her education. While receiving an American university degree may be the ideal for most Panamanian Chinese, it is not always an option for the less privileged, which was the case for Victoria. The cost of living and education in the United States is much higher than in other parts of Latin America. Fluency in English may be another factor. Victoria's story runs counter to the dominant emphasis in migration studies, which stress unidirectional movements from the global South, or developing world, to the global North (i.e., from Panama to the United States). Her migrations *within* the global South exemplify a set of conversations and relationships that are equally important but that have not received adequate attention in our study of global migration.

The differences presented in these life narratives disrupt any fixed notion of what it means to be Chinese in diaspora. Whereas Marco strives to explore all the potential facets of his identity, and extensive travel actually enhances his sense of diasporic belonging, Pedro's high-profile family and his own set of migrations have left him feeling alienated. Also, whereas Fernando asserts his belonging by actively participating in community activities, Victoria holds herself aloof from the Chinese community because she feels it does not accept her. Juxtaposing their migration stories offsets reductionist tropes that homogenize the Chinese experience in diaspora. Indeed, even though all four interviewees have partaken in serial migration, each of their experiences has led to varying formulations of what it means to be Chinese and to belong in the diaspora.

Moreover, what emerges powerfully in these narratives is the way class and gender significantly shape the range of possibilities open to different migrants. Victoria's story underscores this point. Unlike Fernando, Pedro, and Marco, for whom migrating to the United States to pursue higher education was expected and encouraged by their families, Victoria—being a woman and coming from a less-privileged class position—had to seek out opportunities on her own. She sought after fellowships for financial support, and she went to Brazil, a less ideal location to pursue higher education but where an opportunity was available. For Victoria, gender and social class clearly restricted her possibilities for migration.

Despite their differences, however, serial migration emerges as a strategy of self-realization and of seeking the most suitable home amid the constraints and contingencies of national belonging. On one level, the actual practice of crossing borders occurs under a variety of circumstances and for a number of reasons. There are three most salient themes. First, state violence and political persecution are recurrent issues in Chinese migration. Both Victoria and Pedro were forced to migrate because of the political situations in China and Panama. In China, it was communist persecution of the landed class. In Panama, it was President Arnulfo Arias's exclusionist and nationalist agenda that denied the Chinese (and other nonwhite immigrant groups) the right to Panamanian citizenship. Disenfranchisement, persecution, and forced migration have thus been important factors not only in shaping diasporic Chinese subjectivity but also in propelling serial migration. Under these circumstances, migration has served as a strategy of survival.

Second, serial migration is a method of accumulating cultural capital. Aihwa Ong's work with Hong Kong elites and Donald Nonini's study of Malaysian Chinese offer two instances of how differently positioned diasporic Chinese use migration to accrue cultural capital.[28] Beyond the four interviewees presented in this paper, I encountered significant numbers of diasporic Chinese who had attended college or university abroad. The Georgia Institute of Technology, the University of Notre Dame, the University of Chicago, and the University of Florida are a few of the universities they have attended. For most middle-class and upper-middle-class Panamanian Chinese, studying abroad is both a vehicle for social mobility and an emblem of social status. While some choose to stay abroad after graduation, many return to Panama either to pursue careers in their fields of study or, like Pedro and Marco, to manage their family businesses. The fact that not everyone who studied abroad did so for reasons of social mobility suggests that something more is at work, and when I situate this practice in relation to their contingent national belonging, I wonder if this could be a form of preparing for the worst-case scenario. In times of crisis, when one is forced to relocate on short notice, one's educational degree may be the only thing that is transportable across national borders.

Third, I suggest that serial migration is the process by which my interviewees have come to realize where home is or at least have located where they want to commit to making a home. All four of the interviewees discussed in this essay chose to return to Panama for one reason or another. Victoria came back with the intention of creating a family with her husband; Fernando left the United States to re-establish his roots in Panama. Marco and Pedro came back to be with their families and to participate in their respective family businesses. Indeed, my interviewees both symbolically and physically identified Panama as home. This is not to say that their detours did not affect their subject formation. Whether it is the United States for Fernando (as reflected in his play production), Brazil for Victoria (in gaining a sense of economic independence), or Taiwan for Marco (deepening his connection to Chinese culture), these stopovers have informed their sense of who they are. More important, in telling their stories, the interviewees implicitly and explicitly show how their respective migration experiences lead them to make Panama their home, at the same time as they recognize their connection to other places.

On another level, these narratives of serial migration both perform the cultural work of normalizing the ruptures associated with migration and sketch an emergent diasporic identity of Chinese in the Americas. The narratives mark a clear departure from the conventional understanding of migration as a singular and unidirectional movement. Instead, they convey their multiple migrations as if they were ordinary and normal aspects of diasporic life. Over and over again, my interviewees narrated the history of their families' migrations. By tracing serial migration through several generations, the narratives not only reorganize spatial-temporal disjunctures into a continuum but also illustrate how memories of migration influence the way people construct geographies of home, belonging, and community. The mapping of genealogies onto dispersed locales helps transform unfamiliar places into familiar, homely ones. For Marco, weaving together generations of migration has helped him map the various places to which family members have settled. Binding unfamiliar places with kinship ties, he incorporated them into his geography of family and community, thereby bringing them closer to home and making them into possible places of belonging.

Moreover, as I listened closely to their migration stories, I realized that most of my interviewees did not convey the expected feelings of traumatic displacement from an estranged "home." Even for Victoria, who had to leave China in order to survive, migration was portrayed as something necessary, and her idea of home and belonging was never romanticized or fixed. For most, the repeated relocations entailed in serial migration appeared more like normal, matter-of-fact occurrences than like traumatic uprootings. Ironically, even as these narratives show the salience of constant movement and relocation, they simultaneously reveal their ordinariness in the lives of diasporic Chinese. Perhaps the narrative repetition of displacement helps transform it into something seemingly more common. In a sense, my interviewees described their serial migrations as open-ended journeys, in which ruptures were normal, expected, and accepted. It was as if once they had left China, migration became the means of self-realization and of finding the most suitable home, wherever that might be. I have thus come to interpret these narratives as living archives and pedagogical tools. On one hand, these narratives remind Panamanian Chinese that, as people who historically lack full national belonging and citizenship, migration and the disruptions associated with relocation are common aspects of diasporic life. On the other hand, they serve as a collective script that teaches and helps reproduce migration as one possible strategy to achieve belonging. By showing the resilience of diasporic Chinese as they move from place to place, these narratives help transmit cultural knowledge and instill a sense of confidence about migration. Serial migration, hence, is not simply a social phenomenon of crossing multiple borders; it is also a distinct cultural logic that emerges from the experience of living in diaspora.

Lastly, by tracing continuous routes between Panama and the United States, and across different parts of Latin America and the Caribbean, these narratives illustrate their collective identification with the Americas. While all my interviewees have made Panama their home, each of their stories traces a web of connected sites across the continent. For Fernando, the key nodes include Chicago and Jamaica, whereas Marco will always find Miami and Peru important. Meanwhile, Guatemala, Managua, and California remain significant places for Fernando, and Victoria will always remember Brazil. In all four cases, not only have their respective migrations revised their understanding of where home was, is, and can be, but their narratives also convey that even as they live in Panama, they remember and imagine themselves as part of the Americas.

NOTES

This essay is drawn from "Migration Stories: Serial Migration and the Production of Home and Identity in Diaspora" in my book Memories of a Future Home: Diasporic Citizenship of Chinese in Panama *(Stanford, Calif.: Stanford University Press, 2005). A much earlier version of this essay was published in* The Chinese in the Caribbean, *ed. Andrew Wilson (Princeton, N.J.: Markus Wiener Publishers, 2004).*

1. See Paul Gilroy, *There Ain't No Black in the Union Jack: The Cultural Politics of Race and Nation* (Chicago: University of Chicago, 1987); and Paul Gilroy, *The Black Atlantic: Modernity and Double Consciousness,* reissue ed. (Cambridge, Mass.: Harvard University Press, 1993).

2. Anthropologist Keith Basso has written extensively about the significance of place in relation to Native Americans. Here I explore the role and meaning of place in relation to diaspora. The question becomes: If diaspora is about processes of dispersal and displacement, then what is the significance of place for them? What is their relationship to place? In line with his assertion that geographical landscapes are never actually vacant but filled with cultural significance, I am interested in exploring what places are evoked by diasporic Chinese and what significance diasporic Chinese give to those places. See Keith Basso, "'Speaking with Names': Language and Landscape among Western Apache," *Cultural Anthropology* 3, no. 2 (1988): 102.

3. See Sucheng Chan, *Asian Americans: An Interpretive History* (Berkeley: University of California Press, 1991); Madeline Hsu, *Dreaming of Gold, Dreaming of Home: Transnationalism and Migration Between the United States and South China, 1882–1943* (Stanford, Calif.: Stanford University Press, 2000); Adam McKeown, *Chinese Migrant Networks and Cultural Change: Peru, Chicago, Hawaii, 1900–1936* (Chicago: University of Chicago Press, 2001); and Ronald Takaki, *Strangers from a Different Shore* (Boston: Little, Brown, 1989).

4. Lucy Cohen, "The Chinese of the Panama Railroad: Preliminary Notes on the Migrants of 1854 Who Failed," *Ethnohistory* 19, no. 4 (1971): 309–20; Evelyn Hu-Dehart, "Latin America in Asia-Pacific Perspective," in *What Is In a Rim? Critical Perspectives on the Pacific Region Idea,* ed. Arif Dirlik (Boulder, Colo.: Rowman & Littlefield, 1998); Gary Okihiro, *Margins and Mainstreams: Asians in American History and Culture* (Seattle: University of Washington Press, 1994); and Jack Tchen, *New York Before Chinatown: Orientalism and the Shaping of American Culture, 1776–1882* (Baltimore: Johns Hopkins University Press, 2001).

5. The term "Greater China" signifies a social formation and geographical area that includes China, Taiwan, Hong Kong, and Macao. The key places in the Caribbean and the Americas that my interviewees indicated include Jamaica, British Guiana, Nicaragua, Peru, and the United States.

6. Movement from less developed countries to more developed ones is inherent in the concept of step migration, but not in that of serial migration. See Kyeyoung Park, "'10,000 Señora Lees': The Changing Gender Ideology of Korean-Latina-American Women in the Diaspora," *Amerasia Journal* 28, no. 2 (2002): 161–80; and Wang Gungwu, "Upgrading the Migrant: Neither Huaquiao nor Huaren," in *The Last Half Century of Chinese Overseas,* ed. Elizabeth Sinn, 15–34 (Hong Kong: Hong Kong University Press, 1998).

7. Roger Rouse, "Mexican Migration and the Social Space of Postmodernity," *Diaspora* 1, no. 1 (1999): 8–23.

8. James Clifford, *Routes: Travel and Translation in the Late Twentieth Century* (Cambridge, Mass.: Harvard University Press, 1997).

9. Cosmopolitanism historically has been associated with subjects whose freedom to circulate around the world is made possible by their relative positions of privilege. Recently, since the 1990s, a number of scholars have attempted to broaden the concept of cosmopolitanism to include other kinds of travelers, mainly travelers of less privilege, such as merchant sailors, au pairs, and guest workers. To include the experiences of these travelers also means changing the meaning of cosmopolitanism from one that is fundamentally committed to the (assumed) universal interests of humanity as a whole to one that is about the ability to grapple with cultural difference on a transnational scale. See Pheng Cheah and Bruce Robbins, eds., *Cosmopolitics: Thinking and Feeling Beyond the Nation* (Minneapolis: University of Minnesota Press, 1992); Clifford, *Routes;* and Ulf Hannerz, *Transnational Connections: Culture, People, Places* (New York: Routledge, 1996).

10. See, for instance, Gita Rajan and Shailja Sharma, eds., *New Cosmopolitanisms: South Asians in the United States* (Stanford, Calif.: Stanford University Press, 2006).

11. Aihwa Ong, *Flexible Citizenship: The Cultural Logics of Transnationality* (Durham, N.C.: Duke University Press, 1999). The use of snakeheads is one of the most common means of migration for mainland Chinese. I have written about this form of migration in *Memories of a Future Home.* Also see Peter Kwong, *Forbidden Workers: Chinese Illegal Immigrants and American Labor* (New York: The New Press, 1999).

12. See May Joseph, *Nomadic Citizenship: The Performance of Citizenship* (Minneapolis: University of Minnesota Press, 1999); Kyeyoung Park, "'10,000 Señora Lees'"; Joshua Roth, *Japanese Brazilian Migrants in Japan* (Ithaca, N.Y.: Cornell University Press, 2002); and Takeyuki Tsuda, *Strangers in the Ethnic Homeland* (New York: Columbia University Press, 2003).

13. For all interviews, I use pseudonyms to protect the identity of interviewees.

14. Stuart Hall, "Cultural Identity and Diaspora," in *Identity: Community, Culture and Difference,* ed. Jonathan Rutherford, 222–37 (London: Lawrence & Wishart, 1990).

15. See Jeffrey Lesser, *Negotiating National Identity: Immigrants, Minorities, and the Struggle for Ethnicity in Brazil* (Durham, N.C.: Duke University Press, 1999), and McKeown, *Chinese Migrant Networks and Cultural Change.*

16. While *mestizaje* refers generally to racial-cultural mixing, it is also associated with the ideology of racial whitening. For a detailed discussion of *mestizaje,* see Marisol de la Cadena, *Indigenous Mestizos: The Politics of Race and Culture in Cuzco, Peru, 1919–1991*

(Durham, N.C.: Duke University Press, 2000); and José Vasconcelos, *The Cosmic Race/ La Raza Cosmica,* trans. Didier Jaén (Baltimore: Johns Hopkins University Press, 1997).

17. For a more detailed discussion, see Caren Kaplan, *Questions of Travel: Postmodern Discourses of Displacement* (Durham, N.C.: Duke University Press, 1996).

18. See Hall, "Cultural Identity and Diaspora."

19. "Paper sons" came to the United States bearing papers documenting them as sons of Chinese who had returned to China to marry and produce children. The Great Earthquake of 1906 in San Francisco had destroyed immigration records, along with other official records of the U.S. government. In the process of redocumentation, Chinese immigrants falsely reported the number of children they had in China in order to get papers for others to immigrate.

20. Janet Wolffe, *Resident Alien: Feminist Cultural Criticism* (New Haven, Conn.: Yale University Press, 1995).

21. It was my uncle Armando in Nicaragua who had first mentioned this quarantine station in Panama. He called it the "wooden house" in Cantonese and compared it to the immigration station on Angel Island in San Francisco Bay, California. When Pedro mentioned the quarantine station again, I decided to go look for it. After a thorough search in the former U.S. Canal Zone, I was unable to locate the actual structure of the station or find any documentation connecting it to Chinese immigration to Latin America. Nonetheless, several of my interviewees who immigrated to Latin American before World War II vividly remember this "wooden house," the quarantine station that served as an immigration processing point for Chinese going to various destinations in Latin America.

22. See Tchen, *New York Before Chinatown,* and Mary Lui, *The Chinatown Trunk Mystery: Murder, Miscegenation, and Other Dangerous Encounters in Turn-of-the-Century New York City* (Princeton, N.J.: Princeton University Press, 2005).

23. Pedro refers here to the first Chinese school that was established in the 1930s, which has since been destroyed. It was a primary school that taught Cantonese in addition to the regular Panamanian curriculum and was attended mostly by children of Chinese descent living in the Chinatown area.

24. Ong, *Flexible Citizenship,* 112.

25. La Chorrera is a suburb west of Panama City, across the Bridge of the Americas. Since the 1980s, La Chorrera has become the city with the largest percentage of Chinese immigrants in Panama. Most of the Chinese there are Hakka speakers from Canton and immigrated to Panama during the Manuel Noriega military regime. The Chinese living in La Chorrera are primarily involved in distribution, small retail businesses, and restaurants. As the next largest city west of Panama City, La Chorrera serves as a major transit point between the capital and the smaller towns in the interior of Panama (the provinces of Coclé, Herrera, Los Santos, and Veraguas). Because of its central location, La Chorrera has become a central distribution center for produce and commercial products to both Panama City and the interior.

26. Kath Weston, *Families We Choose: Lesbians, Gays, Kinship* (New York: Columbia University Press, 1991).

27. The term "Asian American" emerged during the 1960s to mobilize a political coalition of the different ethnic Asian groups in the United States. By asserting a collective identity, it helped articulate shared experiences of racial oppression. Since such a movement did not take place in Panama, a collective "Asian Panamanian" consciousness was never achieved. Indeed, ethnicity and nationality remain the central frameworks in which Panamanians categorize difference.

28. See Ong, *Flexible Citizenship,* and Donald Nonini, "Shifting Identities, Positioned Imaginaries: Transnational Traversals and Reversals by Malaysian Chinese," in *Ungrounded Empire: The Cultural Politics of Modern Chinese Transnationalism,* ed. Aihwa Ong and Donald Nonini (New York: Routledge 1997).

CHAPTER SEVEN

Building Associations

Nineteenth-Century Monumental Architecture and the Jew in the American Imagination

MARTIN A. BERGER

Diaspora studies emerged in the final decades of the twentieth century as an academic discourse concerned to explore the social formation of various ethnic, religious, and racial groups violently dispersed from their traditional homelands. With its focus on disempowered peoples whose relocations were forced by intergroup conflict, economic hardship, war, or political instability, diaspora studies followed in the wake of many revisionist historical inquiries of the last century that sought to give voice to those individuals and groups whose stories had previously been at the margins of historical inquiry. In attending to the social and psychological conditions of diasporic peoples, scholars in a range of academic disciplines have devoted much attention to identity formation, foregrounding the complex negotiations in which displaced peoples engage to balance their identifications with old and new homelands and countrymen.[1]

I share with scholars of diaspora studies an interest in addressing the complexity and site-specificity of identification, foregrounding the material repercussions of one's identity choices and illustrating how the negotiation of identity impacts disempowered peoples. But rather than focus on the actions of displaced peoples per se, my efforts as a historian of visual culture have frequently centered on reconstructing the *idea* of particular diasporic peoples in the imaginations of society's most empowered groups and in considering how perceptions of such peoples aided the powerful in conceptualizing their own identities. My attention to the identity making of empowered peoples is not an effort to re-center their lives at the heart of the writing of history; rather it is an attempt to illustrate the complex process by which "identification" works, the ambivalent attitudes held toward diasporic peoples and, hence, to highlight the lived complexities faced by such peoples in defining themselves within a context in which they are both denigrated and admired.

Whenever empowered peoples imagine the identities of less-empowered groups—and especially when they make use of such imagined traits in fashioning their own identities—scholars frequently respond as if such acts of identification are somehow inauthentic. It is one thing for nineteenth-century Jewish Americans, for example, to identify with the promised land and Old Testament prophets and to express a longing for "return," but quite another for Christian European Americans to long for a return to the "primitive" exoticism and opulence of Oriental Jews. Although Jewish immigrants to America were many generations removed from firsthand knowledge of their "homeland," academics tacitly treat their acts of identification with an imagined past as a reasonable expression of identity, notwithstanding the virtually universal acceptance by historians that ethnic and religious identities are socially produced. Without making claims for the legitimacy of particular longings (or identities), and never losing sight of who pays the psychological and material costs for such identifications, I seek to illustrate the ways in which Christian European American longing for "Jewish" attributes has both played a role in fashioning the real-world identities of Christians and complicated the lived experience of Jews. If Jews (and Muslims, Catholics, Native Americans, African Americans, Asian Americans, Latinos, and gays, for that matter) have long found their assertions of identity complicated by the hatred of the dominant culture toward their groups, the often-expressed desire of empowered peoples for elements of identity supposedly possessed by these same groups has served as no less of a complicating factor.

In this essay, I examine how the radical Pennsylvania Academy of the Fine Arts building, erected in Philadelphia by Frank Furness and George Hewitt between 1872 and 1876, drew much of its cultural significance from its symbolic association with various diasporic peoples whom the directors of the academy surely preferred not to meet in the street. This exclusive structure that stood for the highest cultural aspirations of Christian, white Philadelphia, resonated with viewers precisely for its ability to draw on various associations with Jews and other nonwhite peoples. The architects and their patrons fashioned a paradigmatically "white" structure from architectural motifs and historical narratives closely linked to some of the least white peoples then residing in Philadelphia. In a kind of feedback loop, white Christians imagined who they were by selectively appropriating the symbols used by American

Jews to consolidate their identity as diasporic subjects. In this way, the stone, steel, and marble of the academy building gives material form to the fluid processes of identity formation.

While studying architecture in Paris, Charles McKim received periodic reports from his father on the architectural practice of Frank Furness (1839–1912), a partner in the rising Philadelphia firm of Fraser, Furness and Hewitt. Impressed with the design of Rodeph Shalom Synagogue (1869–70; fig. 7.1), the elder McKim commented in an 1869 letter to his son that "Frank Furness is building a costly Jewish Temple. It is of course in the saracenic style."[2] For McKim and his contemporaries, "Saracenic" or "Moorish" architecture was a Western style adapted from the designs of medieval Muslim builders in North Africa and southern Spain.[3] Such Near Eastern styles were popularized in the nineteenth century by European and American artists like Samuel Taylor Coleridge, Eugène Delacroix, and Washington Irving, and they reached a broad architectural audience through the mid-century publications of the Welsh architect and designer Owen Jones.[4]

Though popular, nineteenth-century Saracenic design was neither as ubiquitous in the United States as either neoclassical or Gothic Revival architecture nor applied as indiscriminately to a range of building types. By the end of the century, for example, the seemingly limitless range of structures with neoclassical designs led an architectural critic to observe wearily that "the country was studded with [neoclassical] 'temples,' from court-houses down to bird-boxes."[5] In contrast, Saracenic designs were applied more narrowly to a particular category of buildings that included synagogues, clubs, department stores, restaurants, theaters, music halls, bandstands, cinemas, exposition structures, and select domestic interiors.[6] European Americans consistently used it for fantastic and transformative structures—for those venues intended to transport viewers from quotidian experiences. The Near East struck audiences as an appropriate reference when the activities associated with the spaces provided an escape from the routines of daily life. But Eastern-inspired designs were also deemed appropriate for use by peoples whose customs seemed rooted in distant, exotic cultures. Just as the style offered Christian European Americans a safe yet foreign outlet from everyday life, it seemed to recreate for Jews, and other alien peoples, more natural, native environments.

Given the novelty of Eastern-inspired synagogues in the United States at the close of the 1860s, McKim's assertion that the design of Rodeph Shalom was "of course" Saracenic reflects less on the inevitability of the style's selection than on his understanding of its ideological fitness for a Jewish place of worship, built for a people whom European Americans thought unable to

Figure 7.1. Fraser, Furness and Hewitt. Rodeph Shalom Synagogue.
Philadelphia, 1869–70.

transcend their alien Eastern character, however long they had lived in the
United States.[7] Period guidebooks described the synagogue as both "peculiar"
and "novel," because of its "elaborate ornamentation," which "contrast[ed]
with the prevailing styles," such contrasts being read by European Americans
as an appropriate expression of Jewish difference.[8] But within the ethnic vocabulary employed by Furness and Hewitt, Moorish designs were also thought

suitable for other exotic peoples who did not necessarily originate in the Near East. Just as Furness's many commissions for Jewish European Americans tended to be built in Saracenic forms (for example, the Jewish Hospital of Philadelphia, whose various structures were built between 1871 and 1907), so the Brazilian pavilion he designed for the Philadelphia Centennial Exhibition (c. 1876) boasted what period commentators knew as a "Moorish style."[9] In determining the appropriateness of Near Eastern forms for particular ethnic or religious groups, European Americans concerned themselves much less with the people's geographic place of origin than with perceptions of their status as an "other."

Architectural historians typically explain the Rodeph Shalom congregation's embrace of Furness and Hewitt's design with reference to the politics of Rabbi Marcus Jastrow, who initiated the synagogue's building campaign. A German-born humanist who earned a doctorate in philosophy, Jastrow surprised his congregants by arguing that men and women should be seated together on the main floor of the new synagogue, separated only by an aisle, and by calling for an organ to be located behind the ark. While the changes instituted by Jastrow surely struck more traditional congregants as radical, they represented another step in a century of reform that brought the religious practices of American Jews more in line with Christian conventions. Many Jewish congregations, equating "reform" with Christian norms, adopted such changes as well as the placement of the ark at the far end of the synagogue, the addition of a pulpit, the establishment of family pews, the introduction of sermons, and the development of a professional clergy.[10] Whether Jastrow's congregants initially interpreted his reforms in a positive or negative light, few could have missed the pull of Rodeph Shalom toward Christian practices of worship. Because Saracenic design was closely associated with both modernity and Reform Judaism in the Germany of Jastrow's youth, the rabbi's politics encouraged his rejection of the classically inspired synagogues that were then the norm in Philadelphia.[11]

The irony is that the architectural expression of reform offered a visual reminder that synagogues were not churches and, by extension, that Jews were not Christians. In discarding older American prototypes of synagogues that appeared stylistically similar to churches embracing Orientalist designs, Reform Jews marked their difference from Christians at the precise moment when their practices became more alike. The Jewish embrace of Saracenic design may be interpreted either as a reflection of the growing comfort of Jews in articulating their differences from other Americans in the late 1860s and 1870s, or as an expression of their emerging concern to assert religious and cultural distinctions they did not want to fully erase. In either case, the adoption of a

Saracenic style for synagogues undoubtedly helped to distinguish Jewish from gentile European Americans.[12]

Less than a year after the synagogue's consecration, Furness and Hewitt abandoned their senior partner and formed their own architectural practice, confident that their social connections and growing reputations might sustain a new firm. The new partnership won a number of design competitions, the most lucrative among them the new home of the Pennsylvania Academy of the Fine Arts (1872–76; fig. 7.2).[13] With its novel design, which bore little stylistic resemblance to any previous museum or school of art, the structure brought together a potpourri of architectural styles, including Venetian Gothic, French Néo-Grec, Ruskinian, French Second Empire, and features at least one critic has interpreted as Native American.[14] But as contemporary architectural historians from James O'Gorman to John Sweetman, and Zeynep Çelik to Michael Lewis, have each observed, the building also made extensive reference to Near Eastern architecture in general and to Rodeph Shalom in particular: in its brilliant color scheme; interior columns capped with diamond-patterned

FIGURE 7.2. Furness and Hewitt, northeast façade of the Pennsylvania Academy of the Fine Arts, Philadelphia, 1876–77. Photographer: Frederick Gutenkunst. Photo courtesy of the Pennsylvania Academy of the Fine Arts Archives, Philadelphia. Granted by PAFA.

detailing; decorative floral patterns; alternating pink and white voussoirs forming arches above the doors and windows; intricate decorative brickwork; a central Gothic arch supported by short columns, displayed on the buildings' facades but also at the head of the academy's second-floor landing; and trefoil arches, evident in the academy over the main entrance and in the borders surrounding the plant motifs in the tympanum of each side-pavilion window, and in the synagogue on its minaret-like tower.[15] While far from carbon copies of one another, the buildings shared obvious Orientalized elements that were all the more noticeable given their proximity on North Broad Street, in a city famously characterized by its unadorned three- to five-story redbrick boxes.

To note the Oriental sources the structures share is not to articulate the ideological work they performed for nineteenth-century audiences. Considerable evidence suggests that while Gilded Age architectural critics saw Near Eastern styles as appropriate for synagogues, they were slightly unsettled to find them used for academies of fine art. One observer, summing up critics' confusion about the Pennsylvania Academy in 1876, claimed that "the style of architecture appears to baffle the critics; one calls it ornamented Gothic; another, modified Gothic; another nearly touches correctness in calling it 'Byzantine or Venetian'; perhaps we may come still nearer the truth in designating it as a combination or patchwork style; we doubt if any known epithet would convey to one who has not seen it a conception of the marvelous incongruities that go to make up the showy exterior of the new Academy of Fine Arts."[16] In the nineteenth century such "bafflement" resulted not from the incoherence of the "combination" or "patchwork" style but from the tendency of old-fashioned architectural critics to interpret eclecticism through the lens of more familiar, yet incompatible, architectural theories.

Confronted with an emergent style that demanded new ways of looking, many critics simply applied the logic of traditional architectural paradigms to eclecticism and misinterpreted the resulting confusion as a failure of the style. This tendency of critics is evident in the controversy surrounding the academy directors' decision to relocate an ancient Greek statue of Ceres from the front courtyard of their previous building to a pedestal above the front portal of the new edifice.[17] As soon as the plans became known, a commentator warned in the press that the colossal sculpture, placed "in an odd incongruity with their facade, . . . will never be regarded, and will probably soon perish of exposure." The reinstallation prompted a second critic to lament that the statue now stood "in odd contrast with the trim freshness of the surrounding architecture" and was located where "few people will wait to study its beauties, and where it will receive more attention from the weather than from the public."[18]

Each critic linked the reinstallation of the statue to its physical destruction and visual neglect, thus implying that Ceres in its old location had been both safe and studied, though the reality was considerably more complex. Moved from the open courtyard to a covered niche at the center of the Academy's Broad Street facade, Ceres was arguably both better protected from the elements and more visible in its more prominent site. No longer relegated to a quiet courtyard, gracing "a silent pale building in the Greek style . . . dedicated to the powers of seclusion and reserve, and only exceptionally approached," the statue was now framed by a large tracery window and centered on a facade fronting a busy Philadelphia street.[19] Had the sculpture remained cloistered in its neoclassical home, the critics never would have voiced discontent; ironically, only when it became all too visible—by its "incongruous" juxtaposition with disparate architectural traditions—did viewers express concern for what they implicitly understood as its new *kind* of visibility. Some of those who disapproved may have held the emerging view of fine art that championed the display of individual sculptures and paintings; the majority, however, were probably more conservative viewers. Their investment in revivalist architecture had conditioned them to expect that the architectural motifs of a structure be drawn from a single national or cultural tradition.

If elite architectural critics articulated no coherent rationale for the academy's Near Eastern eclecticism, the directors and patrons of the academy nonetheless self-consciously promoted the structure's Near Eastern associations. The academy directors fashioned a consecration ceremony for the opening of the building that pointedly connected it to an ancient Jewish past. At noon on April 22, 1876, the academy staged an elaborately choreographed inauguration that included processions, orchestral music, speeches by eminent Philadelphians, and displays of select works of art. The keynote address was delivered by the liberal theologian William Henry Furness, the father of the architect, who dedicated the structure with the words of the Old Testament prophet Moses, the "poet of the Hebrews." Then, dramatically unveiling two marble sculptures—G. B. Lombardi's *Deborah* (c. 1874) and William Wetmore Story's allegory *Jerusalem in Her Desolation* (1873)—the elder Furness declared the building open.[20] Boasting a collection of art whose breadth and quality were then unrivaled in the United States, the institution was consecrated with the presentation of two sculptures that referred explicitly to Old Testament narratives and, so, to an ancient Jewish past.

These sculptures established a transition from opening ceremonies focused on the academy's architecture to the artworks that the academy was designed to house. In transferring the attention of the audience from building to holdings, the sculptures established the artistic benchmark for future exhibitions to follow from this first display. *Deborah* and *Jerusalem* served as literal and figurative progenitors of a long line of academy shows. The two scantily clad female figures, for Gilded Age audiences, alluded to sexuality and to motherhood, but *Deborah,* as the "mother of Israel" in the Book of Judges, made the maternal reference explicit. Having prophesied the military victory of the Israelites over King Jabin of Canaan, Deborah was honored by her people as the mother of their national rebirth.

Jerusalem in Her Desolation depicts a brooding figure who sits amid ruins and contemplates her recent destruction at the hands of the Babylonians, but also a maternal figure giving birth to a new institution. Inaugurating a building that was routinely referred to as a "temple of art" with a sculpture that alludes to the destruction of the Temple in Jerusalem, the directors linked their modern temple to the lost glories of the ancient Israelites. With a symbolism lost on few of the assembled guests, the directors consciously invoked the demise of Jerusalem to mark the completion of their academy, suggesting the cyclical nature of civilizations, the passing of the torch of culture from the Near East to Europe and finally to America, and to the academy's institutional grounding in the wreckage of an ancient past.

Audiences who frequently traced their religious heritage to the biblical Israelites conceived of Jews as the most logical inheritors of the Moorish architectural tradition in the United States, and those who collapsed the distinctions between Israelites and other Near Eastern peoples found it natural to read in Islamic architectural details and Old Testament subjects an affirmation of the academy's ties to a mythic Jewish lineage.[21] For Christian European Americans in the 1870s, the eclectic academy ultimately fused Jewish (but also Islamic, Catholic, and potentially Native American) sources into a structure that embodied the highest cultural aspirations of Quaker, Unitarian, and Protestant Euro-America. From a twenty-first-century vantage, it seems remarkable that such sources might blend together to express the values of an academy of fine art, given that they constituted not just foreign but, I will argue, nonwhite motifs and considering that such academies were among the "whitest" institutions in European American society. (The whiteness of such institutions was overdetermined by the cultural associations of fine art, the historical role and development of museums, the pedagogical function of painting and sculpture in the West, and the historically specific ways in which museums regularized the behavior of their visitors during the final decades of the nineteenth century.)

The suggestion that Jewish sources might meaningfully be termed nonwhite may strike readers as an untenable claim. Some scholars, to be sure, have argued for the nonwhite status of Jews in late nineteenth-century America, but others claim that while Jews (and Irish Catholics and Italians, for that matter) were racialized, there is little evidence to support a claim of their nonwhite status.[22] Protestant European Americans routinely saw Jews, these scholars argue, as inferior in religion, morals, and even race, but never as nonwhite; for unlike Chinese, Japanese, and at times Arab immigrants, they were always granted citizenship based on the understanding that they met the naturalization criterion of being "free white people."[23] To be considered an inferior white is far different from being designated nonwhite.

While I am sympathetic to claims that nineteenth-century American Jews were only "provisional whites," I am not invested in their not-quite-white status. Their designation as racial inferiors raises the important question why elite, Christian European Americans used architectural styles associated with an inferior group.[24] Modern Americans may reflexively assume that one is either white or not, but historians of the nineteenth century generally agree that a European American Jew ranked lower in the white hierarchy than a Protestant of the same national origin. We also know that being Chinese in Gilded Age America never carried the ideological or material consequences of being African American. Asian immigrants, indisputably subjected to withering discrimination, were accorded better job opportunities and enjoyed greater economic mobility than African Americans. Those designated "nonwhite" in American society have never been disadvantaged to precisely the same degree.[25]

Nevertheless, there is evidence that religious and racial forms of otherness were much more closely aligned in the nineteenth century than they appear today. Such alignment stems from the invention of race itself. In his sweeping survey of whiteness in late nineteenth-century and early twentieth-century American culture, historian Matthew Frye Jacobson takes the divide between Christian and heathen as foundational both for determining belonging and otherness in Western culture and for laying the conceptual framework for later racial hierarchies.[26] The historian Thomas Holt takes up this point. Noting that all social constructs must build themselves out of existing traditions, he hypothesizes that race owes a developmental debt to the religious hierarchies from which it grew. The modern concept of race emerged in the late seventeenth and early eighteenth centuries from long-standing conventions for arranging peoples in hierarchies and legitimating those divisions in purportedly objective scientific studies. Most prominently, climatic development theories, predispositions in reading physical appearance, xenophobia, and religious exclusion contributed to the invention of modern race. Holt proposes that European religious criteria were used to distinguish between pure and impure populations, between those who belonged and those who stood in ideological opposition.

To make his case, Holt points to the Spanish expulsion of Jews in 1492 as an expression of protoracial (and protonational) values. Grounded in the rhetoric of "purity of faith," the expulsion was protoracial in the sense that religious prejudices furnished the logic that racial hierarchies would in time adopt. What began as a quest for ideological purity was eventually transformed into a crusade for "purity of blood," as the Inquisition moved to root out biologically inferior Jewish converts who hid their "true" selves behind the mask of Catholicism. Holt argues that prior to its emergence as a coherent category of identity, race took its only possible form (to speak anachronistically, yet historically) in the logic of religious exclusion.[27] Given the ease with which the Spanish transubstantiated ideological distinctions into biological ones, and the impossibility that race could emerge suddenly as a concept unconnected to previous social relations, there is a logic in considering preracial phenomena at least partly in racial terms. But there is even more compelling reason *after* the advent of race to interpret racially the value systems that fed its development, considering their ideological overlap. Racial hierarchies would initially have made sense to Europeans only to the degree that they jibed with pre-existing value systems. Protestant, Unitarian, and even Catholic European Americans who considered Jews and Jewish-inspired designs were likely to have seen people and products foreign to them in religion and nationality but also alien to them in race.

In nineteenth-century America, religious difference was routinely read through the lens of race. The art historian John Davis has explored how American culture has long been infused with symbols linking the nation to a mythic Holy Land, and Christian European Americans to the chosen people. Unconcerned with stylistic accuracy or geographic precision, a wide cross-section of Americans liberally interpreted a host of Near Eastern references as signs of the link between their cultural and religious heritage and an ancient Jewish past. While Davis is concerned primarily with illustrating how Christian European Americans invoked the Holy Land to fashion a usable past, he is sensitive to the anxiety accompanying such associations, offering hints as to its racial grounding. Drawing attention to the European American desire to downplay the presence of indigenous figures in photographs, paintings, and recreations of the Holy Land, Davis explains that Near Eastern Arabs and Jews provided useful evidence of scriptural continuity but only to the extent they were safely distanced in a religious past. Arabs and Jews who were too clearly of the present threatened, in Davis's estimation, the ability of Christian European Americans to take ideological or material possession of the Holy Land.[28]

In many popular outlets, the articulation of this anxiety was explicitly racial. Consider the reaction of Mark Twain's contemporary and sometime collaborator Charles Dudley Warner to the people of Jerusalem, whom he encountered on an 1875 trip through the Near East. Warner's travelogue, *In the Levant* (1877), records his pleasure in connecting the life of Jesus to the landscape before him, but it also registers his mounting unease as his contact with indigenous peoples increased. In particular, Warner frets over his difficulties in explaining why most of the Jews he encountered in Jerusalem possess "the hook nose, dark hair and eyes, and not at all the faces of the fair-haired race from which our Saviour is supposed to have sprung." Unable to accept the origin of his God in such "dark" people, Warner solves his "ethnological problem" by hypothesizing that the "real Jews" from whom Jesus descended possessed "fair skin and light hair, with straight nose and regular features," and that those "debased, mis-begotten" Jews characteristic of the West were the corrupted product of an amalgamation with Assyrian conquerors.[29]

Writing three years after *In the Levant* was published, the Reverend William Henry Poole connected contemporary Christian European Americans more explicitly to ancient Jews by arguing that Anglo-Saxons had descended directly from the lost tribes of Israel. Although Poole's "Anglo-Israel" thesis was never widely embraced, it employed the same defensive gesture evident in more mainstream European Americans texts—forging a link with a biblical past that avoided tying modern Christian European Americans to living Jews. Poole based his genealogical argument on tortured philological reasoning, selective scriptural citation, and a series of myths, but it was ultimately grounded in what for him were elemental biological differences. He argued that the ancient Hebrews must have comprised at least two physiognomically distinct groups, for if the lost tribes had had the obvious physical markers of contemporary Jews, they never would have gone missing. Since the bodies of modern Jews were racially marked, it seemed obvious to Poole—from his Christian Eurocentric perspective—that the lost tribes must have been "unmarked," meaning that they looked both Christian and white. For the theologian, God's master plan for losing the tribes was possible only in a context where they had never possessed "the physiognomy of the Jews."[30]

Had Christians coded Jewish difference in religious or cultural terms alone, there would have been little need to distance Christ from the physiognomy of his ancient progenitors.[31] It is telling, then, that Warner and Poole expressed their discomfort with contemporary Western Jews in exclusively physical terms. Rather than object to theological positions or cultural traits of the people who engendered both Christ and modern-day Anglo-Saxons, they worried about the shape of noses and the color of skin, hair, and eyes. Poole's thesis makes explicit Warner's desire to distance Christ from an inferior race to preserve what both men clearly understood as God's Anglo-Saxon stock. This racial sleight of hand performed significant cultural work, allowing Warner and Poole to uphold an image of Christ as white and to root their heritage in the Old Testament yet distance themselves from ancient "dark" Jews and their modern incarnations. The lengths to which European American commentators went in their efforts to dissociate Christian European Americans from the Jews of Europe and America suggest the ambivalence of patrons of the Pennsylvania Academy about the building's Jewish and Islamic architectural forms.

No doubt the academy's nonwhite associations complicated nineteenth-century European Americans' responses to it, but with eclecticism the dominant architectural style during the 1870s, Philadelphia as its American center, and the immensely popular team of Hewitt and Furness among its leading practitioners, the important racial work of the structure more than compensated for its "paradox." Architects, directors, and patrons of the academy somehow transformed nonwhite elements into the epitome of whiteness. While it is certainly possible that for Americans eclecticism performed symbolic work unrelated to race (and thus helped offset its racial drawbacks), both its popularity and its complexity were firmly rooted in the racial register. To explain how this might be so, I want to turn to the meaning of eclecticism for European American audiences in the postbellum era.

Before anything approximating a national style developed in the United States, culturally chauvinistic European American builders turned to Europe for architectural models. As the architectural historian James O'Gorman explains, reliance on European design in antebellum America was largely manifest in historicist styles, but briefly in the 1870s it found expression in eclectic designs. Historicist building programs reproduced a single architectural style with (supposed) archaeological accuracy; eclectic designs self-consciously assembled motifs from different national and cultural traditions, centuries, and continents.[32] The commingling of styles that Americans had long seen as a sign of architectural ignorance came to represent the height of scholarly practice in the years following the Civil War. Eclectic building design met two important needs of postbellum society: it provided a new national architecture that seemed appropriate to the modern age, and it helped European Americans transcend the oppressive cultural and racial weight of European, Near Eastern, and, later, Asian architectural precedents.

Concerned that the roots of European American culture were shallow, American architectural critics in the 1870s worked to turn this newness to America's advantage by seeing the country's lack of architectural precedents legitimating the selective borrowing from the most valued styles of the past. The prominent architect and critic Henry Van Brunt noted in 1876, "We Americans occupy a new country, having no [European American] inheritance of ruins and no embarrassments of tradition in matters of architecture." Americans, lacking physical reminders of a cultured past, were free to appreciate how "all the past is ours; books, engravings, photographs, have so multiplied, that at any moment we can turn to and examine the architectural achievements of any age or nations." He concludes that "where architectural monuments and traditions have accumulated to the vast extent that they have in modern times, the question is not whether we shall use them at all, but how we shall choose among them, and to what extent shall such choice be allowed to influence our modern practice."[33] Echoing Van Brunt's assessment, an editorial in the *American Architect* in 1877 claimed that the very profusion of sources available to American architects "seems to lay on us the duty of utilizing them."[34] In 1878 the same editors argued that the selective assemblage of older architectural elements "inevitably gathers to itself more or less modern characteristics; and the results are an eclectic work belonging to the latter half of the nineteenth century, as is proper."[35]

The lack of a European American architectural tradition, the plethora of available source material, and the heterogeneity of the U.S. population all seemed to justify architectural eclecticism. As Austin Bierbower wrote in the *Penn Monthly,* a literary journal, "we are in a new country, far off from any other, with new resources and new wants, composed of the people of all other countries, so that there is no reason why there should not be, from this fusion of national elements, a new product in [architectural] style superior to any of the others."[36] Scores of architectural critics embraced Bierbower's sentiment. One observer explained "our present conglomerate of architecture" by the "many different nationalities" that make up the population. Another attributed American eclecticism to "the mixed nationalities and sympathies of our people, and our free intercourse with many nations."[37]

None of the authors I quote here was interested in reviving archaeologically accurate historical styles; for each of them, mining past traditions meant selectively recombining older designs into a national architecture appropriate to contemporary America. As Bierbower explains, in an American style "all the [foreign architectural] elements could be used, in small proportions indeed, but in great numbers and variety" to provide an "appearance of richness."[38] Seeing evidence for a national style in eclectic domestic architecture, another critic claimed that "the combination of [styles] . . . makes the distinctiveness, for the features just named are . . . all derived from European sources."[39] Eclecticism borrowed the forms but not the rules of previous architectural systems so that eclectic structures expressed European American identity in heterogeneity and accumulation rather than in a consistent look. An anonymous critic pleading for eclecticism explicitly addressed its lack of a structuring grammar or vocabulary, noting that "whatever the source from which we borrow our expression, the essential characteristic of our work is modern, and it does not in reality differ so fundamentally from that of our neighbor who selects his form of expression from a precedent as far removed from our own choice as Gothic is removed from Renaissance; . . . they both possess all the distinctive characteristics of that first of the great eclectic eras of architecture, the nineteenth century."[40] Given that we live today in a world still haunted by modernist concepts of originality, it is difficult to imagine how an eclectic amalgam of sources might signal either nationalism or modernity, but for nineteenth-century American and English audiences, buildings such as Furness and Hewitt's Pennsylvania Academy, William Ware and Henry Van Brunt's Memorial Hall at Harvard University (1865–78), and H. H. Richardson's Trinity Church in Copley Square in Boston (1872–77) did just that.

European Americans defending eclecticism frequently denigrated what they saw as "creative," or even "original," architectural paradigms. Because eclecticism was understood to draw from a range of "original" styles, its positive qualities were defined ironically in opposition to the secondary styles from which it drew. Van Brunt saw this architectural opposition in decidedly hierarchical terms, writing that "it must not be forgotten that the most essential distinction between the arts of primitive barbarism and those of civilization is that, while the former are original and independent, and consequently simple, the latter must be retrospective, naturally turning to tradition and precedent, and are therefore complex."[41] In 1878 an anonymous architectural critic implicitly expanded on Van Brunt's ideas, claiming that "only two kinds of originality are possible in [architecture]. One is the originality which begins with no acquirement or habit; develops its own forms and methods in native experimental ways. This is the originality of barbarous art; . . . it is manifestly impossible in any people which has the appliances of civilized life. . . . The other kind of originality, the only kind which is possible or desirable in a high civilization, is that of thoroughly trained artists, whose skill is cumulative, advancing step by step from the mastery of old forms to the development of new."[42] When European American viewers stood before the academy building, they saw a structure whose civilized qualities were signaled by the architects' facility in recombining past architectural precedents *and* by the barbarism resonant in the architectural forms brought together in the structure's design.

The eclecticism of the academy—its assemblage of elements understood as the products of racially inferior peoples—constructed no new system for imagining European American identity. Instead, it provided a new outlet for a long-standing impulse. I have already pointed to John Davis's work, which considers how European American conceptions of Jews and Muslims aided in the construction of American identity, but one might just as fruitfully consider Philip Deloria's analysis of the European American use of Indian symbols and costumes, or Michael Rogin's discussion of the Jewish embrace of blackface, to see the widespread use of racial others in fashioning both American whiteness and nationalism. On the architectural front, the design and arrangement of American expositions increasingly invoked racial others to articulate imperial, national, and racial identity during the time when eclecticism emerged as a dominant style in the United States. Scholars ranging from Robert Rydell to Alan Trachtenberg have detailed the ways in which late-century American fairs articulated a hierarchy of civilizations through the use of particular architectural styles and colors; the arrangement of national displays in racial clusters; the banishment of supposedly inferior cultures to the margins of exhibition halls and fairgrounds; the exclusion of many nonwhite exhibitors, construction workers, and even attendees; and the presentation of nonwhite peoples in ways that confirmed racial stereotypes held by European Americans.[43] In the words of an 1876 newspaper account of the Centennial Exposition in Philadelphia, such fairs managed "to carry the spectator through the successive steps of human progress," with whites, predictably, epitomizing the ultimate step.[44]

The racial politics of international fairs became more pointed in the final third of the century, according to the historian Curtis Hinsley, when national and international expositions routinely included archaeological and ethnographic displays. Augmenting the standard practice of highlighting national aspirations by exhibiting raw materials extracted from distant colonial possessions, fairs now juxtaposed these resources with the manufactured goods produced from them in the home country. Hinsley notes that in a parallel gesture, European and American fairs that followed the Paris Exposition of 1867 supplemented their displays of colonial resources with exhibits of indigenous peoples themselves to visualize their belief in the linear progression of culture and, hence, the superiority of whites. Not only did black, brown, yellow, and red bodies signal everything that whites were not, but, as Hinsley contends, the "exhibition techniques tended to represent [nonwhite] peoples as raw materials" for the creation of civilized societies.[45] In the logic of the expositions, iron ore was to locomotive engines as Filipinos were to whites. By displaying the products and peoples of their own colonies, Europeans and European Americans highlighted the distinctions between nonwhite and white identity and discovered new traits from which they could imaginatively refashion whiteness.

The activities of eclectic architects, blackface performers, and fair orga-
nizers were based on the assumption that European Americans could absorb
and assimilate racially inferior forms and traits before transforming them into
something representative of white culture. A remarkable commencement
address delivered by Dexter Hawkins to the graduating class at Syracuse
University in 1875 voices the unspoken assumptions of whites. He assured his
European American audience that "political power and the arts of civilization
are for the time being entrusted to [our nation]; and while playing its destined
role in the great epic poem of human life, its sister races struggle in vain to
surpass it." He then stated that "the strength of [Anglo-Saxon] blood is manifest in the fact that it crosses with all cognate races, and takes up and absorbs
their good qualities without losing its own identity, or failing to manifest or
obey its own characteristics." In contrast to the Jews described by Warner,
whites, according to Hawkins, had the capacity to intermingle with other
races and emerge enhanced, without their essential nature undergoing change.
In both the architectural and the eugenic rhetoric of the era, European Americans were racial alchemists whose core nature and cultural creations were
simultaneously transforming and fixed.[46]

A number of scholars in recent years, building on the important work of
Edward Said, have argued that the Western fascination with the East should
be read in precisely these terms—less a foil for defining what the West was
not than a means for enlarging its conceptual boundaries. Taking issue with
Said's insistence that Orientalism represented the Western fantasy of an un-
changing East, serving to protect Europeans and European Americans from
the threat of "contamination brought forward . . . by the very existence of
the other," the historian of imperialism John MacKenzie notes that the West
has never read its "others" in exclusively negative terms; they are interesting
for their blend of feared and desired traits. As MacKenzie contends, the use of
Oriental forms illustrates how "the western arts sought contamination at
every turn, restlessly seeking renewal and reinvigoration through contacts
with other traditions" with "both Self and Other . . . locked into processes of
mutual modification."[47] While fashioning a powerful statement of racial imperialism, the academy also tied Christian European Americans to a prized
lineage that stretched back to the founding of monotheism. In so doing, eclecticism communicated the desire of whites to dominate "inferior" foreign races
and to share in various traits associated with those groups. The constitutive
motifs of eclecticism, instead of defining whiteness through its absence, helped
European Americans imagine identity as an amalgam of difference and affinity.

In the case of the Pennsylvania Academy, this dynamic allowed Christian
European Americans to revel in "contaminations," then strongly associated

with Jews and just as forcefully proscribed to proper whites. With Jews as cultural middlemen, Christian European Americans could display furtive, taboo traits whose enjoyment would otherwise have cast doubt on a European American's racial fitness. Much as blacks, historically, have given European Americans access to sensuality and Native Americans have showed them a way to the primitive, Jews have served as an excuse for whites to partake in ostentatious and extravagant display. The architecture and ceremonies of the academy, by invoking Jews—and their attendant stereotypes—could legitimately express an ostentation for which Christian European Americans had previously found fewer outlets.

After parsimony, perhaps no stereotype of the Jew was more firmly ingrained in Gilded Age culture than ostentation. When Henry Hilton famously refused to rent a room in his Saratoga hotel to the Jewish, German-born banker Joseph Seligman in the summer of 1877, he defended his action to reporters by pointing to the Jew's "vulgar ostentation" and "overweening display of condition."[48] The *Nation* did not endorse Hilton's policy of exclusion but supported his racial values, finding that the Jewish "tendency to gaudiness in dress or ornament . . . testifies to the purity of the race and the freshness with which its eye still retains the Oriental passion for brilliancy of costume," and concluding that the resultant "effect in our climate is barbaric and coarse."[49] Two years later Austin Corbin echoed Hilton's logic in explaining his determination to bar Jews from his lavish Coney Island resort: Jews were a "pretentious class" and a "vulgar people," and he had known "but one 'white' Jew in [his] life."[50] In response to the controversy, Corbin created the New York–based *Puck* that produced, in 1879, an image of the Jewish type shunned by fashionable hoteliers (fig. 7.3). During these same years, Nina Morais summed up the late-century attitudes of Christians toward her people, describing in the *North American Review* how "the Jew generically (so runs the ordinary estimate) is an objectionable character, whose shrewdness and questionable dealings in trade enable him to wear large diamonds and flashy clothes. He raises his voice beyond the fashionable key, in a language execrable to the ear of English-speaking people. . . . Mean in pence, he spends his pounds with an ostentation that shocks people."[51]

Several of the most widely reported anti-Semitic incidents in the final quarter of the nineteenth century revolved around admission policies of hotels. During decades when some of the grandest and most opulent structures in the country were built, hotel owners and managers initiated policies to exclude "ostentatious" Jews, who might spoil the pleasure of their white Christian guests.[52] Christian European Americans maintained the symbolic distance between their favorite vacation spots and what they viewed as a racially inferior group, at the moment when the associations of hotels and Jews began

Corbin's "White Jew" and Whiter Jewess.

FIGURE 7.3. Joseph Keppler, Corbin's "White Jew" and Whiter Jewess, detail from "Hints for the Jews, Several Ways of getting to Manhattan Beach." *Puck*, July 30, 1879, 328–29.

to converge, by deeming the gross display of Jews incompatible with hotel life. This symbolic distancing freed whites to disparage the "vulgar ostentation" and "pretentious" nature of Jews and at the same time admire hotels "built of huge slabs of marble in true Babylonian magnificence," where "everything within it simply drips with gold, silk, and velvet . . . and the opulence spill[s] over the brim like bubbles in a glass of champagne."[53] It is revealing that Corbin restricted admission to his Manhattan Beach Hotel, described by contemporaries as "a monster" resort, "the largest sea-side structure in the world, . . . [employing] 1,000 servants and attaches," a place that Theodore Dreiser recalled from his youth as populated by a "prosperous" and "showy" clientele.[54] Not simply lavish, Corbin's hotel exuded a decidedly Oriental flavor because of the architect's decision to place its picnic area in the relocated Moorish fantasy that Furness originally constructed to house the Brazilian Pavilion at the Philadelphia Centennial Exhibition.[55]

In convincing themselves that the most lavish—and often exotic—hotels were not appropriate for Jews, European Americans displaced the negative associations of opulence onto a people who were safely excluded, allowing whites to enjoy their ostentatious vacations without the fear of taint. In the case of the academy as well, Jews offered cultural "cover" for Christians who wanted to break away from the sober simplicity of Philadelphia's architectural heritage and revel in forms that were acceptable largely because they were understood to be other. The often-described "richness" and "enormity" of the academy, with its "elaborately decorated" and "showy exterior," flowing "with veins of gold," would have been difficult to swallow had not it been safely cloaked in the aura of an Eastern fantasy.[56]

Having considered how eclecticism made use of architectural forms associated with racially inferior and nonwhite peoples to serve the interests of Christian European Americans, I want to consider why eclecticism became the dominant style through which whiteness was articulated by Philadelphia architects, patrons, and critics during the 1870s and early 1880s, and how it overcame the potentially destabilizing association of whites with inferior peoples. Since European Americans of the era had recourse to a number of architectural styles that supported their racial interests (even as the racial coding of each was rooted in distinct intellectual contexts), we must consider not simply what made the racial meanings of eclecticism possible but what made them appealing at this particular historical moment. I suspect that the eclecticism of Furness and Hewitt owed its popularity and persistence in Philadelphia to its use of unthreatening national and racial sources. Christian European Americans regarded the sources as benign either because the peoples with whom the motifs originated were seen as white (or white enough) or because they were largely absent.

In her study of how multiracial environments influence white identity, the ethnographer Pamela Perry found that contemporary European Americans think through their identities as white using symbols associated with visible minorities, and that use of such symbols is partially guided by the depth and nature of their day-to-day interactions with minority peoples. Perry set out to explore how intimate, routine processes (rather than structural forces) affect the construction of racial self-identification. She pursued her research as a participant observer at two California high schools during the mid-1990s— one suburban and largely white, and the other urban and racially mixed. European Americans, she found, are much more likely to embrace perceptible signs of black culture, such as hip-hop clothing, rap music, or vernacular speech and manners, when their real-life contacts with African Americans are limited.

For her segregated white subjects, African American styles denoted "toughness" or "coolness" rather than "blackness" per se, and they were adopted with little consideration of their racial implications for minority populations. Most of the white (and nonwhite) students in the predominantly white school accepted the European American adoption of attributes associated with minority cultures as little more than a fashion choice. Careful to examine how racial values spoke through such acts of appropriation, regardless of the students' conscious understandings, Perry illustrates how an individual's racial environment alters expressions of whiteness. European American students in diverse communities appropriated black, Latino, and Asian styles less frequently, but they understood such borrowings as charged with racial overtones—signifying political alliance or sympathetic identification with the minority groups. In settings with significant minority representation, appropriation was a conscious and conspicuous act.[57]

The link Perry discovered between the meaning of appropriated styles and the extent of European American contact with minority peoples may help to explain the Pennsylvania Academy's appeal for whites in the 1870s. Philadelphia, like every other urban center of the era, required a stream of immigrant (and African American) laborers to sustain its industries. But lacking the scale of industrial production that dominated the economies of its northeastern and midwestern neighbors, Philadelphia attracted the smallest percentage of foreign-born residents of any large city in the United States. In 1870, the peak of its immigrant influx, a mere 27 percent of Philadelphia's inhabitants had been born abroad, compared with 48 percent in Chicago, 47 percent in Milwaukee, 44.5 percent in both New York City and Detroit, 42 percent in Cleveland, 35 percent in Boston, and 32 percent in Pittsburgh.[58] Philadelphia had fewer Irish Catholics, Italians, Poles, Russians, and Jews than any other metropolitan area, which led European Americans to refer to it as the most "American" city—meaning, of course, the most white.[59]

Despite a continuous presence in Philadelphia stretching back to the time of William Penn, Jews accounted for less than 2 percent of the city's more than eight hundred thousand residents when Furness and Hewitt's academy opened its doors to the public in 1876.[60] The relative paucity of Jews made the Near Eastern narratives of the academy acceptable to Christian European Americans, for without a significant Jewish presence, Oriental motifs suggested neither the alliance nor an identification of Christians with Jews. Christians were free to revel in architectural, ceremonial, and artistic fantasies of a racial other that expanded whiteness without coupling them to a living people who were habitually disparaged. Recall that Warner was preoccupied with the racial link of Jesus to Jews only as his contact with Jews increased in the Holy Land; at his home in Hartford, symbolic ties to an ancient people surely caused considerably less concern.

Christians may have accepted Saracenic motifs in the academy more readily because there were so few Jews in Philadelphia and because of their relative visibility. This may sound contradictory. Most scholars of American Jewry have argued that German Jews—the majority of Philadelphia's Jewish population during the 1870s—assimilated quickly into American society because their Reform Judaism was palatable to Christians and because they adopted Christian European American customs in dress, social habits, and business.[61] Thus one might claim that the subdued profile of Philadelphia's Jews promoted the Christian European American embrace of an eclectic design that used Oriental motifs. But evidence suggests that in some contexts the *invisibility* of Jews concerned Europeans and European Americans more than Jewish visibility.

The historian Patrick Girard and the sociologist Zygmunt Bauman have both made a compelling case for the link between the rise of anti-Semitism in nineteenth-century Europe and the growing invisibility of Jews over the previous two centuries. Bauman contends that the historical visibility of Jews was crucial to Christians because the observable signs of cultural and physiognomic difference stood for millennia as signs of Jewish estrangement from Christianity, and because such alienation has long been a central means by which Christians have imagined who they were. Consequently, anything that threatened to question Jewish estrangement or reconcile Jews and Christians menaced the very core of Christian identity. When in the eighteenth and nineteenth centuries modernity swept away centuries of legal and social restrictions that had barred Jews from either religious or cultural assimilation, the outward marks of Jewish difference began to wane and Christian self-definition became more problematic.[62]

Philadelphia's small population of German Jews did not simply blend into Christian American society in the 1870s but embraced Saracenic designs to link themselves to an imagined past and perhaps to distinguish themselves visually from their Christian neighbors at a time when their national, cultural, and theological distinctness was eroding. As an unintended corollary, the Jewish acceptance of Saracenic forms aided Christians by reassuring them of their essential difference and by giving them a new architectural idiom that broadened the socially acceptable range of Christian European American attributes. Visibility was reassuring only because Philadelphia's Jewish population was small and sufficiently similar to the larger Christian population to appear nonthreatening. In many ways, the visibility of German Jews was appealing because it belied the reality of racial and cultural sameness. When Polish and Russian Jews flooded into American urban centers roughly two decades later, their visibility caused grave concern, for it was understood to reflect significant cultural, religious, and racial differences. In the 1870s, however, German Jews provided an unthreatening source of raw materials for the evolving construct of whiteness.

Because the spatial dimension of buildings complicates the perception of their formal attributes, to make sense of a structure entails considering how viewers experienced its exterior and interior spaces. Such spatial issues generated one of the earliest controversies associated with the construction of the new Pennsylvania Academy, for as soon as the directors purchased the lot at the southwest corner of North Broad and Cherry streets in 1870, a member of the board resigned in protest. The industrialist and inventor Joseph Harrison, who had favored a location on Lemon Hill in Fairmount Park, claimed that "no one would pass the barrier of the public buildings onto North Broad Street."[63] Harrison's objection reflected the popular perception of a European American elite that the center city region north of Market Street (the main north-south dividing line of Philadelphia) was not an acceptable address for an academy of fine art. The many tourist guidebooks to the city that described the academy and its surroundings in the mid-1870s reinforced such a view. One noted in 1876 that moving just a block or two north of Market,

> one encounters an interruption of the usual magnificent display of Broad Street—a region of warehouses and lumber-yards, which once threatened to be permanent, but to which the removal of the railroad tracks from Broad Street gave a death blow: so that we may now hope to see their places occupied before long by structures in keeping with the magnificent plan of the street. Nevertheless, it must be confessed that, at the present writing, Broad Street from Arch to Callowhill is *not* a pleasant through fare. The new Academy of Fine Arts, at Broad and Cherry, will do much for this part of the street.[64]

Other guidebooks similarly describe Broad Street north of Market as a crude "industrial" region of "warehouses, shops, lumber yards," claiming that "the only building of note in this part of the street is the new *Academy of Fine Arts*."[65]

The late nineteenth-century photographs and prints of North Broad confirm the industrial character of the region. Like the academy building itself, D. P. S. Nichols' Broad St. Horse & Carriage Bazaar was built in 1876 in anticipation of the crowds that were to flood Philadelphia for the centennial celebrations. The stable was located on North Broad just across Cherry from the academy. A block north of the stable, on North Broad, at the intersection of Race, visitors would have found H. Huhr's Sons watch and jewelry factory. And intrepid travelers venturing two blocks farther north would have entered the Bush Hill District, the industrial heart of Philadelphia near the end of the century. Here was the massive terminal of the Philadelphia & Reading Railroad; William Seller's and Company, manufacturer of shafting and large industrial tools; and the Baldwin Locomotive Works, the city's single largest manufacturer, occupying acres of land.[66]

Harrison clearly believed that the region would drag down the institution, while many guidebook authors imagined that the academy might improve the street. In both cases, European Americans perceived a clash between the commercial and industrial identity of the neighborhood and the cultural aspirations of the institution. For the middle- and leisure-class European Americans whose carriages wended through the commercial region to reach their temple of art, the unavoidable juxtaposition of crass commerce and fine art was surely jarring. Modern readers may well think the juxtaposition fitting; how appropriate that the nearly half-million dollars required to construct the edifice came from commercial and industrial profits that a rising generation of businessmen—such as Harrison himself—donated to the academy in the late 1860s and 1870s, and that the physical structure rose from a commercial region that emblematized the source of those funds.[67] Gilded Age audiences, of course, could not have perceived this link; for them the disjunction between commercial and artistic culture was to be resolved by time and the improvement of the street, but also through the design of the building.

Gallery visitors in the 1870s came upon an academy that towered over a sea of unimposing two-story brick commercial structures. A short flight of steps climbs from the street in front of the massive academy to its two entrances (fig. 7.4), on either side of an imposing central column that bisects a shallow arch; nestled on each side of the column are comparatively narrow doorways, each capped with a trefoil arch. Just beyond the doorways is a shallow, dark vestibule that leads, through another bisected arch (fig. 7.5), to a second shallow archway, which, in turn, leads into the massive central stair hall, illuminated by a giant skylight. Intriguingly, the sequence of double and single arches through which one enters from the street is repeated (in reverse) as one passes through the interior vestibule: large shallow arch, then two arches nestled within a bisected arch on the exterior, followed by a second set of bisected arches, which precedes another shallow arch on the interior.

Period audiences knew that the sequence of bisected and shallow arches moved them through space in a manner that had a significant influence on their experience of the academy. After expressing admiration, but also exasperation, with the eclecticism of the building's facade in 1876, one critic concluded that "when we once have passed the impending triple-arch, and

FIGURE 7.4. Furness and Hewitt, northeast façade of the Pennsylvania Academy of the Fine Arts, Philadelphia, 1872–76.

gotten within the building we forget and forgive the absurdities of the exterior in admiration of the perfect and exact fitness of every part of the interior."[68] The critic characterizing the bisected arches nestled within a larger arch (his "triple-arch") as "impending" suggests its menacing quality, probably produced by its unorthodox central column, which hinted at structural instability, and its physical funneling of patrons through a passageway that is surprisingly narrow, off center, and dark, in contrast to the size, symmetry, and brightness of the structure's facade. But having passed through the arch, the critic finds relief in the "perfection" and "fitness" of the interior. Writing in the same year, a second critic focused on the sequence of interior arches: "Once within the vestibule . . . one is seized with a strong desire to knock away a pier which obstructs, in a most unreasonable manner, the view of a

FIGURE 7.5. Furness and Hewitt, detail of northeast interior passage from vestibule to stair hall of the Pennsylvania Academy of the Fine Arts, Philadelphia, 1872–76. Photo courtesy of Ralph Lieberman. Granted by Ralph Lieberman.

really magnificent stairway. It is also impossible to get a full view of the grand hall until the first landing is reached, but, once there, the lofty splendor of the dome and its supporting arcade is very impressive."[69] Focusing this time on the effect produced by the interior arches, this critic also finds both discomfort in the entryway and visual relief in the passage into the stairway.

Rather than take at face value such assertions that Furness and Hewitt's unusual entrance formed an impediment to the enjoyment of the "perfect" and "magnificent" interior, I want to focus on how the awkward entrance contributed to the creation of an admirable interior effect. It seems likely that the discomfort of a dark vestibule, visual obstructions, a hint of structural distress, and the viewer's positioning off the central axis would only have heightened the pleasure of seeing the orderly and brightly lit stairway and galleries beyond. By jarring spectators at the point of entry, Furness and Hewitt made the subsequent "discovery" of the interior space all the more satisfying. But because the interior sequence of arches reverses the order exhibited on the exterior, patrons may have experienced the entrance beyond the once dim vestibule as an "exit" into another kind of *exterior* space. After passing through a dark foyer, the visitor arrives at an imposing, brightly illuminated stairway, which, as the architects Robert Venturi and Denise Scott Brown observe, "is too big in relation to its immediate surroundings," relating instead "to the great scale of Broad Street outside."[70] The grand central stairway mimicked an exterior space because of its oversized proportions, the inclusion of lamps more suited to an outdoor street setting, and the addition of thousands of tiny silver stars to the deep-blue painted well of the overhead skylight.

The awkward transition from exterior city space to "exterior" academy space signals the distance museum visitors have traveled: from a street that displays a crude clash of commercial and artistic cultures to a stairwell that offers a refined blend of eclectic architectural forms and painted and sculpted high art; from a street that is dirty, chaotic, and loud to a stairwell that is clean, ordered, and quiet; from a street that teems with nonwhites to a stairwell filled with only the most privileged European Americans. In providing a strong contrast between the exterior and interior spaces, and by forcing patrons through an entrance that accentuates the border between these two realms, the academy offers an alternative to the imperfect city beyond its walls. Thus the eclecticism of Furness and Hewitt's academy is less usefully read as a reflection of the social or racial heterogeneity of Gilded Age America than as a means of exerting symbolic control over such diversity. The great strength of eclecticism was that instead of ignoring unsettling social and racial realities, it acknowledged their existence and used them as the raw materials for both expanding the identities of European Americans and asserting their cultural and racial dominance over diasporic peoples. Eclecticism nodded to the reality of late-century America while channeling the perceived dangers of difference for European Americans into symbolically useful outlets. Before rising waves of eastern European and Asian immigration toward the century's close made the style untenable—by bringing European Americans into too close proximity with minorities to allow for the "safe" appropriation of minority symbols—eclecticism harnessed the threatening heterogeneity of the street to serve the interests of European Americans both inside and out of their academy.

NOTES

This essay is an abridged and revised version of Martin A. Berger, "Museum Architecture and the Imperialism of Whiteness," in Sight Unseen: Whiteness and American Visual Culture *(Berkeley: University of California Press, 2005), chapter 3. It is reprinted with the permission of the University of California Press.*

1. For essays and volumes that trace the development of diaspora studies and demonstrate the complexity of the discourse, see Khachig Tölölyan, "The Contemporary Discourse of Diaspora Studies," *Comparative Studies of South Asia, Africa and the Middle East* 27, no. 3 (2007): 647–55; James Clifford, "Diasporas," *Cultural Anthropology* 9, no. 3 (1994): 302–38; Kim D. Butler, "Defining Diaspora, Refining a Discourse," *Diaspora: A Journal of Transnational Studies* 10, no. 2 (2001): 189–219; William Safran, "Diasporas in Modern Societies: Myths of Homeland and Return," *Diaspora: A Journal of Transnational Studies* 1, no. 1 (1991): 83–99; and Jana Evans Braziel and Anita Mannur, eds., *Theorizing Diaspora* (Malden, Mass.: Blackwell Publishers, 2003).

2. J. Miller McKim to Charles McKim, August 2, 1869, Charles Follen McKim Collection, Manuscript Division, Library of Congress; microfilm reel 10, frame 657. For other references to the "Saracenic" character of the synagogue, see James D. McCabe, *Illustrated History of the Centennial Exhibition* (Philadelphia: National Publishing Company, 1876, repr. 1975), 29; *Stranger's Illustrated Pocket Guide to Philadelphia and Surrounding Places of Interest* (Philadelphia: J. B. Lippincott & Co., 1876), 44; and William Syckelmoore, *Syckelmoore's Illustrated Handbook of Philadelphia* (Philadelphia: William Syckelmoore, 1874), 21. While few architectural historians have dealt with the links between architecture and whiteness—or even architecture and race—some suggestive studies include Bernard Tschumi, *Architecture and Disjunction* (Cambridge, Mass.: MIT Press, 1994); Lesley Naa Norle Lokko, ed., *White Paper, Black Marks: Architecture, Race, Culture* (Minneapolis: University of Minnesota Press, 2000); and Craig Evan Barton, ed., *Sites of Memory: Perspectives on Architecture and Race* (New York: Princeton Architectural Press, 2001). For the most compelling discussion of which I am aware, see Leland T. Saito, *Race and Politics: Asian Americans, Latinos, and Whites in a Los Angeles Suburb* (Urbana: University of Illinois Press, 1998), 39–54.

3. In nineteenth-century America, the terms Saracenic, Moorish, and Mohammedan were used interchangeably to signify a style of architecture at least loosely inspired by Near Eastern prototypes that were primarily Islamic. Up until the very end of the century, when Americans invoked the Orient, they referred to the peoples, buildings, and cultures of the Near East, and not those of the Far East, with which many Americans associate the term today.

4. For an architectural survey of Orientalism, see John Sweetman, *The Oriental Obsession: Islamic Inspiration in British and American Art and Architecture, 1500–1920* (Cambridge, UK: Cambridge University Press, 1988); for discussion of Oriental-inspired design in the early part of the nineteenth century, see David Van Zanten, *The Architectural Polychromy of the 1830's* (New York: Garland Publishing, 1977).

5. "Progress of Architecture in the United States," *American Architect and Builders' News*, October 1868, 278.

6. While the earliest Saracenic building in the United States was a private home—Iranistan (1848–65; Bridgeport, Conn.) built by the German-Jewish architect Leopold Eidlitz for P. T. Barnum—the style was usually reserved for commercial and religious structures. On those occasions when it was introduced into domestic architecture, it was typically confined to a smoking or billiard room, or to an artist's studio.

7. Rachel Wischnitzer, *Synagogue Architecture in the United States: History and Interpretation* (Philadelphia: Jewish Publication Society of America, 1955), 77. Wischnitzer credits Keneseth Israel (1864) at Sixth and Brown Streets, Philadelphia, with igniting the Saracenic trend for synagogue design in the United States (67). For references to Jews as perpetually alien and outside of historical developments, see Joseph Henry Allen, *Hebrew Men and Times from the Patriarchs to the Messiah* (Boston: Roberts Brothers, 1879), 425; Anna L. Dawes, *The Modern Jew: His Present and Future* (Boston: D. Lothrop and Company, 1886), 41; and David A. Gerber, ed., *Anti-Semitism in American History* (Urbana: University of Illinois Press, 1986), 103–28.

8. *Stranger's Illustrated Pocket Guide,* 98; *Magee's Centennial Guide of Philadelphia* (Philadelphia: R. Magee & Son, 1876), 29.

9. McCabe, *Illustrated History of the Centennial,* 152.

10. Wischnitzer, *Synagogue Architecture,* 60–61; for more on the reforms at Rodeph Shalom, see Malcolm H. Stern, "National Leaders of Their Time: Philadelphia's Reform Rabbis," in *Jewish Life in Philadelphia, 1830–1940,* ed. Murray Friedman, 179–97 (Philadelphia: Ishi Publications, 1983).

11. Michael J. Lewis, *Frank Furness: Architecture and the Violent Mind* (New York: W. W. Norton & Company, 2001), 77–78; James O'Gorman, *The Architecture of Frank Furness* (Philadelphia: Philadelphia Museum of Art, 1973), 32; and George E. Thomas, Michael J. Lewis, and Jeffrey A. Cohen, *Frank Furness: The Complete Works* (New York: Princeton Architectural Press, 1991), 68. Because the commission for the synagogue is likely to have resulted through the familial connections of Frank Furness—not only was his German-speaking brother, Horace, on good terms with the synagogue's new German-born rabbi, but his father was a close friend of Rebecca Gratz, a long-time congregant—it is generally assumed that the firm's senior partner, John Fraser, left the design of the structure to his two junior partners. Lewis, *Frank Furness,* 77; Thomas, Lewis, and Cohen, *Frank Furness,* 68. John Sweetman takes the use of Orientalist forms by European Jews as a statement of pride in a Near Eastern origin and as a means to distance themselves from European traditions. Sweetman, *The Oriental Obsession,* 287, 252–53.

12. In a lecture delivered for the Latrobe Chapter of the Society for Architectural Historians in Washington, D.C., titled "Discourse of Civilizations: 'Islamic' Architectural Forms and Concepts in Western Architecture and Decoration, 1800–1950" (February 12, 2003), the architectural historian Mehrangiz Nikou postulated eight factors influencing the Jewish embrace of what she termed "neo-Islamic" architecture during the nineteenth century: the strong associations of both Gothic and Romanesque architecture with Christianity; the abstract decorative program of Saracenic design, which met the Jewish prohibition of graven images; perception of the medieval Spanish era as a golden age for Jews; desire for a strong architectural expression as the first synagogues were built outside of ghettos; tendency of nineteenth-century audiences to see architecture as an expression of race; the style's appropriateness based on the shared Semitic heritage of Jews and Arabs; desire for a spiritual connection to the Holy Land through geographically appropriate architectural forms; and association of the style with a neonational Jewish identity.

13. Furness and Hewitt's building became the third home of the academy, replacing Richard Gilpin's building (1846–47), which had itself replaced the original structure designed by John Dorsey (1805–06).

14. For reference to Native American rug patterns incorporated into the decorative program of the academy's facade, see Hyman Myers, "Three Buildings of the Pennsylvania Academy," *Antiques* 121, no. 3 (March 1982): 682.

15. O'Gorman, *Architecture of Frank Furness,* 35; Myers, "Three Buildings," 682; Zeynep Çelik, *Displaying the Orient: Architecture of Islam at Nineteenth-Century World's Fairs* (Berkeley: University of California Press, 1992), 168; Lewis, *Frank Furness,* 95; and Sweetman, *Oriental Obsession,* 238. For the most comprehensive consideration of the academy's links to Islamic architecture, see Anne Monahan, " 'Of a Doubtful Gothic': Islamic Sources for the Pennsylvania Academy of the Fine Arts," *Nineteenth Century* 18, no. 2 (Fall 1998): 28–36.

16. "Centennial Exposition Memoranda," *Potter's American Monthly* 7 (November, 1876): 316.

17. Helen Henderson, *The Pennsylvania Academy of the Fine Arts and Other Collections of Philadelphia* (Boston: L. C. Page & Company, 1911), 10; see also "History of the Pennsylvania Academy to 1876" in the "Pennsylvania Academy of the Fine Arts Records, 1805–1976," Archives of American Art, microfilm reel P50, frame 743.

18. *American Architect and Builders' News,* March 4, 1876, 80; *American Architect and Builders' News,* May 6, 1876, 145.

19. "The First American Art Academy: First Paper," *Lippincott's Magazine,* February 1872, 143; also see Fannie Warner Bicknell, "Pennsylvania Academy of the Fine Arts," *The Evening Star,* April 14, 1876, in the clipping file on the Furness and Hewitt building in PAFA Archives, Philadelphia.

20. For the context of Reverend Furness's citation, "Let the Beauty of the Lord our God be upon us," see *Inauguration of the New Building of the Pennsylvania Academy of the Fine Arts* (Philadelphia: Pennsylvania Academy of the Fine Arts, 1876), 18. Reporters following the opening ceremonies showed an invariable interest in the unveiling. The editors of the *American Architect and Builders' News* (May 6, 1876, 145) wrote that "an exhibition of more than usual interest signalizes the opening of the building, of which the most interesting feature is the unveiling of Story's statue of Jerusalem, that has just been presented to the Academy." The *Philadelphia Inquirer* (April 24, 1876, 2) commented that after a speech by Frank's father, the Reverend William Henry Furness, "two magnificent statues, that of 'Jerusalem' by Story, and 'Deborah,' by Lombardi, were unveiled." And the *Art Journal* (2, no. 18 [June 1876], 192) described that "at the conclusion of the address Story's statue of 'Jerusalem,' and Lombardi's statue of 'Deborah,' were unveiled. . . . [*Deborah*] is a beautiful figure, in pearly-white marble, and attracted much attention." See also "The Philadelphia Academy Exhibition," *Art Journal* 2, no. 19 (July 1876): 222–23. There is only one extant photographic illustration of *Deborah* (a currently unlocated work) taken in 1937 after the sculpture was damaged by a hammer-wielding assailant.

21. For the importance of the ancient Israelites to nineteenth-century Americans, see John Davis, *The Landscape of Belief: Encountering the Holy Land in Nineteenth-Century American Art and Culture* (Princeton, N.J.: Princeton University Press, 1996), especially 13–26. During the 1870s, an article appearing in the *Saturday Evening Post* claimed that Moroccan Jews "are the descendants of those Moors whose labors and success . . . are still visible round Grenada," while another noted that the Jews of Syria are "Arabs in language, habits, and occupations, in so far at least as religion will permit." "Return of the Jews," *Saturday Evening Post* 57, no. 23 (December 29, 1877): 8; and "The Jews," *Saturday Evening Post* 55, no. 15 (November 6, 1875): 7.

22. For studies that discuss the nonwhite status of Jews, see Karen Brodkin, *How Jews Became White Folks & What that Says about Race in America* (New Brunswick, N.J.: Rutgers University Press, 1998); and Matthew Frye Jacobson, *Whiteness of a Different Color: European Immigrants and the Alchemy of Race* (Cambridge, Mass.: Harvard University Press, 1998). For arguments disputing the idea that Jews ever occupied a nonwhite identity in American society, see the journal of *International Labor and Working-Class History* 60 (Fall 2001), which is dedicated to a critical reassessment of whiteness studies; especially Eric Arnesen, "Whiteness and the Historians' Imagination," 3–32; Eric Foner, "Response to Eric Arnesen," 57–60.

23. For more on the shifting whiteness of Arabs in United States immigration law, see Ian F. Haney López, *White by Law: The Legal Construction of Race* (New York: New York University Press, 1996), 76, 106, 204–05, 212–13. While granted citizenship, Jews were not necessarily accorded all the rights of citizens. Leonard Dinnerstein notes that a number of eastern states required oaths acknowledging the divinity of Christ for voting up into the nineteenth century. In Leonard Dinnerstein, "Antisemitism in Crisis Times in the United States: The 1920s and 1930s," in *Anti-Semitism in Times of Crisis,* ed., Sander L. Gilman and Steven Katz, 213 (New York: New York University Press, 1991). For a discussion of anti-Semitism in early Philadelphia, see William Pencak, "Jews and Anti-Semitism in Early Pennsylvania," *Pennsylvania Magazine of History and Biography* 126, no. 3 (July 2002): 365–408.

24. The phrase "provisional whites" is taken from Jacobson, *Whiteness of a Different Color.* Also see James R. Barrett and David Roediger, "Inbetween Peoples: Race, Nationality and the 'New Immigrant' Working Class," *Journal of American Ethnic History* 16, no. 3 (Spring 1997): 3–44.

25. See Ronald Takaki, *Iron Cages: Race and Culture in Nineteenth-Century America* (New York: Oxford University Press, 1990), 219–20.

26. Jacobson, *Whiteness of a Different Color,* 23–24. For specific reference to how this dynamic impacted Jews, see 172.

27. Thomas C. Holt, *The Problem of Race in the Twenty-First Century* (Cambridge, Mass.: Harvard University Press, 2000), 37–67. Also see Ronald Sanders, *Lost Tribes and Promised Lands: The Origins of American Racism* (Boston: Little, Brown and Company, 1978), 65–73; and Craig R. Prentiss, ed., *Religion and the Creation of Race and Ethnicity: An Introduction* (New York: New York University Press, 2003).

28. Davis, *Landscape of Belief,* 83, also 84–88. Also see Abigail Solomon-Godeau, "A Photographer in Jerusalem, 1855: Auguste Salzmann and his Times," in *Photography at the Dock: Essays on Photographic History, Institutions, and Practices* (Minneapolis: University of Minnesota Press, 1991), 150–68.

29. Charles Dudley Warner, *In the Levant* (Boston: James R. Osgood and Company, 1877), 42–43; also 44–46. Warner is best known today as Mark Twain's collaborator on *The Gilded Age* (1873).

30. William Henry Poole, *Anglo-Israel or the Saxon Race Proved to be the Lost Tribes of Israel* (Toronto: William Briggs, 1880, repr. 1889), 16–17, 673. Also see Edward H. Rogers, *Law and Love, or, The Resemblance and the Difference Between Moses and Christ with a Prophetic Supplement Concerning Anglo-Israel* (Chelsea, Mass.: E. H. Rogers, 1897); Edward Hine, *Forty-Seven Identifications of the British Nation with the Lost Tribes of Israel: Founded Upon Five Hundred Scripture Proofs* (London: W. H. Guest, 1874); and Edward Hine, *Forty-Seven Identifications of the British Nation and the United States with the Lost Ten Tribes of Israel* (London: W. H. Guest, 1879). For the nineteenth-century tradition of reading Christian Western Europeans as the lost tribes of Israel, see Douglas E. Cowan, "Theologizing Race: The Construction of Christian Identity," in *Religion and the Creation of Race and Ethnicity: An Introduction,* ed., Craig R. Prentis, 113–16 (New York: New York University Press, 2003). For a complementary discussion of how late nineteenth-century Jews understood their identity as racialized and attempted to abandon their "Jewish" bodies, see Sander Gilman, *The Jew's Body* (New York: Routledge, 1991), 169–93.

31. For more on how Christian European Americans conceived of the theological roots of Christianity in Judaism, see Sally Promey's discussion of the controversy engendered by the installation of John Singer Sargent's *Synagogue* (1919) in the Boston Public Library. *Painting Religion in Public: John Singer Sargent's Triumph of Religion at the Boston Public Library* (Princeton, N.J.: Princeton University Press, 1999), 174–225.

32. James O'Gorman, *H. H. Richardson: Architectural Forms for an American Society* (Chicago: University of Chicago Press, 1987), 62.

33. Eugène Emmanuel Viollet-le-Duc, *Discourses on Architecture,* trans. with introductory essay by Henry Van Brunt (Boston: James R. Osgood and Company, 1875), x.

34. "Eclecticism in Architecture," *American Architect and Builders' News,* January 15, 1876, 18.

35. *American Architect and Builders' News,* August 1877, 262.

36. Austin Bierbower, "American Architecture," *The Penn Monthly* 8, no. 1 (December 1877): 937.

37. "Architecture in America: Naissant and Renaissant," *The Architectural Review and American Builders' Journal* (April 1869): 613; "Eclecticism in Architecture"; also see Samuel J. Burr, *Four Thousand Years of the World's Progress from the Early Ages to the Present Time* (Hartford, Conn.: L. Stebbins, 1878), 710.

38. Bierbower, "American Architecture," 939.

39. "An American Style," *Sloan's Architect and Builders' Journal* (November 1868): 336.

40. *American Architect and Builders' News,* August 1877, 262.

41. Van Brunt, introductory essay, *Discourses on Architecture,* x. I do not wish to assert that "creative" and "replicative" practices were firmly linked to inferior and superior racial groups respectively, but rather that this strain of thought could be found in the period discourse. If anything, the *dominant* view linked replicative arts and architecture to female and nonwhite groups. After viewing the Chinese and Japanese displays at the Centennial Exhibition, a Congregational minister voiced the standard European American view in claiming that "Christian nations were 'largely inventive,' whereas Asian nations were 'essentially and laboriously *imitative.*'" Quoted in Robert W. Rydell, *All the World's a Fair: Visions of Empire at American International Expositions, 1876–1916* (Chicago: University of Chicago Press, 1984), 31. For the gendering of this equation, see Rozsika Parker and Griselda Pollock, *Old Mistresses: Women, Art and Ideology* (London: Pandora Press, 1989).

42. *American Architect and Builders' News,* August 1877, 262. For an additional reference to the gradual, evolutionary nature of "proper" architectural development, see James Ferguson, *A History of Architecture in All Countries from the Earliest Times to the Present Day,* vol. 1 (New York: Dodd, Mead, and Company, 1874), 45.

43. Rydell, *All the World's a Fair;* and Alan Trachtenberg, *The Incorporation of America: Culture and Society in the Gilded Age* (New York: Hill and Wang, 1982). For a fascinating contemporary example of how European Americans make use of nonwhite architectural forms to signal whiteness, see Saito, *Race and Politics,* 39–54.

44. Quoted in Rydell, *All the World's a Fair,* 20.

45. Curtis M. Hinsley, "The World as Marketplace: Commodification of the Exotic at the World's Columbian Exposition, Chicago, 1893," in *Exhibiting Cultures: The Poetics and Politics of Museum Display,* ed. Ivan Karp and Steven D. Levine, 345 (Washington, D.C.: Smithsonian Institution Press, 1991).

46. Dexter A. Hawkins, *The Anglo-Saxon Race: Its History, Character, and Destiny: An Address Before the Syracuse University, at Commencement, June 21, 1875* (New York: Nelson & Phillips, 1875), 3, 26; for a related discussion of how Victorians juggled both "civilized" and "barbaric" traits, see Matthew Frye Jacobson, *Barbarian Virtues: The United States Encounters Foreign Peoples at Home and Abroad, 1876–1917* (New York: Hill and Wang, 2000).

47. Edward Said, *Orientalism* (New York: Vintage Books, 1978). Edward Said, *Musical Elaborations* (New York: Columbia University Press, 1991), 52, quoted in John M. MacKenzie, *Orientalism: History, Theory and the Arts* (Manchester, UK: Manchester University Press, 1995), 209. For critiques of Said's work that stress the changing nature and valences of the Orient for the West, see MacKenzie, *Orientalism,* 78, 101, 76–77, 208–15; James Clifford, *The Predicament of Culture* (Cambridge, Mass.: Harvard University Press, 1988), 258, 263–64; and Malini Johar Schueller, *U.S. Orientalism: Race, Nation, and Gender in Literature, 1790–1890* (Ann Arbor: University of Michigan Press, 1998).

48. *New York Tribune,* June 20, 1877, 4.

49. *Nation,* June 28, 1877, 378, quoted in Jacobson, *Whiteness of a Different Color,* 164.

50. Stanley McKenna, "Reviving a Prejudice," *New York Herald,* July 22, 1879, 5; also see *Coney Island and the Jews: A History of the Development and Success of this Famous*

Seaside Resort Together with a Full Account of the Recent Jewish Controversy (New York: C. W. Carleton & Co., 1879). In June of 1879, Hilton and Corbin came together to found the American Society for the Suppression of Jews. In Leonard Dinnerstein, *Antisemitism in America* (Oxford: Oxford University Press, 1994), 40.

51. Nina Morais, "Jewish Ostracism in America," *North American Review* 133, no. 298 (September 1881): 269.

52. David Watkin, *Grand Hotel: The Golden Age of Palace Hotels, An Architectural and Social History* (New York: Vendome Press, 1984), 13–18; and Nikolaus Pevsner, *A History of Building Types* (Princeton, N.J.: Princeton University Press, 1976), 176, 182.

53. This is an 1876 description of the Palmer House hotel in Chicago provided by a European visitor in Charles Morley, ed. and trans., *Portrait of America: Letters of Henry Sienkiewicz* (New York: Columbia University Press, 1959), 50.

54. *Coney Island and the Jews,* 11, 17–18; Theodore Dreiser, *The Color of a Great City* (New York: Boni and Liverlight, 1923), 121.

55. Michael Immerso, *Coney Island: The People's Playground* (New Brunswick, N.J.: Rutgers University Press, 2002), 25.

56. *Magee's Centennial Guide,* 29; Thompson Westcott, *The Official Guide Book to Philadelphia* (Philadelphia: Porter and Coates, 1875), 192; *American Architect and Building News,* May 6, 1876, 145; "Fine Arts: The Pennsylvania Academy," *The Nation,* May 4, 1876, 297–98; "Centennial Exposition Memoranda," *Potter's American Monthly* 7 (November 1876): 316; McCabe, *Illustrated History of the Centennial,* 86–87.

57. Pamela Perry, *Shades of White: White Kids and Racial Identities in High School* (Durham, N.C.: Duke University Press, 2002).

58. Caroline Golab, "The Immigrant and the City: Poles, Italians, and Jews in Philadelphia, 1870–1920," in *The Peoples of Philadelphia: A History of Ethnic Groups, and Lower-Class Life, 1790–1940,* ed. Allen F. Davis and Mark H. Haller, 204 (Philadelphia: Temple University Press, 1998).

59. "Philadelphia: Corrupt and Contented," *McClures,* July 1903, quoted in Golab, "The Immigrant and the City," 203.

60. Murray Friedman, ed., *Jewish Life in Philadelphia, 1830–1940* (Philadelphia: Ishi Publications, 1983), 7, 48; Allen F. Davis and Mark H. Haller, eds., *The Peoples of Philadelphia: A History of Ethnic Groups, and Lower-Class Life, 1790–1940* (Philadelphia: Temple University Press, 1998), 9. Philadelphia's population stood at 817,448 in 1876, according to the city census (conducted to correct undercounting in the national census of 1870), as reported in the *Philadelphia Inquirer,* April 3, 1876, 2.

61. Dinnerstein, *Antisemitism in America,* 39; Friedman, *Jewish Life in Philadelphia,* 6; Louise A. Mayo, *The Ambivalent Image: Nineteenth-Century America's Perception of the Jew* (London: Associated University Presses, 1988), 13–14.

62. Zygmunt Bauman, *Modernity and the Holocaust* (Ithaca, N.Y.: Cornell University Press, 1989), 34–66.

63. "History of the Pennsylvania Academy of the Fine Arts to 1876," typescript in the Archives of American Art, Pennsylvania Academy of the Fine Arts Records, microfilm Roll 50, frame 512. For a brief sketch of Harrison's career in locomotive and

boiler production, and in iron smelting, see his obituary in *Scientific America* 30, no. 16 (November 1, 1874): 248.

64. *Stranger's Illustrated Pocket Guide,* 98.

65. *Syckelmoore's Illustrated Handbook,* 20; McCabe, *Illustrated History of the Centennial,* 29.

66. John K. Brown, *The Baldwin Locomotive Works, 1831–1915* (Baltimore: Johns Hopkins University Press, 1995); Domenic Vitiello, "Engineering the Metropolis: William Sellers, Joseph M. Wilson, and Industrial Philadelphia," *Pennsylvania Magazine of History and Biography* 126, no. 2 (July 2002): 273–303.

67. *Inauguration of the New Building,* 20.

68. "Centennial Exposition Memoranda," 316.

69. "Academy of the Fine Arts, Philadelphia," *Art Journal* 2, no. 19 (July 1876): 202.

70. Robert Venturi, *Complexity and Contradiction in Architecture* (New York: Museum of Modern Art, 1966), 25.

CHAPTER EIGHT

Cultural Forms and World Systems

The Ethnic Epic in the New Diaspora

BETTY JOSEPH

Since the rise of cultural studies, literary critics have shown some discomfort in their conjurings with the novel, especially when trying to get a fix on the contemporary globe. Even within the field of eighteenth-century studies, where immense debates still go on about the origins, prehistories, rise and afterlives of the novel, a scholar has recently suggested that perhaps the attraction of the novel to many literary historians is like that of a "recently deceased dignitary to mourners at a wake, more attractive for past rather than future triumphs."[1] Contributing to this feeling of cultural superseding is the rising tide of multimedia technologies that spell an electronic rather than print future for the book, and the dominance of televisual cultural texts (film and music especially) that seem more adequate to the task of representing the rapidly shifting ground in a globalizing world.

It is not my intention to argue against this trend in this essay or suggest that contrary to these disciplinary musings, the novel is actually getting a new lease on life *somewhere else* as it is undergoing its last gasps in Anglo-American postmodernity. Rather, I will suggest that we may learn something from the partial information the novel provides in its fraught existence in postcolonial and diasporic contexts. The novel, even as it is being picked to pieces by oral and visual technological forms, persists as a cultural form, and its supplementary function vis-à-vis the virtual today reveals what Jacques Derrida has called "a constant reinvestment in the book project."[2] Is there a relationship between the destabilizing tendency of the electronic—virtual borders, identities, and communities—and the seemingly stable immobility of the book in contemporary global cultures?

In this essay, I will look at the continuance of the print novel's cultural functions and its new mutations in diaspora as a setting for reading inadequacies within the new technologies as they try to capture a world system in its totality. Here, in the gaps of representation, we might think of print's supplementary function articulated with and in terms of these new technologies. If the routes of circulation for print capitalism were instrumental in producing the nationalist-imagined communities of the modern era, they still retain a powerful interpellative force for the transnational collectivities of today. Indeed, one might begin to read amidst the more virtualized and shuttling scene of many diasporic collectivities today a continued insistence to write one's displacement and rootedness in the new home through the strategic use of popular print and electronic media. Within these modes of self-expression, the novel and its proponents still retain a symbolic representative power in embodying a so-called collective "experience." However, if there is the hint of a cultural time lag in this proposition (the idea that something survives in diaspora and postcoloniality while it is on its way out in the dominant), the "lag" should not be mistaken as a narrative of "underdevelopment." Rather, I am suggesting that temporal disjunctures are embodied in the very transformations of the novelistic forms themselves and are not to be plotted as the progression of various novelistic forms from simple realism (capitalism) to complex postmodern (globalization). My reading of Canadian-based writer Bhagwan Gidwani's *Return of the Aryans* will thus focus less on the actual content of the novel and more on the curious relationship Indian immigrants in North America have established with it. The novel's avowedly fetish status as the "truth" about ancient India has also provided the occasion to resuscitate old academic debates between historians and literary critics about the fiction/history dyad. It has drawn academic historians and cultural critics into a contest with a particular brand of intellectuals emerging within diasporic communities, like the South Asian Indian, where what might have been considered rigorously researched sources at one time is replaced by websites that circulate doctored images and paraphrased argument from various "experts."

My preliminary questions are these: Why do postcolonial and diasporic contexts seem appropriate breeding grounds for the production of "modern world-epics" (Franco Moretti's phrase) especially when the realist novel, which is hitched to the nation-state's geographical and linguistic boundedness, is still considered the prevailing norm? How do print forms like the novel interface with the supposedly more effective technological media that enable the self-constitution of new diasporas? And finally, how does the novel function as a shuttle between archaic and new forms; between the prenational orality of the epic, for instance, and the transnational, time-space-compressed simultaneity of new technologies like the Internet?

Prenational Communities and Virtual Spaces

As I have stated above, under postmodern globalization the privileged objects of cultural study are increasingly those that have historically superseded older cultural forms like the novel (now commonly associated with the nation-state and national cultures). Because the "shifting demographic frontiers" in the postcolonial and globalizing world do not respect the "territorial frontiers" of capitalism or the modern state, it would seem that telecommunications provide more appropriate forms to fix the virtual, multicultural amalgams of the new "parastate collectivities."³ Yet, as contemporary critics have asserted, in that these parastate collectivities resemble those of prenational, multicultural empires that preceded monopoly capitalism, a historical space opens up where a past is embedded in the present despite the break associated with contemporary globalization. (This break is characterized by the assertion that contemporary globalization is different from the mercantilist world-systems charted, for instance, in the work of Immanuel Wallerstein and Samir Amin.) Furthermore, there is also the obvious question about what allows communities to be fixed for identity politics despite the shifts underway by large-scale migration. In *Specters of Marx,* Derrida offers the term "ontopology" for reading a similar fractured scene: "an axiomatics linking indissociably the ontological value of present-being [*on*] to its *situation,* to the stable and presentable determination of a locality, the *topos* of territory, native soil, city, body in general." It is the "spacing of a displacement [that] gives the movement its start," for all "national rootedness . . . is rooted first of all in the memory or the anxiety of a displaced—or displaceable—population."⁴ The desire to fix being in a place has intensified at the very time that massive dislocations and transfers of peoples have taken place in the twentieth century. This contradictory impulse is one of the ways in which the diasporic may be differentiated from the immigrant.

In the scene of displacement, the immigrant and the diasporic may share a common new home and a country of origin, but they are distinguishable by their distance from the communities to which their belonging is predicated. The immigrant is the one who has come from outside and is still alien or unsettled in the host country, while the diasporic is the one who has left another home, and although interpellated into another community, often parastate, a common experience of parting and scattering from a common place of origin forms the basis of the perceived communal bond. It might, however, be a mistake to imagine that the diaspora is an extension of the old nation of origin, which often successfully continues to call the diasporics to their old community. Indeed what we are seeing now is diasporics who shrink and expand this place of origin and activate several different identities that are not continuous with those in the nation-state. Thus we have a spectrum that may go from South Asian, Indian, Pakistani, Punjabi, or even Sindhi, that is, from subcontinental, national, state, and district groups to linguistic or ethnic groups. Each of these activations will then constitute the diaspora differently for the same person. It is important to emphasize here that the distinction between the diasporic and the immigrant cannot be fully assimilated through the rubric of U.S. multiculturalism (as minority culture), but is a series of negotiations between the loss of the old home and the new one that has not assimilated the immigrant. In this liminal space of belonging and parting, ambivalence can lead to politically progressive strategies or reactionary politics that seek to revert to prenational pasts. In the age of electronic reproduction, the speed and intensity with which ideas and resources cross national boundaries has no doubt created what Arjun Appadurai calls "a new order of uncertainty in social life."[5] In these border crossings, he argues, ethnic groups are not able to fix identities through their mixed cultural styles or media representations; rather the representations only mirror back "profound doubts about who exactly are among the 'we' and who are among the 'they' " (5). The question is whether this uncertainty also indicates an unacknowledged crisis in the ways citizenship has been imagined till late within liberal democratic discourse in Euro-America. Such a line of investigation can displace the often banal assertion of clash of values: that the new waves of immigrants are refusing to assimilate in ways that earlier people with shared European values have done.

Ranajit Guha complicates the notion of the spatial distance between former and new homes when he adds another dimension to the displacement experienced by the immigrant and the diasporic. The displacement, he says,

> is stapled firmly to an accentuated and immediate present cut off from a shared past by the adverbial force of "no longer." A sharp and clean cut, the dismissal leaves its victim with nothing to fall back on, no background where to take umbrage, no actual communitarian links to refer to. For it is in the everyday dealings with one another that people in any society form such links in the present which continually assimilates the past to itself as an experience and looks forward at the same time to a future secure for all. The loss of that present amounts, therefore, to a loss of the world in which the migrant has had his own identity forged.[6]

Being temporally cut off by no longer being part of the present "there" and not yet admitted into the community of the present "here," the diasporic has, Guha adds, "only a prospect which faces him with its undaunting openness" (159). In this "inexorably forward drift," the "past does not float passively as a chunk of frozen time, but functions as experience both activated by and invested in the force of precipitation" (159). Guha rejects any reading of this activated past as "nostalgia," for he argues that this is not a dead past but one that has remained "embedded in its time fully alive like a seed in the soil, awaiting the season of warmth and growth to bring it to germination" (159). As such, this past is nothing other than a "potentiality" ready to be "fertilized" and "deployed" for an anticipated future (159).

This is an incomplete analysis, for Guha does not indicate what utopian deployments of the migrant's past might look like. Instead, he forecloses this "potentiality" by suggesting that all anticipatory and futural deployments are liable to be mistaken for nostalgia and dismissed as alien. The migrant must then "learn to live with this doublebind until the next generation arrives on the scene" (160). What Guha does not also make allowance for in this formulation is the possibility that the diasporic might, in the name of a new community, deploy the past as pedagogy for the new generations in diaspora and, even more so, choose to intervene in the home country that has dismissed him with the adverbial force of "no longer."

In recent years, the growing number of websites and blogs operated by Indian expatriates devoted to debates about the "foreign" versus "indigenous" origins of the Aryan (the Indo-European) inhabitants of the Indian subcontinent indicate that a cultural war of sorts is going on, one that pits people of religion-based politics versus secularists and academics versus organic intellectuals. One of the flashpoints in these debates—the Aryan versus non-Aryan origins of the Mohenjo Daro and Harappa ruins in the Sindh province (in present-day Pakistan)—has set off accusations and counteraccusations between the Indologists and historians (mostly based in elite universities in the United States and India) and the self-appointed "experts" from a ragtag team that historian Romila Thapar describes as "engineers, computer experts, journalist-turned-politicians, foreign journalists posing as scholars of Indology . . . [who] assume infallibility, and pronounce on archaeology and history."[7] It is clear to anyone following Michael Witzel and Romila Thapar's brilliant exposé of one "noted historian's" computer-generated archaeological evidence of horses in Harappa that very often such fabrications are blatant and do not follow any established protocols that govern the rules of research or analysis followed by philologists, archaeologists, or historians. (Horses, an integral part of early Vedic or Aryan culture, have been absent in all archaeological data from these ruins. Thus the evidence of horses, many historians argue, could help establish an Aryan presence there.) The question is why these theories, which attribute an indigenous Aryan Hindu origin to what is properly "Indian culture" (also called "Hindutva history" by scholars who are critical of them), run with astonishing speed throughout cyberspace and find a willing audience that supports the fabrications despite objections from well-respected scholars with credentials that would normally allow them legitimacy as experts. When mainstream, disciplinary history is deemed ideologically biased (or "communist" or "imperialist brainwashing," as the case may be) it is open season for history writing on the Internet. My discussion of Gidwani's novel in this essay intersects with the debate about historical fact versus fiction in a very specific way: *Return of the Aryans,* marketed as "fiction" by Penguin, India, has become a veritable blockbuster among expatriate Indian audiences in North America, and much of the discussion around the book, especially in cyberspace circles, treat it as a history book with little or no reference to its status as a "novel." The Indian immigrants' response to the novel, it seems to me, reveals one important thing: that as far as history making on the Internet is concerned, image enhancements, fabrications, falsifications, simulations, parasiting, and so on do not leave the marks of former erasures—as they might on paper sources or archival documents. Thus versions of history circulate with cut-and-pasted quotations or images without any reference to any original source. The web writers are therefore able to write an eternal history, with a manufactured present, that will forever be new and conveniently available.[8] To tweak the scenario Rey Chow has described in her account of media and migrants in the new diasporas today, historical "reality is now an imperfect copy of its images."[9]

As Michael Witzel's account of the horse hoax tells us, the hoax could play out as long as it did because the original image of the seal that was subsequently doctored was rarely available in library sources anywhere, and it was only by tracking it down and reproducing them side by side that Witzer could finally show how exactly the rump of a bull was modified into a horse![10] But Witzel's response also reveals the supplementarity of print in the electronic world of Hindutva history: the legitimating authority of paper and print remains intact despite Hindutva claims that historical texts are biased. And here we might sense that the Internet mirrors back to its virtual communities the dissipated and potentially disruptive nature of its expansive and expanding boundaries. In this tension between gathering (community) and dispersal (diaspora), the book itself may provide, as Derrida has shown in his discussion of the electronic archive, the appearance of unity and form to the potentially unstable.[11]

Now we turn to a shorthand history of the South Asian diaspora in the United States. This immigrant group has grown in numbers as a result of tele-technological transfers to the West, but the professional base has also meant that the recent pool has activated, with some success, these technological tools for its own identity politics. Because South Asian Indians are a relatively new immigrant group in the United States, access to Internet technologies also makes the connection between "home" and "abroad" subject to new negotiations. In recent studies of the politically energized religious right in India, there is the prevailing argument, by scholars on the left, that just as deindustrialization and marketization have undermined the safeties of the welfare state in Europe, leading to anti-immigrant xenophobia, in the poor, postcolonial South, where such state guarantees were not yet fully established, the collapse of dreams of national progress has led to new strains of old religions. As Achin Vanaik puts it, "the exhaustion of perpetually striving after consumerist goals and the anxiety of never seeing them fulfilled" has produced forms of "consolation" in "aggressive cultural self-assertion."[12] The "opium of the people" is replaced by a slightly different phrasing: "balm for social despair" (55). The challenge for cultural critics then remains at least one—how do we read the function of cultural forms that emerge in this shuttle of globalization, between the dismantling of welfare states here and there that produce similar consequences in the wake of cross-border movements of capital? How do cultural forms of and for diasporic communities form the warp and the woof of other border crossings, this time demographic—of people rather than capital? In that these demographic frontiers can also be imagined as the return of formations more appropriate to precapitalist multicultural empires, how do we capture the semiotic excess that must surely exist in cultural representations that cannot capture this present "realistically"? Is it plausible that cultural forms like the novel or the epic, associated with the national and the prenational formations appearing in new permutations, stage the overlay of an older world-system with the new globalizing world? And finally, what is the residual function of printed cultural forms like the novel in the relay between the orality of the epic and the virtuality of the electronic text—not only in its historically progressive function but also as a way of representing the contemporary globe?

Just as Derrida asserts the startling return of ontopology as an outdated form of grounding identity seemingly incommensurate in the globalizing world, Vanaik talks of the "telescoping" of history by religious right political organizations in India (55). The choice of this metaphor enables us to see the drawing in of the historical past for cultural judgment on people who live in the present. Thus for the Hindu neofascist organization RSS (Rashtriya

Swayamsevak Sangh, or National Volunteer Corps) the imperative is to make present-day Muslims responsible for the Mughal rule of centuries past. This is done partly by summoning ancient emblems into the contemporary popular consciousness; a working mosque was pulled down in 1992 because it was purportedly built on a Hindu temple razed by an intolerant sixteenth-century Muslim ruler. The mobilization to rebuild the temple was seen by many as an attempt to reclaim and overcome that history of religious subjugation in the past. Eighty percent of India is Hindu, and with a religious government that advocated pogroms and systematic suppression of minority identity politics, the decade of the 1990s eroded the power of nationalist secularism as a common ideology in nation building. In other words, one is not only seeing assertions of ontopology but also (to tweak a term from Bakhtin) a chronotopology. In these telescopings, we can also see that the historical imperative for the use of cultural pasts for the present is a phenomenon of its own, and once deflected from its place in the postcolony to its new organizing in the new diasporas, new functions emerge in the self-figurations within cultural forms. Here the Internet as a telecommunicative, cultural form and the epic novel as a sort of chronotopology may run closer than one thinks.

Arjun Appadurai, in charting the "geography of anger," suggests that the "globalization of violence against minorities" enacts a "deep anxiety about the national project and its own ambiguous relationship to globalization" (44). Thus the new kinds of migration, both elite and proletarian, that allow great transfers of capital and labor, contrary to producing more flexible citizenry, are actually creating unprecedented tensions between "identities of origin, identities of residence and identities of aspirations" (44). What Appadurai does not address is how new minorities in the country of residence may direct some of their anger against minorities in their countries of origin. The failure of the second home to slot the newly arrived immigrant from India has created, in recent years, a cultural defensiveness on the part of this largely well-off class (enlarged by the software technology transfers from India in the 1990s). Their minority status in the United States by virtue of religion, race, and language is then exported back to the country of origin. Thus Hindutva politics has always shown a disproportionate Malthusian obsession about Hindus (who are the vast majority of India's population of over a billion people) being overrun by Muslims and other minorities who make up only a small part of the demographic. This minority syndrome among Hindutva sympathizers in the United States (and also Canada) now allows the perception of Hindus back "home" as a beleaguered and endangered species. Although Hindutvas have significant political backing in India, they are exhorted to act like a minority to save Hindu culture, religion, and values. Such a reversal (and this is where Guha comes back into the picture) is also accompanied by a deployment of the past, which eschews the nationalist-secularist, postcolonial project initiated by the Nehru-Gandhi generation and puts in its place a new, purer prenational, precolonial, and "prehistoric" past in order to assert a common "now" that reconnects the motherland with the diaspora. This temporal deployment by the diaspora is what I have called "epic" earlier in this paper. The displacement is also spatial. The past cannot be imagined in a way that is bounded by the modern boundaries of the nation-state drawn by the erstwhile colonial power, Britain. Rather, there are assertions of a community that is parastate as well as prenational in its origin. The imagined community of the epic that predates the nation-state, capitalism, and the realist novel is now realized in the wake of new demographic frontiers that are part of today's "virtual realities." Here the literary form, the novel, as epic, brings back in this repetition with a displacement, the function of the diaspora as a global collectivity that is made possible precisely by virtue of accelerated media technologies that do not have to depend on the circulation of print (as they did for the nation-state). Yet as my discussion of the diasporic novel—Bhagwan Gidwani's *Return of the Aryans*[13]—will show, while the Internet has helped in the creation of a Hindutva political agenda among diasporic South Asians, the novel still actualizes deployments of the prenational, precolonial pasts in the function of an anticipated future in the mother country and in diaspora.

Return of the Aryans

Bhagwan Gidwani, perhaps better known as the author of *The Sword of Tipu Sultan,* now lives in Montreal. A copy of his 1994 novel *Return of the Aryans* was recently donated to the main library at my home institution, Rice University. The donors' inscription on the title page tells us that the benefactors are two physicians of Indian origin and that the book has been "presented" by the American Institute of Sindhulogy. A website is provided for reference in this inscription.[14] If you look at the website, you will see inscriptions and monuments from Mohenjo Daro, the immense complex of urban settlements whose historic origin is still up for grabs, but largely accounted for in textbook histories as evidence of pre-Vedic or non-Aryan peoples in the Indian subcontinent dating back to 5000 BC. Mohenjo Daro now lies in postpartition space, in the district of Sindh within largely Muslim Pakistan and not India. This archaeological site has always been and still remains the focus of heated debates about national origins. The stakes are high because if the Mohenjo Daro civilization is pre-Aryan then the subcontinent cannot be the originary space for upper-caste

Hindus who have been recoded as Sanskritic Aryans by Orientalist philologists and historians since the nineteenth century.

The website of the American Institute of Sindhulogy also lists its main objectives: the "Promotion of Awareness in North America and elsewhere about Indus Valley and Saraswati Civilization and its unique contribution to world culture, education and peace."[15] To aid in this pedagogy, the website has excerpted several sections from *Return of the Aryans*. Included on its website in August 2006 was a review of the novel by a maverick lawyer, Ram Jethmalani, who was once a minister of law and justice in the Indian Bharatiya Janata Party (BJP) government. The title of the review, "An Odyssey," invokes again the epic status of the novel, and the reviewer once known for his provocative interpretations of the Indian constitution is now on record telling his readers, "The story, though not [sic] in the form of a novel, is not fiction."[16] This sort of broad advocacy of truth status for a novel is astonishing, especially given that some of the claims are preposterous to even the non-academic reader. Here's a memorable one: The designs for the Egyptian pyramids were perfected in part by a young Aryan soldier, Himatap, from Bharat Varsha. In a curious but not unusual departure from the standpoint of the historical narrator, Gidwani says after this account of Himatap's wanderings as a consultant in Egypt: "it may be worthwhile for Indian historians to take a trip to Egypt to see if this simple theorem was well within the grasp of those simple people" (779).

The main agenda of the American Institute of Sindhulogy for 2002–2003 was shipping copies of Gidwani's novel from India for distribution in North America. Arrangements for distribution were being made, we were told, "with renewed urgency": 450 copies to libraries, 50 copies to "opinion makers in government and media organizations" by September 2002. The program was expected to continue with the support of new membership and donations. In addition, the website told us, *Return of the Aryans* was provided to all Indian consulates in North America, and the institute was also in the process of securing a website link from the Public Broadcasting Service (PBS) website. As of 2002–2003, the institute next intended to ship the novel to school boards, the public library system in the United States, Indian ministries, and news media.

While the website declared its pedagogical project in the diaspora as the dissemination of the history of Sindh, Gidwani's own lengthy introduction to the book provides a guide to the use of this Anglophone text as a supplement to contemporary Hindutva revisionism in India: "This novel tells the story of the Aryans—of how and why they moved out of their homeland in Bharat Varsha (India) in 5000 BC, their trials and triumphs overseas, and finally their return to India" (ix). Gidwani, a former bureaucrat and fiction writer, is now an amateur historian:

> I must present this as a work of fiction. But fiction is not falsehood. Nor a dream. Nor guesswork. Ideally it should be seen as *fictionalized alternative history* that our mainstream historians have not attempted to write. In order to write the book I've had to rely on the oral history tradition— the songs of the ancients from prehistory which still remain in the traditional memory of the people of Angkor, Sind, Bali, Java, Burma, China, Bhutan, Nepal, Iran, Turkey, Egypt, Norway, Sweden, Finland, Italy, Russia, Lithuania, Germany and India. (ix)

In Gidwani's introduction, a seemingly cosmopolitan Sindh excavated from an old diaspora is something else at second glance. Anglophone interjections operate through various technological shifts as orature from various nations is translated into English, disseminated through print in the *lingua franca* of global English, and finally through the World Wide Web.

I have tried to learn what the revisionist project renarrates by going to the work of Romila Thapar, perhaps the best-known authority on the history of early India. Indeed, the vehement objections to her appointment to the Kluge Chair at the Smithsonian in 2003 by diasporic Indians show that mainstream history like hers provides an important obstacle to the recoding of Indian geographical space as aboriginally Aryan and therefore upper-caste Hindu. In Thapar's work on early India, there is no presupposition of racial categories like Aryan (provided by nineteenth-century German philologists and Orientalists) or Hindu as religious identities that have straight lines drawn from 5000 BC to the twenty-first century BJP articulations of the real Indian citizen. Indeed for her, the demographic reality of early "Vedic" India can only be drawn as a palimpsestic series of arrivals and interminglings ranging from eastern Iran and central Asia to west Asia via the Persian Gulf. The characteristic features of the Harappa and Mohenjo Daro cultures from 5000 BC do not mesh with those of the Vedic texts (dating from the second millennium) associated with the culture of the Indo-Aryan speakers.[17] Furthermore, even the Vedic texts already register the presence of non-Aryan speakers.[18] The emergent picture is of Indo-Aryan speakers who may have been in a "symbiotic relationship with speakers of non-Aryan languages with a mutual adopting of not only vocabulary and linguistic structures in a bilingual situation but also technologies and religious practices and beliefs."[19] And finally, here is the so-called mainstream historian's imagining of this past: "Archaeological evidence from the third millennium [when

Aryan culture is believed to have been dominant] confirms wide-ranging, overland contacts between north-western India, southern and eastern Iran and the Oxus region and maritime contacts with Oman and Mesopotamia. It was clearly a cosmopolitan world with people on the move, making languages mixed too."[20]

It is against this historical evidence of a cosmopolitanism and intermixture in the "origins" of the subcontinental civilizations that Gidwani's book asserts its fictionalized alternative history. In Gidwani's own words his novel is meant to stave off what he terms "a cultural holocaust" (xvii). "We have inherited an ancient culture," he tells his readers, and

> it has faced many waves of invasions, among others, from the Greek, Persian, Pathan, Mongol, French, Dutch and the English. Often with savagery they attempted to suppress our culture; yet the flame of hope burnt brightly against the dark background of foreign rule. Our culture endured, though our land has shrunk to less than half its size compared to the past. But then freedom in 1947 did not bring a fulfillment of our dreams. Day by day, the menace grows from within. In the final analysis, the greatest danger lies not outside our borders but inside, and in our soul and spirit. (x)

Gidwani appropriates postcolonialism as a continuing struggle for the upper-caste Hindu. Now the colonial struggle can be redirected against outsiders in the nation, namely, the non-Hindu minorities who are dangerous residual elements trying to undo the long continuity of Vedic and Aryan civilization.

Thapar is obviously not unaware of these moves in the elite Indian diaspora. In the last chapter of her book *Cultural Pasts,* she refers to the so-called Indo-American school of scholars, which consists predominantly of American-trained Indian professional scientists researching on ancient India as a hobby. These scientist-historians—committed to proving that the Vedic and Harappan culture are the same, that the Aryans were indigenous to India, and that they took the Aryan mission westwards from India into Europe before returning home—draw a tongue-in-cheek comment from Thapar:

> That Indian scientists should take upon themselves the task of proving the Harappan to be Vedic, to having influenced other civilizations such as the Egyptian and that the Aryans proceeded on a civilizing mission out of India and going westwards, can only suggest that the Indo-American school is in the midst of an identity crisis in its new environment. It is anxious to demarcate itself from other immigrants and to proclaim that

the Indian identity is superior to the others who have fallen into the great melting pot.[21]

Diasporic nationalist politics as reverse Orientalism, Thapar reads here, is a symptom of failed multiculturalism in North America. Perceived inferiority as new citizens produces cultural supremacy as a reactive project. But this spatial demarcation of effects or audiences as nonresident Indians fail to become hyphenated Americans is only one part of the reality. The other is that this new demographic is parastate and sees itself as such and effectively wants to intervene in the contemporary Indian scene. These new power lines stretching from the new home to the old home are not addressed by Thapar. For a reading of the structures that have cultivated these cultural maneuvers in the diaspora, it may be useful to look at the work of Vinay Lal, the United States–based historian of South Asia, whose research into the Internet histories of diasporic Hindutvas (as well as his own forays into Internet publishing to expose right-wing revisionist fabrications) has made him the punching bag of the Internet Hindutvas.

Lal has spent much time analyzing the phenomenon of right-wing Hindutva politics among U.S. immigrants from India. In a series of articles published from his UCLA history department website, Lal evokes the term "rhizomatic" to characterize the cyberspace transformation of Hindus into Hindutvas (from a category of religious faith to that of militant identity politics).[22] What is being differentiated here? If the old Indic diasporas were constituted by the seriality and linear nature of shipping routes, mercantilist trade, and labor transfers between colonies, the new Indic diasporas have the overlay of cyberspace technologies to produce what resembles the rhizome-like structures described by Gilles Deleuze and Félix Guattari in *A Thousand Plateaus:* in the principles of connection and heterogeneity "any point of a rhizome can be connected to anything other, and must be."[23] In this assemblage, there are no points or positions, only lines. Because "transversal communications between different lines scramble the genealogical trees," the rhizome is an "antigenealogy."[24] Yet, even as Lal applies this principle to community formation in the diaspora, what we see is that even with territorial expansion of the rhizomatic principle, there is also the active recoding of genealogies and histories, but in a new mode. I will come back to this point soon, but first a segue into the perceived relationship between globalization, nationalism, and this community.

It is now commonplace to argue that tele-technologies are driving globalization and thereby unhinging the power of the nation as the organizing principle of community. In that sense my argument is counterintuitive. On the one hand, the rhizomatic principle of cyberspace has more than anything else produced the *effect* of a global Hinduism—that is, the geographical reach of these technologies produces a sense of global community even though the Indian diaspora is smaller than the Chinese or the African. On the other hand, conspiracy theories as well as the metonymic constructions of worldwide persecution from Uganda to Fiji for instance (represented in newsletters by reports of ruined temples) are also constructing a renewed coding of the nation—the former home as an imperiled space. As such we are seeing the drive to consolidate the community's reach through new political alliances between the diasporic communities and the internal bourgeoisie at home and pedagogical practices initiated in the diaspora. (This is a reversal of Guha's perception that the diasporic is banished from the nation with the dictum "you don't live here any more.") Thus, even as the political party BJP, the power base of the Hindutva movement in India, makes *swadeshi* (self-reliance) its loudest principle, its website is located in the United States, as is the website of its paramilitary organization, the Rashtriya Swayamsevak Sangh (National Patriotism Organization) (RSS). Similarly, the well-known involvement of International Monetary Fund (IMF)– and World Bank–trained economists and technocrats in the drive toward liberalizing the Indian economy in the 1980s, the recent spate of advertisements taken out by diasporic Indians in California supporting the destruction of the Babri Masjid Mosque in 1992, and finally the recent exposés of diasporic-funded "development" agencies funneling resources to Hindutva organizations in India all suggest that the diasporic classes now more than ever can intervene in the political outcomes of their former homes.

The pedagogical function of the Hindutva cyberspace is precisely what interrupts the commonplace notion that tele-technologies are cultural forms that erase space with time. The time-space compression produces, it would seem, a sort of simultaneity of time—the existence of all in a synchronous moment of imagined community. But what it has also engendered is a historical consciousness; it has given rise to what Vinay Lal calls "Hindutva history." Now secularist and nationalist—i.e., the textbook versions are easily recognized as such and now deemed elite, Western, secularist, and thus anti-Hindu— these histories are revised on many websites with common tropes: the cruelty and anti-Hindu policies as well as "genocides" against Hindus by the Muslim invaders who ruled India for six centuries, a history also seen as one of devastation of Hindu temples, forced conversions, and cultural appropriations. In the interstices of this story, Hindu culture is presented as one of survival and reclamation. Here is one example provided by Vinay Lal's scrutiny of these websites: the most famous monument of Mughal architecture, the Taj Mahal, is now renamed "TejMaholay" and presented as the product of Hindu architects, Hindu designs, and Hindu labor. The point is not only that these are obvious fabrications but that the historical archive is now part of the Internet, a virtual medium where archiving never had the reputation of the solidity of print. What is also interesting is the way in which the globalizing community is also universalist and yet is recoding the power of the nation in a global reoccupation of geography; thus the Indian community, still a tiny minority in Anglo-America, shows signs of wanting to be a global phenomenon. In a curious reversal, the long-accepted historical narrative of the Aryan migration to the subcontinent is rewritten as a story of diasporic scattering and return. In this replotting, the Aryans originated in the subcontinent and left their traces throughout Europe before returning to India. The European Aryan, in other words, was originally Hindu. Etymology becomes the recoding tool of choice: Argentina is thus a place where Lord Arjun sojourned while in exile and dairy-rich Denmark is actually a distortion of "Dhenu Marg," or the abode of the cows—all proof that Hindu traditions once thrived there. Similarly, the Red Indians and ViveCanada (Vivekananda) are proof of Hindu reach in North America. When the distinction between "knowledge" and "information" is being undone in dangerous ways, for an interested pedagogy in the diaspora, the distinction between history and literature is also blurred. Here the switchover from Internet histories to the novel *Return of the Aryans* can be seen as a relay between two forms of media that have crosshatched their functions. Each can claim the other as its offspring, but at the same time one cannot ignore that an archival fetish operates so as to give preservation through print texts (i.e., the novel) a moment of cultural dominance in the scene of virtuality. But if the novel is approximating history in problematic ways, such contexts where fictional constructions are producing "effects of the real," the professional historian is often tempted to flex some disciplinary muscle.[25]

Lal, as a postcolonial "new" historian of South Asia, is aware that his discipline is also tyrannical about its epistemological paradigms. He makes much of the fact that mainstream Indian historiography is in a hurry to adopt Western historicist paradigms and in a hurry to give up on earlier forms of historical consciousness that used myth. But in his attempt to legitimize subjugated knowledges like myth—banished by Orientalist, nationalist, and Marxist historians alike—at times Lal comes close to rubbing shoulders with the Hindutvas, whose mythic fabrications he dismisses but within whose reterritorialized space of history he must still battle for a new position. Thus Lal ends one of his Internet essays on the diasporic communities by calling for new forms of cultural histories:

The modern Indian diaspora began in conditions of extreme adversity, and it is incumbent upon us not to allow the accumulated narratives of Silicon Valley "miracles," the masculization of Hinduism among diasporic populations in the Anglo-American world and the musings (and lately rantings) of Salman Rushdie to monopolize our understandings of a diaspora that has also nurtured soft forms of Hinduism, new forms of Chutney music, and even, from within the depths of Ramacaritamanas country in Fiji, the first novel ever written in Bhojpuri. Our Indian diaspora needs a hefty Purana.[26]

Clearly Lal's evocation of the Purana instead of the "novel" is the return of the epic form as an appropriate form for the global Indic diaspora. The Puranas are ancient Indian texts that date back to the first millennium AD and are texts with genealogies and lineage histories now read as the first signs of historical consciousness in that tradition. The Puranas also marked a transition to representations of political control based on legitimacy (lineage), rather than conquest. It is of course tantalizing how the great epic traditions of patrilineal lineage may be redone for a politically progressive diaspora and it is within the spirit of Lal's challenge, and yet it is with a cautionary glance at the one such resuscitation of archaic forms that I now turn to a closer reading of Gidwani's *Return of the Aryans*.

The novel spans a period that is beyond the reach of disciplinary history of early India—from 5068 to 5005 BC—and uses "flashbacks" to go further back to 5086 BC. In this way an epic "absolute past" is put together even as the novel insists on its supplementary role as "alternative fictionalized history." Thus unlike epic conventions, chapter titles have dates. The birth of the hero, Sindhu Putra in 5068, his emergence as the leader of the Aryans, and his death in 5015 forms the dominant narrative strand in the novel. But the real story is that of the mix of people who through Putra's leadership constitute an undivided Aryan identity by leaving behind their multiple tribal pasts to call themselves Aryans and the land they live in "Bharat Varsha," or the land of Bharat (the contemporary Hindi name for India). Here both community formation and nation building are taken away from Mughal pasts and colonial British pasts and yoked to a common origin that precedes the dominant and elite stories of the Indian nation as a violent, constructed legacy of colonial modernity.

The second maneuver in the novel is cartographic. A mythic narrative transforms contemporary North Indian cities like Varanasi and Allahabad into the centers of an epic Aryan diaspora. Furthermore, countries like Turkey,

Iran, and Germany are no longer potential sites from which Aryans dispersed toward the Indian subcontinent (the dominant historical narrative today), but places where the traces of Aryan or Indo-Gangetic civilizations exist because Aryan explorers led "contingents" to those places and left a permanent imprint on those cultures (877). The pedagogical imperative asserts itself by the annotations on the text to actual coordinates on maps, so that readers can trace their fingers across the globe as the Aryan becomes, through progressive chapters, a globally imagined community: "People on the Move," "Hindus All," "We are the Aryans," "Aryans in Iran," "Aryans Everywhere," "Aryans in Europe," "On to Finland, Sweden, Norway," "Aryans in Lithuania, Baltic States and Elsewhere," and "Aryans in Germany." In the epilogue, the last scene of the novel shows the return of Kamalpati with an Aryan contingent from Spain:

> He was back home, back at last!
> Sindhu flowed on.
> Ganga flowed on.
> Saraswati flowed on.
> Kauveri flowed on.
> Kamalpati gazed at the peaceful countryside and felt a glow of happiness and peace within. He was home—in Hindu Varsha, Bharat Varsha! Arya Varsha!
> If there was a dark age to follow, Kamalpati did not know about it.
> But then even today, who in this land—sieged within and without—knows of the dark ages ahead. (944)

The cover of the novel is meant to invoke this moment of return as Kamalpati sits on a horse and gazes over the Saraswati river. (I have already indicated earlier the strategic use of horses in these revisionist Hindutva accounts.) The return of the Aryans from their Eurasian diaspora to the great northern Indian plains of the four rivers that now form the heartland of the popular support for the Hindutva movement in India is a significant sleight-of-hand. It not only provides an undivided origin for the contemporary nation, but also a cultural bedrock from where Arya-Bharat-Hindu can be conflated, thus erasing the existing religious heterogeneity of the subcontinent—the Muslim, Christian, Buddhist, Jain, and the Zoroastrian, as well as the multiple tribal peoples who are non-Aryan and non-Hindu in religious, cultural, and ethnic affiliations. But more significantly, the novel's epic geographical reach into Europe and the return to the subcontinent also rewrites the transcendental homelessness of the novel into that of epic return. This is a point that Georg Lukacs has made in another context—that of the European epic and novel.

In *The Theory of the Novel,* Lukacs presents the typology of novel forms in their relation to "modes of totality." The unbridgeable gap that separates us, the inhabitants of capitalist modernity, from the world of Homer's epic, he asserts, is the impossibility of returning home. In the epic,

> man does not stand alone: . . . his relation to others and the structure which arise therefrom are as full of substance as he is himself, indeed they are more truly filled with substance because they are more general, more "philosophic," closer and more akin to the archetypal home: love, the family, the state. What he should do or be is, for him, only a pedagogical question, an expression of the fact that he has not yet come home; . . . a long road lies before him, but within him there is no abyss.[27]

The fall from this ideal world of essence to representation of "reality" in the art form (the separation of matter from substance) is thus a fall from grace, and the novel form, Lukacs argues, is "like no other [form], an expression of this transcendental homelessness."[28]

It is important to note that Gidwani's novel departs from contemporary diasporic fiction where return to the country of origin is recorded as a sort of failure to assimilate, to globalize, or to redo the diaspora or the Anglo-American metropole in one's own image (Salman Rushdie's call to "tropicalize" London, for instance). Choosing to live away despite its threat to identity and cultural origin is marked as the possibility of the diasporic subject's open-ended agency. In Michael Ondaatje's *Anil's Ghost,* the expatriate overcome by the violence in the former homeland gets on a plane to return to the United States. In Monica Ali's *Brick Lane,* the woman who has negotiated the oppressive life of homeworker in London refuses to return to Bangladesh with her husband. In Zadie Smith's *White Teeth,* a delegated return in the guise of sending children back to the country of origin to be educated in their original culture results in disaster. The Bangladesh-educated son returns to London as an Anglophile with no traces of nativism. In Gidwani's novel, on the other hand, the return of the expatriate is imagined as an epic return. In this narrative reordering, what is also being imagined for the diasporic Hindutva is a plot that neutralizes the adverbial force of the "no longer" that has banished the expatriate into a liminal existence of cultural anonymity, second-class citizenship, and guilt for having left the home country. In Gidwani's novel Anglo-America is but a space for a temporary sojourn for cultural dissemination and pedagogy—for globalizing Hinduism before returning home.

Against these tendencies of telescoped history and the transformation of heterogeneous and cosmopolitan historical pasts into landscapes of purity and undivided origin, it seems more important than ever to assert the potentialities of diaspora. In her eloquent description of her trajectory from nonresident alien, to alien resident, and finally to U.S. citizen, Chandra Mohanty describes how it is precisely living away that has enabled forms of transnational solidarities that has to constitute one of the necessary responses to uneven globalization. "Political solidarity and a sense of family could be melded together imaginatively," she says, "to create a strategic space I could call 'home.'" Here home is not a "comfortable, stable, inherited, and familiar space," but instead a "politically charged space," that enables shared collective analysis of social injustice. By deploying the United States and India as the "two places" she calls "home," Mohanty embodies not only the ways in which technology enables these coincidences for transnational subjects but how they may also enable forms of solidarity that allow actual transnational organizing.[29]

In Houston, where I currently live, I have been fortunate to be part of another diasporic experiment. As a member of a team that hosts a radio talk show called Border Crossings on an alternative station in the Pacifica network, I have experienced in a small way the cosmopolitical potentialities of diaspora. Our team includes a Mexican, a Pakistani, and three Indians—a Hindu, a Sikh, and a Christian. Constituted mostly through professional alliances (three of us are academics at Houston-based universities while the other two are spouses of Indian computer software engineers), the group ironically mimics the Indian state's postindependence pedagogical slogan—"Unity in Diversity"—as it is redone in the United States. But the more significant work of the show has been our use of "South Asia" (an old Area Studies designation) as a subcontinental reference that eschews nationalist agendas and chauvinism while emphasizing a common postcolonial experience and cultural mix in ways that allow us to form a different extended community of listeners who can imagine their coexistence by tuning in, calling in, or sponsoring the show. It is in the North American diaspora, away from the visa restrictions that forbid ordinary citizens of Pakistan and Indian in the subcontinent from meeting each other, that a "South Asia" can be realized in a very real way. And as we connect with local groups that are organizing more and more functions that draw together people from the subcontinent, the diaspora seems to be rerouting some geographies of anger.

The show is in English, although attempts are often made to play music in different languages and translate, wherever possible, some of the texts we discuss on the show. Anglophony is without doubt one of the enabling mechanisms here. If Benedict Anderson is right and temporal imaginings are crucial in the task of creating communities of belonging and exclusion, then such imaginings are equally crucial in inserting the new immigrant within multiculturalism in the nation of arrival as well as for creating new communities of enemies and friends. In the imagining of communities beyond the local—not the universalizing of the great values of neoliberalism—but rather the relationship between particular cultures and mutuality despite mutability, new technologies as well as "global English" can work toward a broader understanding of the human or the planet through the diaspora.

NOTES

1. Srinivas Aravamudan, "In the Wake of the Novel: The Oriental Tale as National Allegory," *Novel: A Forum on Fiction* 33, no. 1 (1999): 5–31.

2. Jacques Derrida, *Paper Machine,* trans. Rachel Bowlby (Stanford, Calif.: Stanford University Press, 2005), 15.

3. Gayatri Spivak, *Death of a Discipline* (New York: Columbia University Press, 2003), 15.

4. Jacques Derrida, *Specters of Marx: The State of the Debt, the Work of Mourning, and the New International,* trans. Peggy Kamuf (New York: Routledge, 1994), 82–83.

5. Arjun Appadurai, *Fear of Small Numbers: An Essay on the Geography of Anger* (Durham, N.C.: Duke University Press, 2006), 5. Further page references are cited parenthetically in the text.

6. Ranajit Guha, "The Migrant's Time," *Postcolonial Studies* 1, no. 2 (1998): 155–60. Further page references are cited parenthetically in the text.

7. Romila Thapar, "Hindutva and History," *Frontline* 17, no. 20 (October 13, 2000): 15–16.

8. For further elaboration of such erasures see Derrida, *Paper Machine,* 24.

9. Rey Chow, *Writing Diaspora: Tactics of Intervention in Contemporary Cultural Studies* (Bloomington: Indiana University Press, 1993), 169.

10. See Michael Witzel, "Horseplay in Harappa: The Indus Valley Decipherment Hoax," *Frontline* 17, no. 20 (October 13, 2000): 4–14.

11. Derrida, *Paper Machine,* 13–15.

12. Achin Vanaik, "The New Indian Right," *New Left Review* 9 (2001): 43–67. Further page references are cited parenthetically in the text.

13. Bhagwan Gidwani, *Return of the Aryans* (New Delhi: Penguin, 1994). Page references to the novel are cited parenthetically in the text.

14. The website of the American Institute of Sindhulogy, http://www.sindhulogy .org/.

15. "About/Mission," http://www.sindhulogy.org/DynImageContent.aspx?pid=3 &xmlpath=Mission&xsltpath=std01 (accessed October 6, 2010).

16. Ram Jethmalani, "An Odyssey," review of *Return of the Aryans,* by Bhagwan Gidwani, the website of the American Institute of Sindhulogy, "News/Return of the Aryans Review," http://www.sindhulogy.org/DynImageContent.aspx?pid=26 &xmlpath=News05&xsltpath=std01 (accessed January 23, 2011).

17. Romila Thapar, "Imagined Religious Communities? Ancient History and the Modern Search for a Hindu Identity," in *Cultural Pasts: Essays in Early Indian History* (New Delhi: Oxford University Press, 2000), 981.

18. Ibid., 982.

19. Ibid.

20. Romila Thapar, "The Theory of Aryan Race and India: History and Politics," in *Cultural Pasts: Essays in Early Indian History* (New Delhi: Oxford University Press, 2000), 1121.

21. Ibid., 1125. As Thapar points out, it is ironic that the current Hindutva theory that the Aryans were the progenitors of the European civilization was first put forward by a sympathetic European: Colonel Olcott of the Theosophical Society in Bengal.

22. Vinay Lal, "India and Its Neighbors," last updated July/August 2009, http://www.sscnet.ucla.edu/southasia/.

23. Gilles Deleuze and Félix Guattari, *A Thousand Plateaus,* trans. Brian Massumi (Minneapolis: University of Minnesota Press, 1987), 7–8.

24. Ibid.

25. For a more detailed discussion of this point see Gayatri Spivak, *A Critique of Postcolonial Reason* (Cambridge, Mass.: Harvard University Press, 1999), 203.

26. Vinay Lal, "Diaspora Purana: The Indic Presence in World Culture," http://www.sscnet.ucla.edu/southasia/Diaspora/indic_presence.html (accessed October 6, 2010).

27. Georg Lukacs, *The Theory of the Novel* (Cambridge, Mass.: MIT Press, 1990), 33.

28. Ibid., 41.

29. Chandra Mohanty, *Feminism Without Borders: Decolonizing Theory, Practicing Solidarity* (Durham, N.C.: Duke University Press, 2003), 128, 136.

Afterword

Diaspora and the Language of Neoliberalism

AIMS MCGUINNESS AND STEVEN C. MCKAY

Some categories of analysis are useful for gathering together or cutting apart. Others work better for dissolving received ideas and misconceptions. One solvent that scholars found particularly useful in the late twentieth century was the adjective "global." Following the breakup of the Soviet Union and the obsolescence of the paradigm of three worlds, commentators turned to "global" and other alternatives such as "transnational" to help them think beyond the limits of deeply ingrained biases of the nation and area studies. "Global" and "transnational" worried away not only spatial but also disciplinary barriers. Calls to uncover the workings of global or transnational phenomena gave an urgency to interdisciplinarity that interdisciplinarity lacked when it was invoked as a virtue in and of itself.

The weaknesses of the "global" and "transnational" as key words became more apparent when the terms were used not as adjectives but as nouns. The placement of a definite article in front of "global" and "transnational" ("the global" or "the transnational") represented an attempt to imagine novel spatial units of analysis. "Global" and "transnational" became labels that functioned in a way that resembled how nations and world regions, or "areas" such as Latin America or the Middle East, had previously served to clump scholars together along spatial lines during the Cold War. This transmogrification from adjective to noun has too often resulted in the unfortunate and unintended effect of robbing these terms of their virtues as solvents. As useful as "global" and "transnational" were as antidotes to the rigidities of national and area studies, they were too vague and amorphous to be useful as replacements for those rigidities. To say that "the global" or "the transnational" were not national was both to say too little and too much. The vague and shifting morass that lay "beyond the nation" lacked sufficient definition to be productive as a framework for analysis. The term "transnational" in particular assumed the nation as the fundamental unit of political organization, creating a constant temptation for anachronism. Rather than a space to be investigated, "the global" and "the transnational" became catch-alls, receptacles for whatever remnants of history happened to exceed borders.

Even more problematic was the term "globalization," which underwent a rapid transformation in the 1990s from a compelling subject of research to a piece of intellectual furniture that no discipline could do without. Rather than a vehicle capable of transporting critique to new places, globalization too often came to function as a place for weary heads to rest worn arguments. The concept of globalization created a false dichotomy by opposing a supposedly "preglobal" past with a putatively global present, reducing history to a linear process in which the beginning and the end were essentially assumed. Ephemeral policies, such as the reduction of trade barriers, were spoken of as if they were historical inevitabilities. The "end of history" was assumed to be foreordained, and globalization was the teleological highway that led to that end. An ill-conceived set of historical assumptions was misconstrued as the distillation of an actual historical process.[1]

Efforts to add nuance to debates about globalization by adding an *s* (from "globalization" to "globalizations") succeeded only in pluralizing the teleology that was the root of the problem in the first place. To speak of the globalization of a given place was to imply that previous to globalization, the place in question was somehow disconnected from the rest of the globe. But almost always, this maneuver proved to be a mystifying oversimplification. To speak of the globalization of, say, Bolivia as if it were a novel development peculiar to the late twentieth century was to ignore how Bolivia had been linked previously to places such as Spain, China, or India nearly five centuries before.

As an explanation of historical change, globalization was even worse. Every moment of friction, resistance, or negotiation in the history of capital was written off as no more than a pause on the road toward the inevitable, globalized future. All nuance was lost in the rush to smash history into two boxes—the globalizing "now" and the yet-to-be-globalized past. History in such hands took the form of a straw man constructed for the purpose of supporting breathless assertions about the unprecedented nature of the present.[2]

As Frederick Cooper notes in his own critique of "globalization," to which the foregoing analysis is indebted, the concept of "diaspora" retains a utility in the present that concepts of "the global" or "the transnational" lack.[3]

And as noted in the introduction to this volume, "diaspora," in contrast to "globalization," does not contain any assumption of its own inevitability. It focuses the attention of the investigator on particular collectivities or groups of people without relegating those people to the status of pawns in some imagined, overarching historical process. Like "transnational," the adjective "diasporic" may be applied to phenomena or communities that span nations or other political units, but its meaning does not derive solely from that quality. Diaspora draws attention to networks that could be characterized as "global." But it does not refer to *every* global network. This limitation—or, better, specificity—is a sign not of the weakness of diaspora as a concept but rather of the richness of the possibilities it entails.

The essays in this book can be described as being global or transnational in their focus, but they go beyond simply gesturing vaguely at whatever lies beyond the nation. Each of them is concerned in some way with locating collectivities that the neoliberal language of globalization too often obscures. Together, the authors in this volume demonstrate that the ongoing power of "diaspoetics" or diaspora studies lies precisely in its practitioners' capacity to balance and hold in creative tension "diaspora" as broad analytical lens and "diaspora" as historically and materially grounded experience.

If creative tensions are what render the diasporic approach both meaningful and productive, then the future of diaspora studies may lie with continuing to explore and explicate such dialectical tendencies and not necessarily trying to resolve them. As others have similarly noted, we need to continue the shift away from thinking of diaspora as a category, typology, or even a process, but instead approach diasporas as contested historical practices.[4] Thus we should approach the study of "diaspora" the way we have already learned to study the "nation"—as imagined yet quite real political projects that may have the potential to cross borders yet remain rooted in ways that adjectives such as "global" or "transnational" can only begin to describe.

NOTES

1. The classic formulation of this teleology—since qualified by its author and cited far more by its legion of critics than by any admirers—is Francis Fukuyama, *The End of History and the Last Man* (New York: Free Press, 1992).

2. The most popular manifestation of this mode of telling the past was Thomas Friedman, *The Lexus and the Olive Tree* (New York: Anchor Books, 2000). Although Friedman was dismissed as overly simplistic by academics, the basic historical assumptions at work in this and later of his works such as *The World Is Flat* (New York: Farrar,

Straus, and Giroux, 2005) can be found in much, if not most, scholarship that takes "globalization" as its object of study.

3. See Frederick Cooper, "Globalization," in *Colonialism in Question: Theory, Knowledge, History* (Berkeley: University of California Press, 2005), 95–112.

4. See Ien Ang, "Beyond 'Asian Diasporas,'" in *Asian Diasporas: New Formations, New Conceptions,* ed. Rhacel Salazar Parreñas and Lok C. D. Siu, 285–90 (Stanford, Calif.: Stanford University Press, 2007); and Rogers Brubaker, "The 'Diaspora' Diaspora," *Ethnic and Racial Studies* 28, no. 1 (2005): 1–19.

CONTRIBUTORS

Sukanya Banerjee is Associate Professor of English at the University of Wisconsin–Milwaukee and author of *Becoming Imperial Citizens: Indians in the Late-Victorian Empire*.

Crispin Bates is Reader in History (Classics and Archaeology) at the University of Edinburgh. He is author of *Subalterns and Raj: South Asia since 1600* and editor of *Beyond Representation: Colonial and Postcolonial Constructions of Indian Identity*.

Martin A. Berger is Professor of History of Art and Visual Culture and Director of the Visual Studies Graduate Program at the University of California, Santa Cruz. He is author of *Seeing through Race: A Reinterpretation of Civil Rights Photography*, *Sight Unseen: Whiteness and American Visual Culture*, and *Man Made: Thomas Eakins and the Construction of Gilded Age Manhood*.

Rachel Ida Buff is Associate Professor of History at the University of Wisconsin–Milwaukee. She is author of *Immigration and the Political Economy of Home: West Indian Brooklyn and American Indian Minneapolis, 1945–1992* and editor of *Immigrant Rights in the Shadows of Citizenship*.

Marina Carter is Research Fellow, Centre for South Asian Studies, in the School of History (Classics and Archaeology) at the University of Edinburgh. She is author (with James Ng Foong Kwong) of *Abacus and Mah Jong: Sino-Mauritian Settlement and Economic Consolidation*, of *Companions of Misfortune: Flinders and Friends at the Isle of France, 1803–1810*, and (with Khal Torabully) of *Coolitude: An Anthology of the Indian Labour Diaspora*.

Betty Joseph is Associate Professor of English at Rice University and author of *Reading the East India Company, 1720–1840: Colonial Currencies of Gender*.

Aims McGuinness is Associate Professor of History at the University of Wisconsin–Milwaukee and author of *Path of Empire: Panama and the California Gold Rush, 1848–1856*.

Steven C. McKay is Associate Professor of Sociology at the University of California, Santa Cruz. He is author of *Satanic Mills or Silicon Islands? The Politics of High-Tech Production in the Philippines*.

Parama Roy is Professor of English at the University of California, Davis. She is the author of *Alimentary Tracts: Appetites, Aversions, and the Postcolonial* and *Indian Traffic: Identities in Question in Colonial and Postcolonial India.* and is a co-editor of *States of Trauma. Gender and Violence in South Asia*.

Jenny Sharpe is Professor of English at the University of California, Los Angeles. Her books include *Ghosts of Slavery: A Literary Archeology of Black Women's Lives* and *Allegories of Empire: The Figure of Woman in the Colonial Text*.

Todd Shepard is Associate Professor of History at Johns Hopkins University and author of *The Invention of Decolonization: The Algerian War and the Remaking of France*.

Lok Siu is Associate Professor of Anthropology at the University of Texas at Austin. She is the author of *Memories of a Future Home: Diasporic Citizenship of Chinese in Panama*.

INDEX

Page numbers in italics refer to illustrations.

Dirks, Nicholas, 118n20

discourse: analysis, 6, 73; colonial, 70; of democracy, 125, 211; of diaspora, 2, 5, 123, 173; foreign policy, 123; on freedom and unfreedom, 69, 73; of French citizenship, 10, 56; of immigration, 76, 125–126; of indenture, 69; of ingestion, 99; nationalist, 15, 73, 75, 123; racial, 15; of U.S. citizenship, 127; of U.S. imperialism, 12, 123; of U.S. security, 124; Victorian, 88

displacement, 2, 4, 7, 168, 209–211, 216; in diasporic identity, 9–10, 31; forced, 14; repeated, 146; shared experience of, 144; significance of place in, 169n2

Distant Shore, A (Phillips), 26–34, 40, 42n13

Dreiser, Theodore, 191

Du Bois, W. E. B., 130

Duff, Alexander, 108

dyaspora, 39–40

East India Company, 95–97, 100, 118n20

eclecticism (architectural style), 179–180, 185–192, 196, 199. *See also* architecture

Edwards, Brent Hayes, 8, 18n24, 41n3

Elias, Norbert: *The Civilizing Process,* 102

epic (noun), 15–16, 208, 209–210, 214–216, 223–225. *See also* novel

Equiano, Olaudah, 30–31, 42n15

Evian Accords, 45, 56–58, 65n57

exodus: from Algeria, 10, 44, 46–61; from Haiti, 34

Fanon, Frantz: *The Wretched of the Earth,* 100

Farber, David, 136

Fouchet, Christian, 57

Fraser, Furness and Hewitt, 175. *See also* Rodeph Shalom Synagogue

French Republic, 46, 49, 57–58, 60

Furness, Frank, 174–178, 185–187, 192–193, 197–199, 202n13

Furness, William Henry, 180, 202n20

Furness and Hewitt, 176, 178, 192, 197–198. *See also* Pennsylvania Academy of the Fine Arts

Gandhi, Mahatma, 73, 83; *satyagraha,* 131

Ghosh, Amitav: *Sea of Poppies,* 87

Ghosh, K., 73, 83

Gidwani, Bhagwan, 216–217; *Return of the Aryans,* 15, 209, 213, 216–219, 222–225; *The Sword of Tipu,* 216

Gilded Age, 179–182, 190, 196, 199

Gilroy, Paul, 2, 26, 36–37, 144; *The Black Atlantic: Modernity and Double Consciousness,* 2, 26, 155. *See also* Black Atlantic

Girard, Patrick, 194

Glissant, Édouard, 25, 39, 43n35

globalization, 5, 214–215, 226, 231n2; of commodity culture, 32; as different from diaspora, 1; disembodied nature of, 7; driven by tele-technologies, 220; flexible citizenship as a response to, 159; as postmodern, 209–210; transformation of the term, 230–231

Guha, Ranajit, 119n35, 211–212, 216, 221

Guinin, 37–38

Hadrami diaspora, 5

Haitian diaspora, 9, 39

Hall, Stuart, 9, 31, 150

harkis, 10, 13, 58–62, 66n67

Harris, Wilson, 25

Harrison, Joseph, 195–196

Hawkins, Dexter, 189

Heart of Darkness (Conrad), 32, 42

Hernandez, Philippe, 51–52

Hewitt, George, 174–178, 185, 192, 197–198

Hilton, Henry, 190, 205n50

Himid, Lubaina, 25

Hinduism, 221, 223, 225

Hindutvas: as diasporic, 225; history of, 213, 220–222, 228n21; and the Internet, 220–221; politics of, 215–216, 220–221; as religious faith, 220; revisionism, 217, 224; sympathizers in North America, 215, 220. *See also* BJP (Bharatiya Janata Party); Gidwani, Bhagwan; Lal, Vinay; *Return of the Aryans* (Gidwani)

Hinsley, Curtis, 188

Hirai, Kowashi, 136–137

Ho, Engseng, 5

Stokes, Eric, 102
Stoller, Ann, 11, 138n8
Story, William Wetmore: *Jerusalem in Her Desolation* (sculpture), 180–181
subaltern networks, 67–68, 70, 82–83, 85
Sugishita, Robert, 133
swadeshi, 221

Taj Mahal, 221–222
Taylor, Diana: *The Archive and the Repertoire: Performing Cultural Memory in the Americas,* 36, 43n28
Thapar, Romila, 212, 218, 228n21; *Cultural Pasts,* 219–220
Tinker, Hugh: *A New System of Slavery: the Export of Indian Labour Overseas, 1830–1920,* 69–70
Tölölyan, Khachig, 1–2, 16n1
Trachtenberg, Alan, 188
transnational (noun), 4–5, 16, 229–231
transnationalism, 4, 18n16, 18n20
Trevelyan, George Otto: *Cawnpore,* 110, 112, 115–116
Truman, Harry S., 126–127, 129–131, 137
Turner, J. M. W., *The Slave Ship (Slavers Throwing Overboard the Dead and Dying, Typhoon Coming On),* 37

Ujaama, James, 124

Van Brunt, Henry, 186–187, 205n41
Vanaik, Achin, 214
Venturi, Robert, 199

Wallerstein, Immanuel, 210
war brides, 125, 127, 137
Ware, William, 187
Warner, Charles Dudley: *In the Levant,* 184–185
whiteness, 15, 185, 192–195, 203nn22–23, 205n43; and architecture, 200n2; in European American culture, 181–182, 188–189. *See also* eclecticism (architectural style); identity; nonwhiteness
Witzel, Michael, 212–213
Wolff, Gérard, 49
Wood, Marcus: *Blind Memory: Visual Representations of Slavery in England and America,* 37
World War II, 12–13, 46, 125–129, 135–137, 171n21

Yang, Anand, 74

Zong incident, 29, 37, 39, 41n10